regional shopping centres

BRENT CROSS CENTRE, LONDON.   The model is of the proposed regional shopping centre at the intersection of the M.1 extension and the North Circular Road, with two department stores, over 100 other units and parking for nearly 3,000 cars.

REGIONAL SHOPPING CENTRES

Their location, planning and design

Colin S. Jones

Dip. Arch., Dip. T.P. (Dist.), A.R.I.B.A.

with a Preface by

F. B. Pooley.,

C.B.E., F.R.I.B.A., F.R.I.C.S., A.M.T.P.I.

BUSINESS BOOKS LIMITED

LONDON

First published 1969

© 1969 COLIN SEYMOUR JONES

S.B.N. 220.79930.x

This book has been set in 10 on 13 pt Univers light: printed in England
by Page Bros. (Norwich) Ltd., Norwich for the publishers, Business
Books Limited (registered office: 180 Fleet Street, London E.C.4),
publishing offices: Mercury House, Waterloo Road, London S.E.1.

MADE AND PRINTED IN GREAT BRITAIN

acknowledgements

I should like to express my thanks to J. Koek Esq., A.B. Urbanism (Brooklyn College), M.C.R.P. (Harvard University), Senior Lecturer at the Nottingham School of Town and Country Planning, for his advice and assistance in the preparation of the original thesis on which this book is based, and to other members of the Staff of the School for their comments and recommendations. In addition to the other individuals and organizations acknowledged in the Appendix, I am especially indebted to the following for the valuable information and assistance that they afforded me:

A. W. Anderson Esq., for C. and A. Anderson, developers of the Breda Centre, Belfast.

S. J. Beaven Esq. and K. G. Grey Esq., and the Market Research and Modern Merchandising Methods Department of the National Cash Register Company Ltd., London.

P. R. East Esq., B.Sc., A.R.I.C.S., the Hammerson Group of Companies.

R. W. Evely Esq., Development Analysts Ltd., London.

R. A. Parry Esq., and the Second Covent Garden Property Company Ltd.

K. F. Russell Esq., the Murrayfield Real Estate Company Ltd.

P. C. Waldock Esq., and the Metropolitan Estate and Property Company of London and Dublin.

P. J. B. Wilkinson Esq., Arndale Developments Ltd., Bradford.

Finally, I wish to thank F. B. Pooley Esq., C.B.E., for kindly agreeing to provide the Preface, and also my wife, for her assistance and fortitude during the preparation and reproduction of the original text and of the book.

July, 1969.   C.S.J.

contents

PART ONE: HISTORICAL DEVELOPMENT

PART TWO: LOCATIONAL REQUIREMENTS

list of figures

list of plates

PLATES IN APPENDIX A

list of tables

preface

This is an age of intense planning activity; more houses are being built than ever before; the renewal of urban areas gathers momentum; more new towns are springing up and new large cities are about to come on the scene.

Added to all this, social patterns and habits are changing. We are moving into an age of greater leisure time and people are demanding more mobility and freedom of choice.

All these factors have a bearing on the future of shopping centres. Britain is known as a nation of shopkeepers and this is clear for all to see in the distribution and types of shops in our old towns. But the advent of the co-operative, the departmental store, the multiples and now the self-service supermarket show that change is taking place. What is the future?

Even those who spend their lives and money specializing in shopping developments seem to be confused about the future. This book will be a help not only to students but also those who want to stand back and see what a new pair of keen research eyes make of it all. The book covers the complete spectrum ranging from the history of shopping and the decline of central areas, to such matters as the statistical survey of frequency of shopping trips related to public transport services, the assessment of locational potential, the economics of individual sites and the way in which physical development should proceed. All the research has been thorough and the facts are presented in a clear and logical fashion.

Mr Jones has taken an objective new look at this absorbing subject and his work will be of interest not only to the student but to the practising town planner and economist alike.

July, 1969

F. B. POOLEY

introduction

The regional or out-of-town centre, so prevalent in the United States, is a relatively new phenomenon in the British retailing scene; it is a concept on which many people have widely diverging and conflicting opinions, often based on preconceived and sometimes misinformed notions. In fact, the name itself is something of a misnomer, and has fostered the popular misconception that, in America at least, such centres are invariably located close to the intersection of turnpikes, and set in totally rural surroundings several miles from the nearest house. In reality, the great majority of regional centres is situated in suburban areas, closely related to residential districts, and often on subsidiary roads having only limited access to motorways. Their development arose as a direct consequence of the prevailing conditions of our time—conditions brought about by continual changes in population, economic prosperity, living and shopping habits and in rising car ownership. These factors encouraged the steady growth of regional centres in America and Europe, and their more recent introduction into Britain has emphasized the essential problems inherent in their location and design in the compact nature of this country; it is these problems which are considered in this book, rather than the implications of such developments on the town centre itself.

In this connotation, the term 'shopping centre' is taken to imply a peripheral or suburban location, as opposed to the central area, and as being a planned project by one developer to provide a complete range of integrated services and predetermined parking facilities; this definition places no limitation on the size of the centre, but stresses the importance of co-ordinated planning, when compared with the gradual accretion of the multitudes of independent and unrelated outlets over a number of years. This same broad definition implies that the location and design of centres will encompass several different activities and involve many allied specialists; this fact, combined with the wide variations in sites and building forms, means that no 'hard and fast' rules are applicable to every project. Consequently, it is the main purpose of this book to outline the various basic criteria which have been developed and employed in the past few years, both in America and in Britain, to assess the merits and disadvantages of particular systems and to analyse the facilities and relative success of a number of different centres.

Using the above terms of reference, a brief summary of the historical development of such centres in America and Europe is given in Part One, together with the particular reasons for their growth and the trends in design in each case. This summary is prefaced by a short analysis of traditional shops in Britain, since many such outlets are the potential tenants of these new suburban projects. The ultimate success of any new centre is dependent on expert and realistic market assessment, and Part Two considers the accepted classification of different centres and their locational requirements, and enumerates the many elements that developers and local authorities should include in the preparation of an economic analysis. This implies that the developer should not necessarily be required to produce such an analysis independently and in isolation, and that the local authorities should not accept these analyses verbatim, but should themselves undertake research into the viability and implications of any project. For this reason, some of the accepted techniques of market evaluation are also considered, ranging from the customary projection methods to the more recent computer systems, together with the question of their application for peripheral locations.

The formulation of a detailed market analysis presumes the prior planning of the complete centre, and for this reason, questions of importance both to developers and to local authorities, concerning site economics, neighbouring uses and the availability of willing and suitable tenants, are dealt with in Part Three, together with the types of traders at present operating in British out-of-town centres. Finally, in Part Four, the particular requirements for sites are discussed, consideration being given to the principles of the retailing layout, to the detailed design of the areas allocated for different uses, such as pedestrian zones, parking spaces and storage areas, and to the three dimensional aspects of design.

In each of the four parts, the formulation of rigid principles has been deliberately avoided, and a selection of various alternatives and solutions discussed and evaluated, with their particular suitability for differing locations and site conditions. Thus, the planners of future centres may refer readily to the appropriate sections for a comparative synopsis of previous and current practice, both in Britain and abroad. In such a wide ranging subject, it has not been possible to include the complete analysis and conclusions from all of the many relevant books, papers and articles, and therefore detailed references have been given in each case, together with a comprehensive bibliography indicating the major sources of information for topics considered in the text.

Despite the shortage of eminently suitable sites, and the unpredictability of social and economic factors, a number of out-of-town centres are being planned at present in this country, some by concerns with little experience or expertise in this form of development. As will be shown subsequently, many of the more important socio-economic circumstances will prompt an increasing demand for further sites and centres, and it is the primary intention of this book to set out the main factors which should be considered, by architects, planners, developers and local authorities, in the location, design and assessment of such centres as may be proposed in the future.

PART ONE:
historical development

1
traditional shops

Shopping locations stem from historic or geographic precedent, with the gradual accretion of altered or purpose built premises around the medieval market place and alongside the main routes, thus constituting the 'High Street'. The stalls of the traders who congregated in these traditional situations developed into more permanent open fronted shops, the elevations of which did not assume their modern aspect until the introduction of plate glass in the nineteenth century. The growth of retailing and business emphasized the nucleated nature of many town centres, in which accessibility became a vital factor, and in which the motor vehicle has become a major visual and physical intrusion. The resulting danger and lack of parking detracted from the economic success of the traditional centres. Consequently, the massive expansion into suburban areas after 1920, and especially in the 1930s, was followed by the development of extensive shopping parades close to the new housing districts, which can be regarded as the precursors of out-of-town centres.

1.1 FUNCTION AND LOCATION

Before considering the reasons for the growth of out-of-town centres, brief mention must be made of the types of retail outlet at present operating, since they form either the components or the competitors of such centres. In 1966, retail trade amounted to almost £11,000 million, with 498,000 units employing over $2\frac{1}{2}$ million people, or over 10 per cent of the total working population, while expenditure on new buildings rose by over £150 million between 1959 and 1965.[1]

1.2 TRENDS IN RETAILING SINCE 1945

Prior to 1939, the independent trader formed 90 per cent of all retail outlets, but this percentage had dropped to 84 per cent in 1957 and to 83 per cent by 1961. In 1966, this figure had fallen to 79 per cent,

INDEPENDENT TRADERS

representing almost 400,000 outlets and a turnover of £6,082 million or 55 per cent of all retail expenditure. Many of these units are very small (in 1961, there were 178,000 with a turnover of less than £5,000 per annum, accounting for only 5 per cent of retail trade), and these shops are gradually yielding before the competition from the larger undertakings.[2] Over 81,000 independents closed their doors between 1957 and 1966, while during the same period, turnover rose by only 13 per cent compared with an almost 50 per cent increase for multiple chains.

DEPARTMENT STORES Department stores transact a volume of trade out of all proportion to their numbers—there were only 784 in Great Britain in 1961, but they transacted 6 per cent of national turnover, or 11 per cent if food retailing is excluded.[3] In a shopping centre, their presence is a virtual guarantee of success for adjacent shops, though department store groups have tended to merge, as well as adopting self-service methods in some sections. Despite this streamlining of techniques, these stores lost some of their trade between 1961 and 1966, compared with a 23 per cent rise in national retail trade.

MULTIPLES A noticeable advance in retail trading has been achieved by multiples and chain stores, which now attract 27 per cent of expenditure, compared with 20 per cent in 1957. Despite the increased turnover induced by self-service techniques, quality tends to be good and its control strict. The total number of multiples rose from 59,000 in 1957 to nearly 74,000 in 1966, and since 1961 have experienced a 60 per cent increase in food sales turnover.

CO-OPERATIVES Co-operatives, who opened their first supermarket in 1949, have not made similar progress to multiples—in fact, their percentage of national turnover fell from almost 12 per cent in 1957 to 9 per cent in 1966, when profits were £3·4 million. In 1967, sales fell by £17·6 million to £494 million, and incurred a loss of over £500,000. Since then, reorganization has continued, linked with the withdrawal of the traditional dividend system and the opening of the computer controlled warehouse in the North East.

SELF-SERVICE AND SUPERMARKETS Development of self-service selling is almost entirely postwar, while supermarkets did not prosper until the abolition of rationing in 1953, from when their growth has been most marked. In December 1967, there were almost 20,000 self-service outlets, of which over 17,000 were self-service shops and about 2,850 were supermarkets. Between December 1965 and December 1966, over 190 new or converted premises were opened each month, of which over 30 were supermarkets. A supermarket is defined as having over 2,000 square feet of selling area, with at least two checkouts, and selling a broad range of groceries and meat, with non-food sales not exceeding 50 per cent of turnover. The average supermarket originally stocked between 7,000 and 8,000 separate items, though this has now been rationalized to around 5,000 to 6,000 items. Average sales per square foot rose from 24*s* per week in 1960 to 27*s* in 1967, with an average gross profit of 19 per cent, or 2–3 per cent net profit.[4] Self-service and supermarkets now account for over 50 per cent of all grocery turnover, and are experiencing increasing patronage—a recent survey indicates that 65 per cent of all shoppers visit a supermarket at least once a week, that 75 per cent have a supermarket within easy shopping distance, while 54 per cent have two supermarkets within easy shopping distance.[5] These survey findings emphasize the spread of this form of retail outlet into suburban locations, closer to the main residential areas, and consequently easily accessible to many pedestrian shoppers, at the same time as being able to provide better parking facilities than many central areas.

The preliminary results of the 1966 Census of Distribution indicate an overall drop in grocery outlets from 151,000 in 1961 to 122,000 in 1966; of this 29,000 decrease, 24,000 were independents, 2,000 were multiples and about 1,200 were co-operatives. However, turnover rose by almost 22 per cent during the same period, from £2,366 million in 1961 to £2,871 million in 1966.

Plate 1.1 GEM STORE, DUNDONALD STREET, PRESTON, LANCASHIRE.   A typical discount house location and building in an 'off-peak' area on the fringe of the town centre.

DISCOUNT HOUSES Discount houses represent a logical extension of supermarket trading, being introduced into Britain in 1959. (See Plate 1.1.) Supermarket techniques are applied to all goods, ample parking space is provided to encourage bulk buying, and therefore premises and land need to be cheap. Consequently, discount houses are frequently located in blighted or 'off peak' areas, especially in converted warehouses and cinemas, where rents are low.[6] (See Plate 1.2.) Owing to imprecise definition of the term 'discount house', reliable figures are not available for current turnover.

Plate 1.2 GEM STORE, PRESTON.   The interior before its takeover and modernization by the Gem organization.

MAIL ORDER SHOPPING The growth of mail order shopping has been more than double that of other retail outlets, rising from £45 million in 1950 to £226 million in 1961, and amounted to over £488 million in 1966. Between 1961 and 1966, mail order business rose from 2·5 per cent to 4 per cent of the total retail trade, and as such will provide a considerable threat in the future, especially to department stores.

REFERENCES   1 Board of Trade, *Preliminary Results of the Census of Distribution and Other Services*, 1966.
Board of Trade Journal, 23 Feb. 1968, p. 582–589.
These references also supplied other statistical data in Chapter 1.

2 Northumberland C.C. *Trends in Retail Distribution*, p. 4.
3 Northumberland C.C. op. cit., p. 6.
4 *Self-Service and Supermarket Journal.* Supermarket Association, March 1967, p. 19.
5 Index of Marketing Trends, *Supermarkets and the British Housewife*, 1966.
6 Northumberland C.C., op. cit., p. 42.
  Other Sources
  E. Beazley, 'Super-markets' *Architectural Review*, Nov. 1966.
  W. Burns, *British Shopping Centres*.
  O. Marriott, 'When the city centre boom falters', *Sunday Times*, 31 Oct. 1965, p. 29
  Self-Service and Supermarket Journal March 1964, p. 5–7. Oct. 1965. July 1966, p. 30–32. Dec. 1966,
  p. 44–45. 29 Feb. 1968, p. 31.
  N. A. H. Stacey and A. Wilson, *The Changing Pattern of Distribution*.
  Stores and Shops Journal, Feb. 1965, p. 28–31.
  R. Troop, 'The big shopping explosion' *Sunday Times*, 20 Nov. 1966.
  W. L. Waide, *Changes in Shopping Habits* T.P.I. Summer School Report 1962, p. 86–87.

2

the growth of the out-of-town centre in America and elsewhere

The shopping centre movement is only one phase of what has been called the 'retail revolution' —some elements of which have been visible for many years. Indeed, the first recognizable out-of-town centre, the Country Club Plaza, Kansas, opened in 1923.[1] In terms of 'planned' centres however, only seven centres out of a total of over 160 analysed in 1957 were opened prior to 1950, and none of these was a regional centre.[2] By 1965, well over 8,000 centres were in operation (with 10 per cent added during that year) and accounting for 35 per cent of all retail sales in the United States.[3] One of the major department stores in these centres (Sears Roebuck) now transacts £2,000 million worth of trade each year and will open 40 new stores each year for the next three years, estimating that turnover will reach £3,500 million by 1970.[4] Major centres, such as Northland, Detroit, provide over 1 million square feet of space, on a 160 acre site, with over 10,000 parking spaces.

Shopping centre types, ranging from 20,000 to 1 million square feet, are analysed in Part Two.

Of a total population increase of 18 per cent between 1950 and 1960, about 11 per cent occurred in central areas, while 49 per cent occurred in the major metropolitan suburbs.[5] Similarly, Hoyt estimates that, of the $14\frac{1}{2}$ million new houses built between 1947 and 1962, 10 million or 62 per cent were in the suburbs.[6] This migration to the fringes of metro-politan areas has occurred mainly among the middle class white residents, thus placing the most prosperous consumers further from the main shopping districts.

Between 1940 and 1961, purchasing power doubled in real terms, greatly increasing the level of retail sales. In Cincinnati, for example, the

8

market value in constant dollars rose 122 per cent between 1929 and 1960.[7]

In 1963, 76 per cent of all families in the United States owned cars, or 353 cars per 1,000 population. About 13 per cent owned two cars. Possession of a motor vehicle ('a shopping basket on wheels') has had a profound effect on shopping habits—in major centres, 20 per cent of all journeys starting from home were shopping trips.[8] Longer shopping hours encourage family excursions, often only once a week and during the evening, while the deep freeze and the larger type of American cars (17 per cent of which are 'station wagons') enable larger quantities of goods to be stored and carried. The retailer is obliged to carry larger and more varied stocks to cater for this 'one stop' shopping, and compound retailing or 'crossed lines' transforms many modern units into old fashioned general stores.

Reliance on the motor car has been accentuated by the absence, or at the expense of, public transport, which between 1953 and 1956 lost over £30 million.[9] Many 'bus routes, on radial routes direct to city centres, do not encourage intersurburban movement, and difficulties in handling large parcels rules out their use for one stop shopping. Table 2.1 indicates the predominance of private transport for out-of-town shopping in America.[10]

Table 2.1   METHODS OF TRANSPORT USED FOR SHOPPING TRIPS U.S.A.

Methods of transport used	To town centres (%)	To shopping centres (%)
In own car	27·3	82·7
Car of other family	5·5	7·3
Public transport	63·3	5·5
Walked	3·9	4·5

Since it has been estimated that there will be 100 million cars by 1980, and 160 million by 2000, there seens no logical reason why these trends should not continue.

One of the main reasons for the decline in central areas has been best expressed by Richard Nelson in *Selection of Retail Locations* who stated:

> By moving to a non-retail location about 1 mile from the centre, stores voluntarily gave up all of the business which might be generated for them by neighbours .... Other things being equal, stores would do more business in the central area. The move was made because other things were not equal. Downtown parking was inadequate and expensive for customers. The business lost in the cental area was more than made up by self-generated business and through stepping-up advertising and giving a large amount of free parking.

The shoppers' desire for wide selection and comparison of goods is countered by a dislike of inconvenience, which more often than not means traffic congestion, lack of parking space and poor public transportation. The increase in mobility made possible by the car has not increased the number of people coming into central areas.[11] Indeed, a simple formula states 'For each additional car penetrating the heart of a city, one visitor or inhabitant of that heart is lost'. In order to match facilities offered elsewhere retailers have been forced to provide more parking space—in the most extreme case, two thirds of the central area of Los Angeles is given to the motor car in one form or another. Table 2.2 indicates the relative importance given to the various factors contributing to central area decline, as revealed by a survey of members of the American National Retail Merchants Association.[12]

Table 2.2   CAUSES OF CENTRAL AREA
            DECLINE U.S.A.

Cause	Percentage
Lack of parking	81·3
Traffic conjestion	78·6
Antiquated buildings	38·2
Poor retail promotion	27·3
Slums around central area	16·4

AVAILABILITY OF SUITABLE SITES

The foregoing conditions, coupled with massive capital investment, led to the introduction of out-of-town centres. Large areas of land were available at relatively cheap prices at nodal points on the road system, particularly where major roads intersected, at the junction of radial roads and 'ring' roads. Frequently, several ring roads were constructed, and centres developed on all routes. The proliferation of centres without adequate control led to newer centres being in direct competition with the older. The continued growth and success is due to many factors, notably the delay in central area renewal, which nevertheless exercises considerable attraction, especially for selection of goods, as indicated in Table 2.3, which may be compared with Table 5.17. (See page 54).

Table 2.3   MOTIVES FOR PREFERENCE:
            TOWN CENTRES v. SHOPPING
            CENTRES U.S.A.[13]

Motive	Town centre percentage of customers	Shopping centres percentage of customers
Selection	44·2	7·5
Convenience	28·9	65·3
Parking	0·6	17·5
Enjoys experience	24·8	14·7
One stop shopping	0·5	7·6
'Sales' and bargains	3·3	1·2
Other	1·4	1·7
No definite motives	3·5	8·4

Major out-of-town centres have been built, on the American pattern, especially in Canada, but also in Australia, Germany and Sweden—the largest in Australia (located outside Sydney) provides 1½ million square feet of space. The first major German centre, at Main-Taunus (Frankfurt) is the model for five others now being planned at Hamburg, Bochum, Stuttgart, Cologne and Bonn. Development of shopping centres in Sweden has often been combined with residential districts, especially in the new suburbs of Stockholm, such as Vallingby, where a total of 100,000 people have a multistorey shopping centre within 25 minutes of the city centre by underground. Similar centres are being built outside other cities, one already being in operation at Uppsala.

2.3 DEVELOPMENT OF SHOPPING CENTRES ELSEWHERE

Plate 2.1 FROLUNDA TORG CENTRE, GOTHENBURG, SWEDEN.   This is the largest shopping centre under one roof in Europe, with over 613,000 square feet gross floor space, including 54,000 square feet of offices. It has car parking for 3,000 vehicles, and is planned to serve a catchment population of 100,000 people, 60,000 of whom are within comfortable walking distance.

REFERENCES

1 E. Kelly, *Locating Controlled Regional Shopping Centres*, p. 73.
2 Urban Land Institute, *Shopping Centres Re-studied*, p. 7–8.
3 *Self-Service and Supermarket Journal*, Jan. 1966, p. 52, 57. June 1966, p. 44.
4 *Stores and Shops Journal*, Nov. 1965, p. 27.
5 Manchester University (Dept. of Town and Country Planning), *Regional Shopping Centres, a Planning Report on North-West England*, 1964, p. 10, (hereinafter referred to as the *Haydock Report*).
6 H. Hoyt, 'The effect of the automobile on patterns of urban growth,' *Traffic Quarterly*, April 1963, p. 296.
7 W. L. Waide, 'Changing shopping habits and their impact on town planning'. *T.P.I. Journal*, Oct. 1963, p. 258.
8 Manchester University, *Haydock Report*, p. 11, quoting W. Smith.
9 National Cash Register Co. Ltd., *Shopping Centres in America and Britain*.
10 W. L. Waide, op. cit., p. 262.
11 S. C. McMillan, 'Recent trends in the decentralisation of retail trades', *Traffic Quarterly*, Jan. 1962.
12 O. Luder, 'Out-of-town shopping—solution or mistake?, *Estates Gazette*, 20 Feb. 1965, p. 651.
13 W. L. Waide, op. cit., p. 261.
    Other Sources
    J. Alevizos and A. Beckwith, 'Shopping attitudes', *Business Week*, 24 Oct. 1953.
    G. Baker and B. Funaro, *Shopping Centres—Design and Operation*, p. 16.
    V. Gruen, *The Heart of our Cities*, p. 79 and 96.
    R. L. Nelson, *The Selection of Retail Locations*, p. 39.
    J. P. Reynolds, 'Suburban shopping in America',*Town Planning Review*, April 1958, p. 43–59.
    Self-Service and Supermarket Journal, Dec. 1964, Feb. 1965.
    Stores and Shops Journal, March 1965, p. 22 and 24.

3

the growth of the out-of-town
centre in Britain

The idea of a covered, controlled environment for shopping was realized by Ebenezer Howard, who proposed a circular 'Crystal Palace'—'in wet weather one of the favourite resorts of the people'—which represents a combination of the traditional arcade with Paxton's 1851 exhibition building, and being within 600 yards of every inhabitant.[1] It is noteworthy that some of the present New Towns, especially Stevenage, are exercising an 'out-of-town function', in which precincts, first proposed by Alker Tripp in 1942, are an accepted principle.[2]

The first genuine move of out-of-town locations came in 1954, when Finnegan's, the Manchester department store, decided to move to Wilmslow, 12 miles south of the city, from where they estimated 65 per cent of their custom derived.[3] This actual development, completed in 1956, coincided with the theoretical proposal, sponsored by the Glass Age Development Committee, for the High Market scheme, containing 1 million square feet of shopping space and parking for 3,500 cars, located so as to supplement the facilities of Birmingham, Wolverhampton, West Bromwich and Walsall.[4] (See Plates 3.1 and 3.2.)

Since that date, a series of schemes have been put forward, notably the proposal to build a regional shopping centre costing £10 million at Haydock, Lancashire which was rejected by the Minister of Housing and Local Government.[5] (See Fig. 3.1.) Other centres now in operation are the Gem Supercentres (at Nottingham and Leeds), the Newtown Breda Centre (Belfast), Stillorgan (Dublin), Yate (Gloucestershire), Elephant and Castle (London) and the Hampshire Centre (Bournemouth), which also contains a Woolco store similar to those at Leicester and Thornaby on Tees. A comparative analysis of centres is given in Appendix A.

Plate 3.1 THE HIGH MARKET SCHEME. An aerial view of the Glass Age Development Committee proposal to supplement the shopping facilities of the West Midlands with a major regional centre.

Most of these schemes are 'fringe surburban', rather than true out-of-town, and key locations, such as junctions on ring roads around major cities, are also being developed rapidly. Many larger 'satellite' suburbs, such as Cowley (Oxford), Ormesby (Middlesbrough) (see Plate 3.3 and Fig. 3.2), Tolworth (Kingston), Solihull, Aston, Tivoli, Erdington, Perry Barr and Norton (Birmingham), Cross Gates (Leeds), Bootle (Liverpool) and Walkden (Manchester), are or have developed major shopping facilities in competition to the city centres.

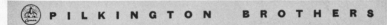

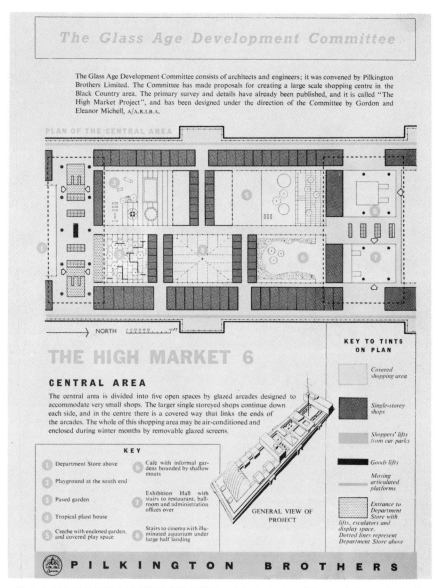

Plate 3.2 THE HIGH MARKET SCHEME.   A typical plan of the central area, indicating the comprehensive nature of the proposal.

3.2 REASONS FOR DEVELOPMENT

The reasons for the growth of out-of-town centres are largely those applying in the United States, and can be similarly analysed.

POPULATION GROWTH AND MIGRATION

The total population has grown from 50 million in 1951 to 52 million in 1961, and reliable sources estimate a total population of 70 million by 2001. This growth has been accompanied by considerable expansion in suburban areas, both from central districts and rural areas.

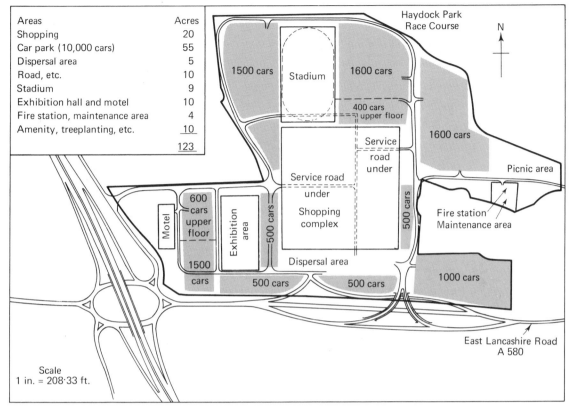

Areas	Acres
Shopping	20
Car park (10,000 cars)	55
Dispersal area	5
Road, etc.	10
Stadium	9
Exhibition hall and motel	10
Fire station, maintenance area	4
Amenity, treeplanting, etc.	10
	123

Fig. 3.1 HAYDOCK SHOPPING CENTRE.   This outline plan of the original proposal shows the suggested layout and the junction of the M.6 and the East Lancashire Roads.

The growth of real incomes is reflected in the increase in retail sales INCREASED SPEND-
between 1951 and 1961, from £5,000 millions to £8,949, or sales of ING POWER
£102 per head in 1951 to sales of £174 per head in 1961. This 71 per cent
increase in turnover was handled by about the same number of shops
and staff.[6]

The continuing increase in incomes was typically indicated in the
Family Expenditure Survey for 1965, which showed that the average
family income rose from £23 12s 0d per week in 1964 to £24 13s 0d in
1965. The average family also spent 35s per week more than in 1964,
of which 10s was on transport, 6s each on housing and food, 5s on
clothing and 2s on fuel.[7] There is little doubt that much of the 10s spent
on transport went on private cars.

In September 1966, there were 13 million registered vehicles of which CAR OWNERSHIP
9 million were private cars, representing 1 car per 5·9 people, compared AND SHOPPING
with 1 per 6·4 in 1964. Between 1954 and 1962, vehicles per road mile HABITS

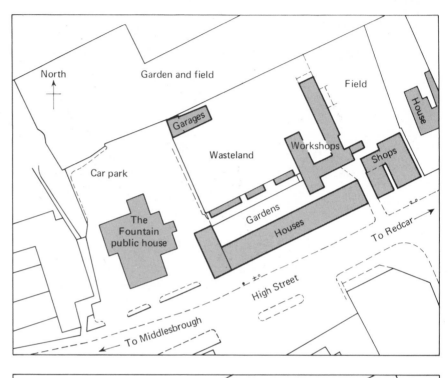

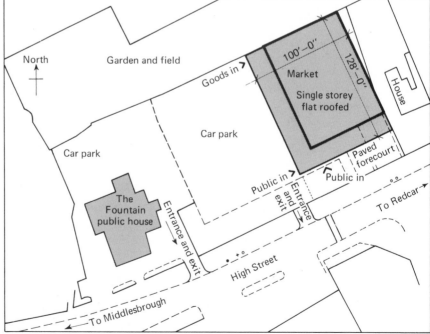

Fig. 3.2 ORMESBY CENTRE, MIDDLESBROUGH. The site plan before and after development of the project, indicating the 'backland' later used for car parking.

Plate 3.3 ORMESBY MARKET, MIDDLESBROUGH. A suburban centre of 13,000 square feet of covered shopping with an estimated 12,500 potential customers. The car park, with over 100 spaces, is amalgamated with that of an adjoining public house.

rose from 22·3 to 40·9, an 83 per cent increase, and the Ministry of Transport then estimated that a rise of 160 per cent in vehicle ownership would occur by 1980, and that saturation level should be taken as 0·4 private cars per person. The marked effect on shopping habits and travelling distances is indicated in the survey undertaken by Kent County Council, who established that 42 per cent of all weekly shopping trips were made by car,[8] and by Stone, in his analysis of Wilmslow, as set out in Table 3.1.

Table 3.1   METHODS OF TRANSPORT AND DISTANCE
            TRAVELLED TO WILMSLOW STORE[9]

| | Forms of transport used | | Distance travelled | |
	Tues.	Sat.	Tues.	Sat.
Car	74·3%	81·2%	7·0 miles	6·3 miles
Bus	14·6	9·4	3·0	3·6
Foot	7·6	5·7	0·4	0·6
Train	2·1	2·5	10·8	8·8
Other	1·4	1·2	—	—
All forms			6·4 miles	6·2 miles

The Gem Centre, Nottingham, states that 60 per cent of all customers arrive by car. Shopping habits have also been influenced by the national ownership of domestic refrigerators, which rose from 34 per cent in mid-1964 to 44 per cent in March 1966, and would reach 75 per cent by 1970 if this trend continued. In fact, ownership has already reached 70 per cent in the London area, but is only 28 per cent in Yorkshire.[10]

Plate 3.4 PICCADILLY, LONDON. The familiar scene of traffic congestion, parking restrictions, danger to pedestrians and intrusion into the environment.

Plate 3.5 HIGH STREET, INVERNESS.   At peak shopping hours, pedestrians jam narrow pavements and themselves cause further traffic hazards and congestion .

This trend has not been so marked as in the United States, but obsolete CENTRAL AREA and antiquated premises, combined with increasing traffic congestion, DECLINE are now affecting the economic success of the town centre. (See plates 3.4 and 3.5.) A recent survey indicates that 20 per cent of Edinburgh's motorists avoid their town centre because of parking difficulty, in Nottingham 19 per cent, Cardiff 17 per cent, and in Leamington Spa 16 per cent. In assessing the resultant loss of shopkeepers, it was estimated that a 1 per cent drop on shopping traffic incurred a loss of £2,600 in Edinburgh, £1,500 in Cardiff and £1,100 in Norwich.[11] An earlier survey indicates that, in London, the average speed for a 5 mile journey, including parking, is no more than 8 miles per hour, and 5 miles per hour for a 'bus.[12] It seems unlikely that future demand can be satisfied by present planning solutions. Indeed, the Leicester Traffic Plan states that only one third of the total of 64,000 private cars in the city will have central area parking space, and new methods of control, such as road pricing, are now being considered for future national policy.[13]

Proposals are in hand for a major centre at Brent Cross, in north London, **3.3 FUTURE** and for a further Woolco store at Edinburgh; future Woolco schemes **OUT-OF-TOWN** may well depend on the success of their first three centres. The Southland **CENTRES** Corporation of Dallas has announced its intention of purchasing a group of British retail outlets, prior to establishing a chain of convenience stores in this country, and further surburban developments by subsidiaries of other American companies may be expected, probably similar to those of the Safeway Group.

The advantage of out-of-town or major suburban centres may result in many more such schemes being proposed. Indeed, both planners, such as Wilfred Burns, and retailers, such as Lord Sainsbury, anticipate that a limited number could be built at suitable locations.[14] The chief obstacle to their development is the lack of such suitable sites—Gem Supercentres stated that 300 sites were inspected in 3 years, and 30 investigated closely.[15] The scarcity of sites means that each must be analysed carefully before development, and the basic methods employed in this assessment are considered in Part Two.

REFERENCES 1 E. Howard, *Garden Cities of Tomorrow*, p. 54 (1964 edition).
2 A. Tripp, *Town Planning and Road Traffic*, 1942.
3 E. M. Stone, 'Traffic generated by a Wilmslow store', *Town Planning Review*, July 1963 p. 119.
4 Pilkington Brothers Ltd., The High Market, 1956.
   W. Burns, *British Shopping Centres*, p. 104.
5 Manchester University, *Haydock Report*, Lancashire County Council: The following reasons were given for the refusal of planning permission:
   1 The proposed development would not conform with the zoning provisions of the County Development Plan, which indicates that existing uses of the land in this area are intended to remain for the most part undisturbed.
   2 The proposed development would have an adverse effect on the productive capacity of Haydock Park Farm and Dean Dam Farm, and the Ministry of Agriculture, Fisheries and Food raise objection on agricultural grounds.
   3 The trunk roads have insufficient reserve capacity to enable the vehicles likely to be attracted by the proposed development to enter and leave the site without prejudicing the safety and convenience of other road users (this reason given in accordance with a Directive issued by the Ministry of Transport).
   Northumberland C.C., *Trends in Retail Distribution*, p. 59.
   Self-Service and Supermarket Journal, Feb. 1965, p. 95.
6 W. L. Waide, 'Changing shopping habits and their impact on town planning', *T.P.I. Journal*, Oct. 1963, p. 254–264.
7 Ministry of Labour, *Family Expenditure Survey*.
8 Manchester University, *Haydock Report*, p. 295.
   Kent County Council, *The Influence of Car Ownership on Shopping Habits*, 1964.
9 E. M. Stone, *op. cit.* p. 119–145.
10 Birds Eye Foods Ltd., *What's in Store ?*, 1966.
   Self-Service and Supermarket Journal, March 1966, p. 19.
11 Automobile Association, *Parking—Who Pays ?*, p. 41.
12 R. J. Smeed, 'Traffic problems in towns', *Town Planning Review*, July 1964, p. 133–158.
13 W. K. Smigielski, *Traffice Plan for Leicester*.
   Ministry of Transport, *Better Use of Town Roads*, 1967.
14 W. Burns, *op. cit.* p. 103.
   R. N. Percival, 'Shopping centres in Britain', *T.P.I. Journal*, Oct. 1965, p. 329–333.
   Sainsbury, Lord, 'Chaos or order?' *Stores and Shops Journal*, Feb. 1965, p. 29.
   Self-Service and Supermarket Journal, 8 Feb. 1968, p. 16.
15 *Stores and Shops Journal*, Nov. 1965, p. 33.
   Other Sources
   Alfred Bird and Sons Ltd., *Mrs. Housewife and her Grocer*, 1966.
   C. D. Morley, 'The future of central retail cores', *T.C.P.A. Journal*, Sept. 1962.
   Self-Service and Supermarket Journal, Feb. 1965, p. 92–93. Dec. 1966, p. 18–19.
   Shop Review, July 1960, p. 5. Sept. 1961, p. 21.

PART TWO:

locational requirements

4

classification and regional location

There are two basic methods of classifying centres:

1 By types of goods and shops included.
2 By trade area.

In the former method, centres are divided into two types; those selling 'convenience goods', notably food items, toiletries, hardware and a limited range of service trades, and those selling 'durables', such as clothing, household appliances, furniture and other more specialist items, in addition to a small number of convenience shops. In the latter type, greater emphasis is generally placed on higher quality goods, the customer being offered a greater range of styles and prices.

The latter method, by trade area classification, is the more common system. Confusion arises from the trade area having a large number of characteristics not subject to exact definition. For example, a 'neighbourhood' centre is difficult to distinguish from a 'district' centre.[1] Nevertheless, recognizable types and classifications have emerged, those given by the Urban Land Institute, as the result of a national survey, being the most comprehensive and reliable.[2] (Variations on these basic types, quoted by different authorities, are tabulated in Appendix B.)

1 *Neighbourhood centre* This provides mostly for convenience goods and personal services, for the day to day needs of between 7,500 and 20,000 people, either within walking distance, or within 6 minutes driving time by car. The average building area is 40,000 square feet, planned around a supermarket as the main occupant, on a site of between 4 and 10 acres, with about 360 car spaces. The variation in the number of units provided is given in Table 4.1.

Table 4.1   NUMBER OF UNITS:
            NEIGHBOURHOOD CENTRES[3]

Number of units	Percentage
Less than 10	18·6
10–15	30·5
16–20	28·8
Greater than 20	20·3
Not reported	1·8
	100·0

2 *Community centre* In addition to convenience goods and services, the community centre also provides for the sale of some clothing and appliances, and offers variety in convenience items. (See Fig. 4.1.) It serves 20,000–100,000 people, with an average building area of 150,000 square feet on sites varying from 10 to 30 acres, with about 1,300 car spaces. The major tenant is a variety store, such as Woolworths, or a Junior Department Store, in addition to a supermarket. The variations in the number of units provided is as set out in Table 4.2.

Table 4.2   NUMBER OF UNITS:
            COMMUNITY CENTRES[4]

Number of units	Percentage
Less than 20	16·6
20–30	33·3
31–40	18·4
Greater than 40	10·0
Not reported	21·7
	100·0

3 *Regional centre* This class of centre provides all forms of general merchandise, apparel and furniture, and almost all those retail facilities available in the town centre. A population of at least 100,000 to 250,000 is required to support such a centre, which varies in building area from 400,000 to well over 1 million square feet (though the average is just over 400,000 square feet). The minimum site area is about 40 acres, with an average of 4,000 car spaces. Approximately 45 per cent of the gross rentable area in regional centres is occupied by the department store(s), and the variation in the number of units provided is as tabulated in Table 4.3.

Table 4.3   NUMBER OF UNITS:
            REGIONAL CENTRES[5]

Number of units	Percentage
Less than 40	27·2
40–60	40·8
61–80	13·6
Greater than 80	6·9
Not reported	11·5
	100·0

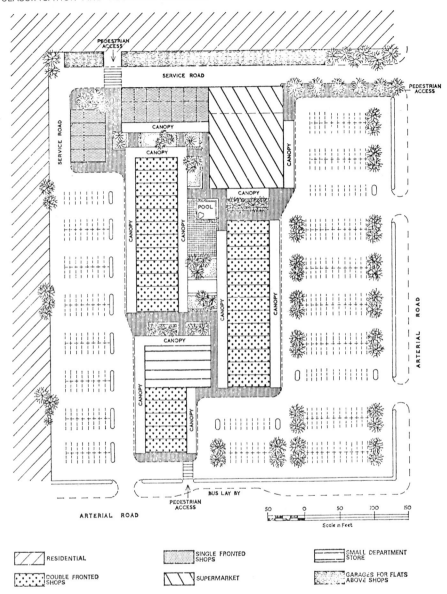

RESIDENTIAL

DOUBLE FRONTED SHOPS

SINGLE FRONTED SHOPS

SUPERMARKET

SMALL DEPARTMENT STORE

GARAGES FOR FLATS ABOVE SHOPS

Fig. 4.1 COMMUNITY CENTRE. A theoretical plan for a centre to serve up to 15,000 people, with a junior department store, a supermarket and 41 shops.

A further variation of this classification is adopted by Hoyt, and is dependent on the type of major tenant as follows:

Class 1: Regional Centre with 1/2 Department Stores.
Class 2: Centre with Junior Department Store.
Class 3: Centre with Variety Store.
Class 4: Centre with Supermarket.[6]

All the above definitions apply to 'conventional' out-of-town centres, for the most part having unenclosed pedestrian areas. More recently, the 'supercentre' has been developed, comprising one large building shell of about 100,000 square feet in area, containing all the separate departments on one level and designed to serve between 75,000 and 100,000 people.[7]

4.2 CLASSIFICATION OF CENTRES IN BRITAIN

The pattern of centres in America evolved from the particular conditions and forces prevailing, and the misuse of the foregoing American classifications is already apparent in this country. On the definitions previously given, no regional centres have yet been built—the proposal to provide 1 million square feet of retail space at Haydock was refused after an appeal and that for Brent Cross (originally for 750,000 square feet) is still at the planning stage.

Comparing the centres planned or operating in this country with similar centres in America, the overall site areas are considerably smaller, reflecting the higher cost of land and the smaller amount of space devoted to car parking. Of the centres tabulated in Appendix A, only Yate, Nottingham, Oadby and Bournemouth provide more car spaces per 1,000 square feet of retail area than the comparable average American example, and those centres in Britain which experience large proportions of pedestrian trade (Elephant and Castle and Cross Gates) have a correspondingly lower than average allocation of parking space.

No definite pattern has yet emerged in Britain, except the supercentres developed by Gem and Woolco, both of whom provide over 80,000 square feet gross building area, and require about 1,000 car spaces. Apart from these projects, only the Elephant and Castle and Cross Gates offer total air conditioned enclosure, all other schemes being variations of the more conventional precinct or mall layout, normally associated with central area redevelopment.

It will be shown in Chapter 11 that the key tenants, such as department stores, occupy proportionally less of the total rentable area than in American centres. The major proportion of space in British centres is devoted to independent retailers in small units, which correspond in size and type to those found in the town centre. These traders offer a complete range of services, whereas in America the tenants of smaller units offer specialist services only, such as high class jewellers or photographic goods.

In view of the small number of centres in operation in Britain, and the absence of accurate and comparable population figures, classification by trade areas is not yet possible, but estimated trade area populations for selected centres are listed in Appendix A.

The term 'retail location' in its geographical sense indicates the general **4.3 LOCATION IN** area in which to select a shopping centre site. A distinction is necessary **THE REGIONAL** between unplanned suburban locations and the normal out-of-town **CONTEXT** centre on the perimeter of the built up area, and also between these locations and the regional centre linked by a motorway and set in open countryside.

Recent applications for major surburban schemes have been scattered and spasmodic, and considered in relation to local circumstances. Local authorities have granted permission without evidence of the economic viability of the project, its repercussions on the regional retailing patterns, and without prior consultation with neighbouring authorities. The present administrative procedure does not require the submission of proposals to other interested parties, either local authorities or private concerns, who may, however, be represented at any appeal which may follow. Any proposal may require the approval of the Ministry of Transport, in the case of trunk roads or motorways, and may also be submitted to the regional planning board. The latter may give their recommendations, but have no authority to veto any such application.

With the proposals for the much larger regional centres at Haydock, Brent Cross and others at the planning stage, the implications for regional planning are further emphasized, raising the possibility of a major new form of land development. As the Haydock Report pointed out, an out-of-town centre might attract many other regional facilities which demand a central location and good vehicular access, or at least be close to the preferred site for such facilities.[8]

The disadvantages of such centres are:

1 They divert commercial prosperity away from the town centre.
2 They divert people coming into the town for other functions.
3 With this 'draw', other functions also tend to fragment.

The Haydock Report estimated that, should the centre be built, Liverpool, Manchester and Bolton would lose about 12 per cent of their actual retail trade in 1971, and that Warrington would lose 46 per cent, Wigan 41 per cent and St. Helens 34 per cent.[9] It was on these grounds, rather than for traffic considerations, that the application was refused. Nevertheless, it should be recognized that many existing towns are in fact decreasing in importance, while others may remain constant over a number of years. The out-of-town centre might be advantageous if it stimulated better facilities generally, and could be used to stimulate growth zones if it were sited on a motorway or major road as part of a regional plan. In addition the character of historic towns, like Cambridge, York, Norwich or Chester, could be retained without the excessive redevelopment necessary to meet commercial demands, if out-of-town centres were strategically located close to these cities. These centres would be complementary to the existing facilities, not in competition.[10] The local authority's share in the profits of such centres, in the form of ground rents, or rates, could contribute towards the cost of central area redevelopment or the less remunerative civic functions.[11] This might mean that the local authorities should themselves sponsor such developments, so designed that they do not overlap in their spheres of influence, both in terms of position and function. This also raises the possibility of granting permission for a limited period, long enough to allow the developer a reasonable profit and also for the necessary central area redevelopment to be carried out. The recent restrictions on building contracts over £100,000 have caused many sites to be investigated in the Development Areas, notably in the north east, but this does not preclude potential developers from submitting applications throughout the country in anticipation of a relaxation of these limitations.

All these considerations emphasize the importance of a regional plan, and the futility of trying to decide developments of regional importance without reference to the wider context. The Haydock Report lists the following five major conditions to which all future applications of regional importance should be subject:[12]

1 The long term strategy for regional development must first be decided; that is, the broad redistribution of population and employment that is desirable. This strategy must include decisions on the location of regional shopping facilities.
2 Cost-benefit analyses should be undertaken to compare the advantages of the out-of-town centre with those of converting a nearby existing centre into a regional shopping centre, or of expanding an existing regional centre itself.
3 The function of nearby shopping centres likely to be affected by the out-of-town centre should be decided, and the scale of redevelopment in these centres established so as to avoid wasteful use of resources.
4 A detailed plan (similar to a town map or a New Town master plan) should be prepared showing the shopping centre site; the land to be used for regional offices and other sources of employment; the supporting residential and ancillary uses; the communications needed to serve all proposed activities in the area, including the centre; and the supporting services and utilities.
5 The responsibility for implementing the plan referred to in (4) must be decided at the same time as permission is given for the development for the out-of-town centre.

REFERENCES 1 R. Nelson, *Selection of Retail Locations*, p. 175–176 and 179.
2 Urban Land Institute, *Shopping Centres Re-studied*, Vol. 1, p. 9–10.
3 Urban Land Institute, op. cit., Vol. 2, p. 11.

4 Urban Land Institute, op. cit., Vol. 2, p. 11.
5 Urban Land Institute, op. cit., Vol. 1, p. 9 and Vol. 2, p. 11.
6 H. Hoyt, *Design for Modern Merchandising*, p. 152.
7 *Stores and Shops Journal*, March 1965, p. 22–24.
8 Manchester University, *Haydock Report*, p. 4.
9 Manchester University, op. cit., p. 38.
10 *Architects Journal*, Planning Forum, 30 Dec. 1964, p. 1533.
    W. L. Waide, 'Changes in shopping habits', *T.P.I. Summer School Report*, June 1962, p. 87.
11 J. V. Butterfill, 'Out-of-town shopping—solution or mistake?' *Estates Gazette*, 13 March 1965, p. 943.
12 Manchester University, op. cit., p. 54–55.

5
factors affecting locational analysis

5.1 GENERAL A retail location is any fixed place for shopping purposes; it is specific and therefore unique. Nelson defines the two main types of location as follows:

1 *Generative* A generative location is one to which the consumer is directly attracted from his home, as the principal purpose of the trip. Such a location is expressly selected to be easily accessible to the greatest proportion of persons who leave home for shopping.

2 *Suscipient* A suscipient location is one to which the consumer is impulsively or coincidentally attracted while out on another primary purpose, and which receives rather than generates business.[1]

Most out-of-town centres are generative, though occasionally suscipient trade may be obtained in large centres offering other attractions, such as entertainment or medical facilities. In preparing an economic appraisal of a potential location, it is necessary for a conceptual image of the completed centre to be formulated, either on an actual or on an unknown site, in order to assess the various factors comprising the analysis. This image should include consideration of likely tenants, and especially of major tenants (many of whom may enter agreements to manage stores in the completed centre before the economic analysis is commenced).

Once a shopping centre site has been selected, it is possible to estimate the total trade that may be expected, as well as the gross floor space necessary to generate such trade. In a detailed analysis, the floor space can be subdivided between the various trades, both convenience and durables, and the unit rentals calculated from the overall development costs and the return required.

In Britain, owing to competition for land, feasible sites are often purchased before any economic analysis is undertaken. Lack of expertise, stemming from inexperience, often results in the purchase of poor sites, and the selection of a site from alternatives is rarely possible. In this case, the analysis will indicate whether the site is viable, and if the amount of building and land area required to produce a satisfactory return can be accommodated on that site.

Whether the site is already purchased or is still under investigation, the economic analysis involves the consideration of the following factors, many of which are subject to complex interdependence. The principles of site economics, on which the ultimate feasibility of any site depends, are considered in Part Three.

The trade or catchment area is defined as the area of influence from which **5.2 THE TRADE** a shopping centre could expect to derive 80–90 per cent of its total **AREA** sales volume, this area often being subdivided into primary, secondary and occasionally tertiary zones, depending on the method of analysis.[2] Although the trade area is in fact determined by the other factors considered in this chapter, it is necessary to evolve in advance a tentative trading area, on which the analysis of these factors is based —this conceptual image should not entail the study of areas so remote that research techniques will be unable to assess them, but it is preferable to consider a trade area that is slightly too large, and subsequently to reduce it if necessary.[3]

The basic techniques used to delineate trade areas are: TRADE AREA
                                                                                  TECHNIQUES

1 Analysis of shopping habits, by reference to public transport demand, in centres of comparable status and conditions.
2 Analysis of retail expenditure in comparable locations.
3 From theoretical formula.

The last, known as gravity models, was first used by W. J. Reilly in 1929, the method being termed 'The Law of Retail Gravitation'.[4] This 'Law' states that two towns will attract trade from any intermediate point in direct proportion to the population of the respective towns, and in inverse proportion to the square of the distance that the intermediate point is from either town, as expressed in the formula:

$$\text{The number of miles from larger centre A to the outer limits of trade area (computed on major roads)} = \frac{\text{Mileage on road to adjacent smaller centre B}}{1 + \sqrt{\left(\dfrac{\text{Population centre B}}{\text{Population centre A}}\right)}}$$

More recently, the population factors have been replaced by the floor space of two major stores in each centre or by sales of durable goods in centres of equal grade offering similar facilities, the mileage factor being

expressed in terms of driving time. While this is an easy method of calculating the trade area, it was originally intended for 'rural' rather than 'urban'
centres, and is limited, since trade accruing from pedestrian shoppers, or
the quality/quantity/value factor, are not considered.[5]

In Britain, trade areas have generally been delineated by an analysis of the
Local Accessibility Map, last published in 1955 by the Ordnance Survey.
This map, by correlating shoppers' travel patterns and public transport
usage, establishes hierarchies of centres and their hinterlands, the latter
being based on the demands for 'bus services between major and lesser
centres.

DEVELOPMENT OF THE PRINCIPLES OF HIERARCHY
Both Reilly's model and the Local Accessibility Map indicate a relatively
fixed perimeter to the trade area. In reality, however, the trade area varies
considerably depending on the type of retail outlet and on the goods
offered, and this is best indicated by a series of concentric rings of irregular
outline. The profile of these varying zones will depend on the degree of
attraction exerted by the shopping centre, and on the relative accessibility
and distance between neighbouring centres. Consequently, the trade
area of the major unit, such as one department store, will enclose entirely
those of smaller units requiring less patronage for their support, such as
supermarkets. Similarly, the trade area of the department store will itself
be contained within that of a group of larger comparable outlets which
demand a larger regional hinterland. Thus, the King's Lynn Study established five zones of attraction based on different categories of shops: this
method, though in itself a measure of accessibility, did not consider
driving times.[6]

THE DRIVING-TIME TECHNIQUE
In America, the dependence of the genuine out-of-town centre on the
motorized shopper has led to the definition of trade area boundaries
solely in terms of driving time, in preference to calculations concerning
graded centres. The early use of the 'concentric ring' technique has now
been replaced by the isochron or isopleth method, with 'contour' lines
linking places of equal driving time from the subject location.[7]

GRADING OF CENTRES
Using the driving time technique, and modifying Reilly's original formula,
the Haydock Report was able to establish four recognizable grades of
centre. The Report considered that average sales of durable goods were
a more reliable measure of scale and attraction of a centre than population
and the formula, expressed in terms of driving time, was revised as
follows:[8]

$$D1 \rightarrow IIA = \frac{t}{1 + \sqrt{\dfrac{SIIA}{SI}}} = x \text{ minutes}$$

where $D1 \rightarrow IIA$ is the position of hinterland boundary moving from a grade I centre.

t is the distance in minutes between centres.

$SIIA$ is mean durable sales in grade II centres.

$S1$ is mean durable sales in grade I centres.

Application of this technique to the north west Region established the following characteristics in each grade:

Grade I Centre. This provides the complete range of shopping services, including the most specialized services, offering a choice in any particular type of goods. The hinterland population is about 2 to 3 million; annual sales are about £50 million, of which over 90 per cent is durable goods sales.

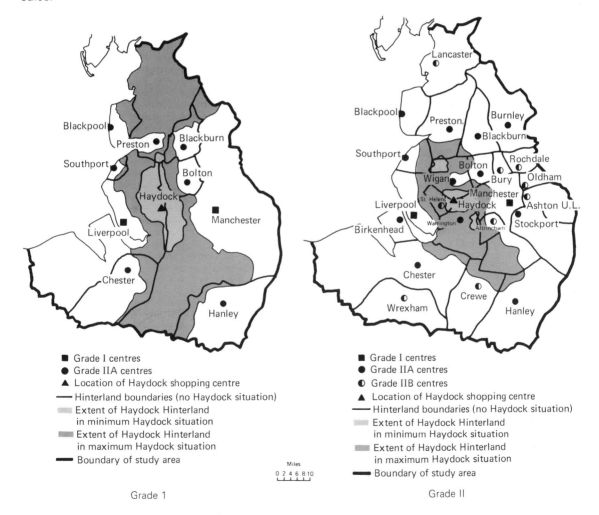

■ Grade I centres
● Grade IIA centres
▲ Location of Haydock shopping centre
— Hinterland boundaries (no Haydock situation)
▨ Extent of Haydock Hinterland in minimum Haydock situation
▨ Extent of Haydock Hinterland in maximum Haydock situation
▬ Boundary of study area

Miles
0 2 4 6 8 10

Grade 1

■ Grade I centres
● Grade IIA centres
◑ Grade IIB centres
▲ Location of Haydock shopping centre
— Hinterland boundaries (no Haydock situation)
▨ Extent of Haydock Hinterland in minimum Haydock situation
▨ Extent of Haydock Hinterland in maximum Haydock situation
▬ Boundary of study area

Grade II

Fig. 5.1 HAYDOCK SHOPPING CENTRE with the Grade I and Grade II hinterlands in 1971, indicating the extent of the catchment areas of the maximum and minimum range of facilities at Haydock.

Grade II *Centre.* This provides nearly the full range of shopping services, but is unlikely to offer a choice of the more specialized shops, including department stores. Two levels were recognized:

Grade IIA *Centre.* This has a hinterland population of between 240,000 and 350,000 people, with sales of £10 million to £17 million, or £8 million to £10 million without Class 1 trade.

Grade IIB *Centre.* This has a hinterland population of between 100,000 and 175,000, with Class 2 trade of £5 million to £8 million, of which 65–75 per cent is durables.

Grade III *Centre.* This has between 30,000 and 100,000 people in its hinterland, with sales of about £2$\frac{1}{2}$ million.[9] Further factors concerning accessibility and competitive facilities are considered later in this chapter.

SUBDIVISION OF TRADE AREA Once the tentative trade area has been established, it must be subdivided for population counts and economic analysis, generally by one of the following methods:

1 *By street blocks* This is normally adopted for central area stores, and possibly suburban locations, but is likely to involve excessive research and detail for most out-of-town centres.

2 *Octant-segments* The trade area is subdivided into quadrants by north–south and east–west lines, and into octants by diagonals, and a series of concentric rings drawn around the subject location, at radii varying from $\frac{1}{2}$ to 20 miles, and possibly 40 miles. The advantages of this method are the creation of the smallest analysis areas closest to the subject location, making for greater accuracy among the majority of potential customers. The errors likely to occur in larger areas further from the centre are less vital, since possibly only 1 per cent of potential sales may come from beyond the 20 mile zone. The standardization of this method for several projects results in improved efficiency in data gathering, and in the emergence of recognizable trade patterns. The main disadvantage is that the segments are arbitrary and not homogeneous, combining several characteristics, possibly both urban and rural.[10] The division of segments without regard to administrative boundaries necessitates the apportioning of statistical data collected by the administrative authority.

3 *Local Authority Districts* While the sole use of administrative boundaries may be convenient in regional analyses, the areas so defined are arbitrary and not homogeneous in many cases, the zones closest to the subject location possibly being as large as those at the extremities of the trade area. Nevertheless, the correlation of statistical material is considerably facilitated by the use of such subdivision.

4 *Census Districts* Owing to the availability of comparable and relatively accurate data from the Census, most economic surveys on this country have subdivided the trade area in accordance with Census districts. The size of the trade area will determine the scale of sub-division employed. Urban areas can be assessed as wards or polling districts, rural areas as parishes. This technique has the advantage of flexibility, in that smaller survey districts may be used closest to the subject location, with several areas being combined at the extremities of the trade area. Where Local Authority or Census districts are employed, the tentative perimeter of the trade area, generally assessed in terms of driving time, should be adapted to comply with the boundaries of those adjacent districts.

Within the trade area, the strongest influence will be exerted closest ZONING to the site, and account should be taken of this diminution of influence by further subdivision into 'radial' zones, previously referred to as primary, secondary and tertiary, at varying distances from the subject location. This system of zoning represents the application of hierarchical principles to various types of shops and goods. For example, it is unrealistic to assign to a supermarket the same trade area as a department store. In these smaller trade areas, such zoning provisions are unnecessary unless wide divergencies exist in population, expenditure or accessibility.

In larger trade areas, zones are delineated according to the extent and nature of facilities planned for the new centre, and various percentage ratings assessed for different types of goods in each zone. Hoyt recommends that three zones should be established.[11]

Zone 1 (Primary) This is the area immediately surrounding the centre, the latter containing the convenience goods shops nearest to the population in that area. Hoyt suggests that over 50 per cent of all food expenditure in this zone will go to the new centre, while Larry Smith recommends a weighting of 100 per cent be assigned for all types of business.[12]

Zone 2 (Secondary) This area would already possess convenience goods stores, such as food, chemist and service shops, nearer to the residents than those at the new centre, but lacks department and clothing stores of equal merit to those in the centre. For this reason, total food expenditure of the population at the new centre is not likely to exceed 10–15 per cent.

Zone 3 (Tertiary) This area is a 'fringe' zone, the degree of attraction being dependent on the existing facilities in that zone and on the quality of services to be provided at the new centre. Any food sales to this zone will be to shoppers attracted to the centre by shoppers' goods items; sales of the latter may be equal to those in zones 1 and 2.

The establishment of these zones, together with the discounts attached to them, can only be assessed on the basis of local circumstances, the actual delineation being based on an analysis of incomes, accessibility and competitive facilites, as well as the boundaries of areas suitable for data collection.

5.3 POPULATION AND EMPLOYMENT

Population within the trade area should be considered as that living in private households, since the population count is used in conjunction with the calculation of expenditure on retail goods taken from the Family Expenditure Survey, from which expenditure by institutions such as schools, hotels and military establishments are omitted, since many of them purchase their goods through wholesale outlets. All population figures should be calculated for the two previous census dates, observing and allowing for changes in Census district boundaries, as listed in the county reports. Where hinterland boundaries cut across Census areas the population should be apportioned according to its detailed distribution in that area.[13]

ANALYSIS OF POPULATION FIGURES

The gross figure for each area must also be subdivided as follows, for each of two decennial Census returns:

1 Number of private households.
2 Age/sex ratios, either in total numbers or per thousand population, with the classification of all persons below school leaving age or over 60 or 65 years of age.
3 The number of persons per household.

In America, it is customary to enumerate all households within about 3 miles of a major shopping centre, but recent British practice has generally limited the area of detailed analysis to approximately 1 mile, depending on the nature and extent of potential competition.

CHANGES IN POPULATION

These occur through natural increase or decrease (the ratio of live births to deaths), or through migration. Apart from the Census, latest figures are available from the Mid-Year Estimates (each June) and further information may be obtained from local Register Offices, or from the District Medical Officers' reports, collected by the County Medical Officers of Health.

FORECASTING POPULATION

The analysis of shopping at a target date requires the provision of population estimates at a Local Authority level of detail, in order that a reasonably accurate picture of shopping hinterlands can be established. There are two main methods of estimating population:

1 *By projection* This system used by the Registrar-General's Office, involves the examination of the existing age/sex structure and

expected natural change, with past trends projected to the target date. This method does not take into account increase or decrease due to migration movements, which are considered as static in this case.

2 *By forecast* Apart from natural change and the age/sex structure, migration trends both past and future are analysed. The extent to which migration is 'planned' or voluntary will depend on national and local policy and circumstances, notably such factors as slum clearance and redevelopment, industrial redundancy or under-occupation.

Certain basic assumptions may apply to both methods of forecasting future population, such as:

ASSUMPTIONS IN FORECASTING

1 Economic and social factors will remain the same: for example, that the birth rate trends will not be altered radically by birth control; that opportunities for full time further education and earlier retirement owing to automation will be continued.

2 National policy on employment and housing. Forecasting must, in the light of other evidence, assume a continuation of present trends and levels of government intervention in the location of employment (considered below), in the rates of subsidy in Development Areas, or in action taken under the New Towns and Town Development Acts.[14]

Detailed information on local factors is obtained from different departments of local authorities, and forecasts derived from Census material should be amended in the light of the following factors:

LOCAL FACTORS AFFECTING POPULATION FORECASTS

1 *Housing sites* The number of sites scheduled for redevelopment and slum clearance; the number of conversions and infilling sites, and new sites for residential use in the Development Plan. The latter should be tabulated in terms of area, average density, accessibility to and distance from the subject location.[15]

2 *Education* Census figures and projections can be checked against local education authority estimates of the required number of school places, and proposed further education facilities. The size and grading of educational establishments will affect the numbers of pupils staying on after normal school leaving age, and also those able to proceed to further education within the area.

3 *Other land uses* Analysis should be made of other land uses in the trade area, and Local Authority provision for future suburban retail facilities in particular. For 'genuine' out-of-town centres in Britain, this will also involve an examination of agricultural and Green Belt policies.

The analysis of employment within the region of trade area links population figures with income and expenditure, since the future spending power available to a new shopping centre will be related to these factors. The measure of employment is the activity rate, which is the number of workers in a population, or in a specific age group, divided by the total population, expressed as a percentage. The demographic factors considered above, notably higher birth rates, full time further education and earlier retirement, will cause a fall in activity rates. However, if the economic prosperity of any area was to rise more rapidly than previously, thereby reducing migration, a rise in activity rates would occur.[16] A higher activity rate indicates a greater potential income capacity for any area, in that a greater percentage of the population is wage earning.

STRUCTURE OF EMPLOYMENT The existing structure of employment should be examined on the basis of the Standard Industrial Classification, for each of the 24 listed categories.

FORECASTING EMPLOYMENT As a measure of future potential earnings in the trade area, each industry should be examined separately, on the basis of changes in the national or regional levels of employment, and the forecasts made by the government for national growth rates. The Haydock Report used three different situations as the basis for forecasting future employment:

Projection 1 The National Economic Council's forecast of a 4 per cent annual growth in the gross domestic product, which could be achieved by an annual regional increase in employment of 0·8 per cent.

Projection 2 Since the national growth rate between 1957 and 1962 was only 2·7 per cent, the annual regional increase was based at 0·45 per cent.

Projection 3 Since the actual regional growth rate between 1957 and 1962 was 0·2 per cent per annum, this percentage was used for the third projection.

These three projections of employment were then used to estimate the population that the various levels of employment will support at the activity rate for the region (47·5 per cent in the case of Haydock). These populations were then subtracted from the projection of change by natural increase, the difference being the migration from that region. The subtraction of the natural increase from the projection would, of course, give the immigration into a region.[17]

LOCAL FACTORS AFFECTING FORECASTS For major regional shopping centres with a large catchment area, a wide range of local factors will affect the existing employment structure, whether diversified, as in conurbations, or highly specialized, as in areas dependent on one major industry, such as motor vehicles.

1 *Unemployment* Account should taken of local unemployment. The total of unemployed at the target date, assessed from projections based on current trends, should be deducted from the estimated total employment at that date. The analysis of current trends should consider the present nature of the local unemployment, whether it is 'hard core' or seasonal, and if further rises can be anticipated, as in the case of pit closures, or the iron and steel or textile industries.

2 *Character of employment* Account must be taken of the incidence of shift work, including the hours worked, since these may affect local shopping hours. Similarly, the extent of part time and casual labour should be assessed, especially for female workers who are earning, but who may be obliged to shop at unusual hours or close to their place of work.

3 *Journeys to work* Total journeys to work and movements between Local Authority areas should be tabulated from census and survey material. Total flows generated by major employers should be measured in terms of the number of employees using private cars and public transport, as well as the peak flows caused during rush hours.

4 *Future location of industry* Major new industries under construction and those for which planning permission has already been granted should be assessed in terms of type, location and number and type of workers. Consideration should be given to government or regional policies for planned industrial development, the extent of subsidies for the relocation of industries in Development Areas, and the effect of government controls on all new contracts over £100,000 and the location of offices, under the Control of Offices and Industrial Development Act 1962.

SOURCES OF INFORMATION

The Census of Population 1961 (Industrial Tables) gives employment by local authorities. This means that for certain local authorities, mainly in rural districts, employment has to be apportioned on the basis of local knowledge. The Ministry of Labour Gazette (March issues) gives regional analyses of the age/sex structure of employment and interregional migration, based on a 1 per cent sample of workers. Employment Exchange Returns of the Ministry of Labour exclude about 5 per cent of total employment, namely those whose National Insurance cards are exchanged in London rather than at the local exchange. In the case of Haydock, these 'absent' returns are concentrated in the agricultural and service trades, and a correction has to be made for this deficiency. Since changes occurred in 1958 in the Standard Industrial Classification, the 1951 figures have to be corrected for comparison with the latest available figures and, since 1959, the *Annual Abstract of Statistics* has given employment figures for both classifications for easier comparison. The correcting factors for these classifications, and for the employment exchange deficiences are listed in Table 5.1, as given in the Haydock Report.[18]

Table 5.1   CORRECTION FOR EMPLOYMENT DATA

Standard industrial classification 1962	Change in S.I.C. (applies to 1951 data)	Employment exchange deficiency (applies to 1962 data)
I Agriculture	1·00	1·31
II Mining	1·00	1·00
III Food, drink and tobacco	0·87	1·00
IV Chemicals	0·96	1·00
V Metal manufacture	1·04	1·00
VI Engineering and electrical	0·96	1·00
VII Shipbuilding and marine engineering	1·00	1·00
VIII Vehicles	0·70	1·00
IX Other metal goods	1·00	1·00
X Textiles	1·00	1·00
XI Leather goods	1·00	1·00
XII Clothing	0·88	1·00
XIII Bricks, etc.	1·00	1·00
XIV Timber and wood products	0·97	1·00
XV Paper and printing	0·98	1·00
XVI Other manufactures	0·97	1·00
XVII–XXIV Services	1·05	1·12

5.4 INCOMES, EXPENDITURE AND RETAIL FLOOR SPACE Most of the important data required for the measurement of incomes, retail distribution and turnover is obtainable from two major sources, namely the Department of Employment and Productivity's Family Expenditure Survey, and the Board of Trade's Census of Distribution. The Department of Employment and Productivity Survey analyses the pattern of family expenditure of individuals (earnings, status, distribution of earnings and the age/sex ratios in regions), information on households (character, income and type of dwelling) and gives an income and expenditure analysis by households for 1960–62, 1961–63, 1962–64, etc.

To correlate both surveys, elements in the Family Expenditure Survey should be adapted and combined to approximate the categories in the Census of Distribution, to allow for the division of the retail trade into convenience and durable goods—the former includes foods, alcoholic drinks and tobacco, the latter includes clothing, footwear, household and other goods.

INCOME In its detailed analysis of incomes and other benefits listed in the Family Expenditure Survey, the Haydock Report states that the range of family incomes is wider than that of the corresponding per capita incomes, suggesting that the number of income earners in a family is a more significant determinant of family income than is the actual level of earnings of the individual earner. Similarly, the differential incidence of taxation, insurance and personal savings ensures an even smaller variation in per capita expenditure than in per capita income. Average figures taken from a small range of figures will be more reliable than from a wide range; hence per capita values of income and expenditure are the main measures used.[19]

Unless the appropriate figures for any region are used directly from the Family Expenditure Survey, sample surveys should be undertaken in each subdivision of the trade area, to establish income, occupation of the head of the household and the number of wage earners. These incomes should be tabulated according to the income groups listed in the Survey and by occupation, i.e. professional, clerical, manual or retired, so that the total expenditure by the number of persons in each group and in each sub-division may be calculated. These occupational classes should be classified according to the socio-economic groupings as set out in the Census of Distribution.

The total retail expenditure, together with other calculations should be analysed for the two previous Census returns:

PRESENT RETAIL EXPENDITURE

1 Total retail expenditure per annum on all goods (retail and service trades) for the trade area, and for each subdivision. This is calculated by multiplying the number of persons of similar status and income groups by the average retail expenditure of persons in that group, as given in the appropriate regional column of the Survey.

2 Total retail expenditure per annum on each good, and for each good in each subdivision in the trade area. These can be calculated by multiplying the number of persons of similar status and income groups by the average retail expenditure of persons in that group on each separate good.

3 Sales per head of population, in terms of total expenditure per year, and for each good in each subdivision, including the service trades. These can be calculated by dividing the results of (1) and (2) by the estimated trade area population. The resultant sales per head can be

Table 5.2   PROPORTIONAL CHANGES IN SALES PER HEAD 1951–1961[20]

	1951		1961		1951–61	Percentage total sales	
	Sales (£m)	Sales per head (£)	Sales (£m)	Sales per head (£)	Increase in sales per head (%)	1951	1961
Total all sales	5,057	103·26	9072	177·00	71·41	100·00	100·00
Total retail	5,000	102·09	8949	174·60	70·04	98·87	98·64
All food	2,220	45·36	4155	81·00	78·57	43·90	45·80
Confectionery	503	10·26	801	15·62	52·24	9·95	8·83
Clothing	930	18·98	1350	26·30	38·57	18·39	14·88
Household goods	537	10·96	1040	20·02	82·66	10·62	11·46
General stores	374	7·63	681	13·29	74·05	7·40	7·51
Other non-foods	436	8·90	922	17·99	102·13	8·61	10·16
Boot/shoe repairs	19	0·39	25	0·49	25·64	0·38	0·28
Hairdressers	38	0·78	98	1·91	144·87	0·74	0·83

checked against the national or regional sales per head as can the percentage change 1951–1961 as given in Table 5.2.

It must be recognized that various assessors have interpreted the Census of Distribution results on a different basis. Bliss, for example, in her analysis of regional variations in expenditure indicates an increase in £10 per head per person for food sales when compared with Table 5.2.

Table 5.3   REGIONAL VARIATIONS IN SALES PER HEAD 1961–1962[21]

	London, S.E.	North Midlands Midlands, Eastern	North, East and West Ridings	South, S.W.	Wales	Scotland	Averages
Food	100·4	91·1	89·8	90·9	89·2	85·6	91·0
Alcoholic drinks	11·3	11·6	11·7	11·0	9·5	10·1	10·8
Tobacco	19·9	17·2	18·5	15·3	17·4	20·5	18·1
Clothing and footwear	33·6	29·1	27·1	25·6	27·3	29·7	28·8
Household goods	26·7	20·9	20·4	18·8	17·7	15·6	20·0
Other non-foods	25·5	24·2	20·3	25·9	19·1	18·0	22·1
Total	217·4	194·1	187·8	187·5	180·2	179·5	199·8

The Haydock Report, using the 1961 Census of Distribution categories, the 1962 Family Expenditure Survey and later corrections, lists per capita expenditure as in Table 5.4.[22] For comparison, the correction factors used in the Report have been applied to the results of Table 5.3, from which it can be observed that the difference in results falls from £4·2 to £3·5 after correction and both figures relate closely to that given by Waide in Table 5.2.

Table 5.4   COMPARATIVE ANALYSIS OF SALES PER HEAD 1962

	1962 Expenditure Haydock	Bliss	Correction factor	1962 Corrected expenditure Haydock	Bliss
(a)	(b)	(c)		(d)	(e)
Food	92·9	91·0	−7·5	85·4	83·5
Alcoholic drink	11·5	10·8		2·8	2·8
Tobacco	18·5	18·1	−0·1	18·4	18·0
Convenience goods	122·9	119·9		106·6	104·3
Clothing and footwear	28·9	28·8			
Durable household goods	20·3	20·0	+1·2	73·3	72·1
Other goods	22·9	22·1			
Durable goods	72·1	70·9		73·3	72·1
Total expenditure	195·0	190·8		179·9	176·4

In Table 5.4, column (a) gives the Census of Distribution categories; column (b) is derived from the Family Expenditure Survey; column (c) is transferred from Table 5.3; columns (d) and (e) show the results of the application of the following corrections for differences in the classifications between the two sources, derived from the Board of Trade Journals, 8th February and 4th October, 1963, as follows: some food is sold in department and variety stores, classified as durable goods, amounting to £0·5 in both cases; food sold in fish and chips shops and restaurants, equal to £6·5, is not included in the Census; this Census only includes alcoholic drink bought in off licenses, equal to £2·8, and in department stores, equal to £0·1; some tobacco, equal to £0·1 is also sold in department stores.[23]

Apart from the regional variations in expenditure per head, as indicated in Table 5.3, further differences occur in retail spending between urban and rural areas, as shown by Table 5.5. These are brought about by the higher wages and prices prevalent in urban areas, and by variations in shopping habits.[24]

URBAN/RURAL
EXPENDITURE
PER HEAD

Table 5.5 URBAN/RURAL DIFFERENCES IN SALES PER HEAD
1961–62

	Greater London	Urban areas 100,000 +	Smaller	Rural areas
Food	101·7	88·5	85·4	85·4
Alcoholic drink	10·7	12·0	10·3	8·7
Tobacco	20·3	18·1	17·0	16·1
Clothing and footwear	34·1	29·0	27·9	29·1
Durable household goods	28·6	18·1	20·1	20·3
Other non-foods	24·9	19·8	22·8	20·8
Total	220·9	185·5	186·5	180·4

Table 5.6 NATIONAL FLOOR SPACE REQUIREMENTS BASED ON 1961
CENSUS OF DISTRIBUTION

	Sales per head of population (£ per year)	Sales per square foot (£ per year)	Gross floor space requirements (square feet per head)
Food	81·4	36	2·26
Confectionery/tobacco	12·0	24	0·50
Clothing	27·2	21	1·29
Hardware	15·4	14	1·10
Books/stationery	4·6	16	0·29
Chemists	5·1	29	0·18
Furniture	7·8	19	0·41
Jewellery and leather	1·7	15	0·11
Catering	25·2	16	1·58
Motor vehicles	18·5	115	0·17
		Total	7·89

The existing net retail area should be considered in terms of square footage. While this survey may not be directly required in an analysis for out-of-town centres, it can be used to ascertain the turnover, i.e. the sales per square foot applicable in the trade area, or conversely, the square footage required to support such a turnover. The national retail floor space requirements have been estimated by Clarke on the basis of the 1961 Census, and are listed in Table 5.6.[25]

The division of national expenditure among different types of shops is given in Table 5.7.

Table 5.7   PERCENTAGE OF SALES
BY RETAIL GROUPS
1961[26]

Retail groups	Percentage of all sales
Food shops	45·0
Hardware shops	2·6
Chemists	3·7
Variety stores	4·2
Department stores	5·8
Clothing shops	9·4
Furniture and electrical shops	4·7
Other shops	24·6
	100·0

The assessment of sales at any target date, assuming no new centre has been built, is relatively straightforward. For each subdivision of the trade area, the population at the target date is multiplied by the per capita expenditure, both in total and for each good. Allowance should be made for differential changes in the rate of per capita expenditure on durable goods, which may be expected to rise more rapidly than that on convenience goods.[27] Table 5.8 shows the retail sales in Great Britain based on 1964 prices, with projections to 1970.

Table 5.8   RETAIL SALES IN GREAT BRITAIN, 1957–1970[28]

Sales (£m 1964 prices)				Annual average increases (%)		
1957	1961	1964	1970	1957–61	1961–64	1964–70
8,490	9,674	10,254	12,080	3·3	2·0	2·0

Social class, indicated by the occupation of the head of the household, is responsible for considerable variations in income and expenditure. Using Family Expenditure Survey, the Haydock Report divided households into two groups; those whose head is either an employer, a professional person or a wealthy retired person (with income more than £10 per week), or those whose head is a clerical or manual worker or a relatively poor retired person. The difference in patterns of consumption between these two types of family is shown in Table 5.9.[29]

Table 5.9 PATTERNS OF CONSUMPTION BY SOCIAL CLASS 1962

Class of expenditure	Per capita income and expenditure in a low class family expressed as a percentage of those in a high class family
Convenience goods	87
Durable goods	64
Total retail	77
Housing (including mortgages and fuel)	52
Motor vehicles	52
Services	48
Taxation, insurances and savings	42
Income	61

In the lowest income group, retail expenditure accounts for a considerable amount of the family income, the proportion of this amount decreasing with the corresponding rise in incomes and depending on the type of trade. For example, the Haydock Report stated that convenience goods purchases accounted for about half the retail expenditure of the lower income group, falling to about a fifth in the highest income group, while both groups spend about a fifth of incomes on durable goods. Considering the prevalent trends of rising incomes and falling percentages in expenditure on retail goods, it was stated that much the same differences will exist between each income group in 1971 as occurred in 1961.[30] The viability of a major regional centre is dependent almost entirely on sales of durable goods, apart from a small suscipient sales by convenience outlets, such as supermarkets. Consequently, greater reliance is placed on purchases of durable goods by the higher income groups, which have a greater percentage of car owners and more flexibility in shopping habits.[31] The special importance of these factors to out-of-town shopping centres is emphasized by American practice, where potential trade from very low income groups is often disregarded in the economic analysis, even if this amounts to over 50 per cent of the trade area.[32]

Table 5.10 RETAIL PRICE INDEX 1950–61 (1950 = 100)

	1950	1952	1956	1961
Food	100·0	122·0	153·0	166·9
Tobacco (and alcohol 1950/52)	100·0	103·2	106·2	125·0
Clothing and footwear	100·0	122·8	121·2	128·0
Durable household goods	100·0	121·6	124·6	125·0
Miscellaneous goods	100·0	121·4	129·4	160·8
Average	100·0	116·7	138·4	150·9

E

ALLOWANCES
FOR INFLATION
The retail price index, adapted from the Interim Index (1950–56) and the Index of Retail Prices (1956–61), gives an indication of the allowances that must be made for the fall in value in money, as listed in Table 5.10.[33] Using this index to convert sales in 1950 to 1961 prices, and comparing the results with sales in 1962 for the whole of Great Britain, Bliss has estimated the approximate increases in the real value of goods sold to be as in Table 5.11.

Table 5.11   INCREASES IN REAL VALUE OF
GOODS SOLD 1950–61

Retailer type	Increase (%)
Grocers and other food	11·7
Confectioners, tobacconists, newsagents	27·3
Clothing and footwear	12·5
Household goods	54·8
Other non-food and general stores	23·0
Total retail	18·9

FUTURE RETAIL
SPACE REQUIRE-
MENTS
Once the total target population, sales per head and sales per square foot have been calculated, the floor area required at that date can be assessed for each good, from the formula, assuming a target date of 1981.

$$\text{Floor area (1981)} = \frac{\text{Sales per head} \frac{£(1969\ value)}{} \times \text{Total population (1981)}}{\text{Sales per square foot (1981)} \frac{£(1969\ value)}{}}$$

In this, the 'sales per square foot' factor is an important element, since it is affected greatly by the increasing efficiency in the use of shopping floor space. This greater efficiency, in terms of turnover per square foot, may well lead to a shrinkage in the required floor space in areas of modest population growth.[34] For this reason, the prevailing higher sales per square foot factor should be used. While more research is required into such factors, which vary considerably in different regions, Table 5.12 serves to indicate the approximate sales per square foot figures as suggested by independent analysts.[35]

CENTRAL v.
SUBURBAN SALES
The floor areas calculated from the previous figures give the total selling area required within the trade area at the target date. Depending on the type of centre and the method of analysis, it may be necessary to apportion sales between the central area and the rest of the city or trade area. The Haydock Report and Percival[36] suggest that about two thirds of all sales take place in central areas and one third in the suburbs. However, wide variations occur, depending on the type of goods, as indicated in Table 5.13, as given for Cambridge.[37]

Table 5.12 SALES PER SQUARE FOOT FIGURES (CONVERSION FACTORS)

	Revised Cumbernauld Report	R. K. Cox	C. Clarke	National Cash Register Co.		E. L. Cripps		
	Sales per square foot gross (£)			Sales per square foot selling area (£)				
				Mean	High average	Low	Mean	High
Food	—	—	36	68	78	50	83	150
Grocery	32	40	—	—	—	—	—	—
Other food	30	35	—	—	—	—	—	—
Confectionery/tobacco	26	22	24	—	—	—	—	—
Clothing	25	20	21	—	—	23	41	67
Footwear		—	—	28	40			
Men's wear	—	—	—	31	41	—	—	—
Women's wear	—	—	—	27	36	—	—	—
Hardware/household goods	20	15	14	18	24	18	27	35
Furniture	—	12	19	21	27	—	—	—
Textiles	—	—	—	24	34	—	—	—
Radio/electrical	—	—	—	26	39	—	—	—
Other non-foods	20	—	—	—	—	25	30	35
Chemists	—	30	29	45	57	—	—	—
Books/stationery	—	—	16	29	44	—	—	—
Jewellery/fancy goods	—	—	15	29	38	—	—	—
Services	25	—	—	—	—	—	—	—
Gas/electricity showrooms	25	—	—	—	—	—	—	—
Motor vehicles	20	—	115	—	—	—	—	—
Catering	20	—	16	—	—	—	—	—
Miscellaneous, inc. laundrettes	20	—	—	—	—	—	—	—

An analysis of King's Lynn, Bedford, Cambridge and Norwich indicated that migrant shoppers, i.e. those from outside those towns, accounted for 55–57 per cent of durable goods sales, and between 11 and 19 per cent of convenience goods sales as indicated in Table 5.14.[38]

Table 5.13 PROPORTION OF SALES AND TURNOVER SUPPORT FIGURES (CAMBRIDGE)

	In city centre Proportion of sales (%)	Turnover per square foot (£)	Rest of city Proportion of sales (%)	Turnover per square foot (£)
Total sales	53·8	7·81	46·2	6·38
Total retail	57·2	9·26	42·8	7·36
All food	25·0	9·76	75·0	10·07
Clothing	76·3	12·62	23·7	10·01
Hardware	47·4	6·28	52·6	5·74
Furniture	67·9	8·31	32·1	2·73
Department stores	84·4	7·30	15·6	2·20
Total services	37·6	3·59	62·4	4·47

The calculations for sales and floor areas make no provision for storage/ TOTAL RETAIL AREA warehouse space. The amount of space required for these uses will depend on the method of trading, the retailer's distribution and central warehousing

Table 5.14   SALES OF DURABLE AND CONVENIENCE GOODS 1961

	King's Lynn		Bedford		Cambridge		Norwich	
	£'000	Percentage	£'000	Percentage	£'000	Percentage	£'000	Percentage
Total durable sales	4,548	100	9,423	100	15,179	100	18,607	100
Durable sales to migrants	2,608	57	4,965	53	8,466	56	10,166	55
Total convenience sales	3,158	100	7,156	100	10,348	100	12,650	100
Convenience goods sales to migrants	595	19	1,204	17	1,384	13	1,380	11

arrangements. The first West Midland Shopping Study, in collating results for eight Midland towns, showed that the selling area varied between 49 per cent and 63 per cent of the total floor space in seven centres, but was as high as 76 per cent in the other, though marked variations occurred between individual trade categories. The Study recognized a distinct tendency towards a 60:40 ratio between selling and storage space in both existing and new centres.[39] Latest available figures indicate that, in self-service stores, the sales area occupies 53 per cent of the total area, whereas in supermarkets it occupies 59 per cent of the total area. The wide variation between different types is apparent in Table 5.15.[40]

Table 5.15   SALES AREA IN SELF-SERVICE STORES AND SUPERMARKETS

	Sales area as percentage of total area	
	Self-service stores	Supermarkets
Co-operatives	55	63
Multiples	53	51
Unaffiliated independents	42	58
Voluntary group members	64	53
Average	53	59

More recently, Rhodes and Whitaker have published the results of their survey of the subdivision of sales and storage space in 17 central shopping areas, obtained by special floor space surveys.[41] (See Table 5.16.)

From an analysis of estimated sales per square foot in 1961 and of Table 5.16, it was found that those centres with a high percentage of ground floor space in use as selling area also experienced high sales per square foot (gross).

5.5 ACCESSI-BILITY The success of a particular centre is dependent on minimum distribution costs for the trader and on its central location in relation to the most productive area within its trading hinterland. Consequently, the relative accessibility of a hierarchy of shopping centres is reflected in their spatial

Table 5.16   USE OF SHOPPING FLOOR SPACE – SELLING SPACE/TOTAL RETAIL SPACE (%)

	Food trades (All floors)	(Ground)	Non-food trades (All floors)	(Ground)	Total retail trade (All floors)	(Ground)
Catford	42%	54%	57%	79%	54%	72%
Deptford	47	61	51	80	50	75
Edinburgh	38	68	58	83	52	78
Edmonton (Lower)	33	45	54	72	48	64
Enfield	41	52	56	72	54	68
Exeter	37	61	50	75	48	72
Grimsby	37	63	56	80	60	72
Hereford	28	52	55	70	48	65
Leamington	46	n.d.	59	n.d.	57	n.d.
Lewisham	41	66	66	83	63	80
Newton Abbot	45	56	49	68	48	65
Paignton	42	57	55	75	52	69
Palmers Green	47	61	64	73	59	70
Peckham	40	49	57	74	55	69
Swindon	47	60	63	80	60	75
Torquay	47	63	n.d.	n.d.	53	72
Totnes	39	43	56	63	50	57

disposition, and in the road usage by private cars and public transport vehicles.[42] Accessibility itself is dependent on journey times, road capacities and usage, car ownership and public transport services, the importance of each being relative to the type of centre envisaged.

Experience in the United States shows that a major suburban regional centre with a department store will obtain most of its business from residents within a distance of 5 to 20 miles, whereas a neighbourhood centre, serving the daily needs for food, drugs and similar convenience items, will probably draw its business from within a distance of 2 miles.[43]

JOURNEY TIMES AND DISTANCES

It has been found that the majority of customers is prepared to travel up to 30 minutes to reach major centres, though 6 minutes was the maximum time travelled to neighbourhood centres. Because of the absence of major out-of-town centres in Britain, comparable data is not available, though sources suggest that distances are not in excess of those in America, but that journey times may be greater — the Haydock Report estimated that the further reaches of its hinterland could be between 30 and 60 minutes driving time from the centre, depending on the relative attraction of the facilities provided.[44] (See Fig. 5.2.)

For analysis purposes, journey times should be calculated with a stopwatch, and map points plotted on all major routes for 5, 10, 15, 20 and 30 minutes travelling time outwards from the subject location, the test driving being done during normal hours, avoiding rush hours and clear periods, and observing all posted speed limits. The original plottings should be checked on the inward journey to the centre.[45]

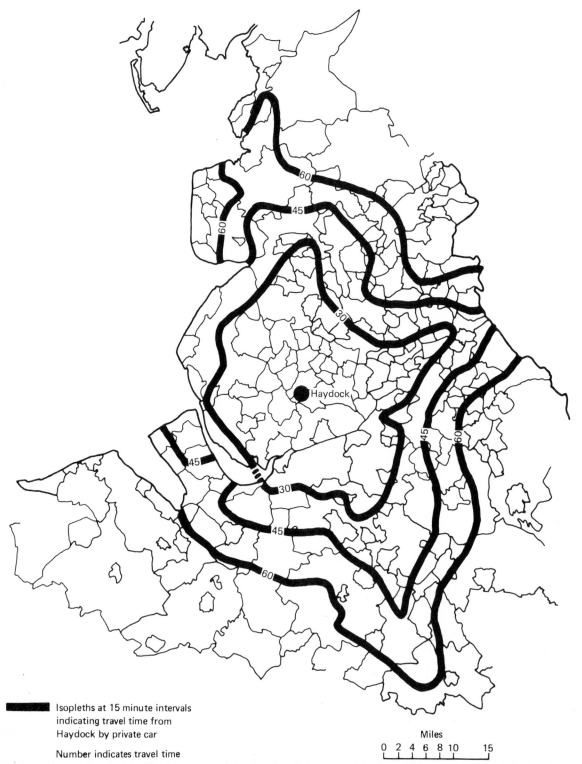

Isopleths at 15 minute intervals
indicating travel time from
Haydock by private car

Number indicates travel time

Miles

0 2 4 6 8 10   15

Fig. 5.2 HAYDOCK SHOPPING CENTRE indicating the relative accessibility of the hinterland to the subject location.

Driving time depends predominantly on the exisiting road network, ROAD USAGE
with the chances of planning permission and possibly the future success or AND CAPACITIES
failure of the centre being crucially affected by road capacity. Major
regional centres are large traffic generators, which could give rise to acute
difficulties if heavy concentrations occurred on roads of inadequate
capacity or at unsuitable points. In assessing the road pattern within the
trade area, the following must be considered:

1 *Vehicular traffic arteries* The width, direction and number of lanes of
   all major routes.
2 *Intersections* The location, nature and capacity of all major intersections within the trade area, and of all intersections close to the
   subject site.
3 *Traffic flows* Traffic counts, together with origin/destination/
   purpose surveys, should be taken on all major routes, for normal and
   peak hours, on week days and weekends. The merits of each route
   may be assessed by the application of a 'congestion factor', this being
   the number of cars passing the survey point in a peak hour divided by
   the number of effective lanes.
4 *Speed limits* Statutory limits should be recorded, together with other
   controls, such as traffic lights, halt signs or tolls, and also routes where
   no such restrictions exist.
5 *Other mobility factors* Limits on mobility, such as poor road surfacing,
   steep hills, corners, and congestion due to periodic on-street parking
   should be noted; also assets such as attractive scenic areas.
6 *Accessibility of major routes* Areas possessing good access to major
   routes should be considered, especially to motorways or motorway
   class roads. These access points should be tabulated according to
   capacity and distance from the subject location.
7 *Future roads* Roads under construction or planned should be evaluated under the headings listed above.[46]

In assessing road capacity, consideration must be given both to traffic ROAD CAPACITY
volume (the number of vehicles per hour passing a given point), and to AND LOCATIONAL
traffic density (the number of vehicles on any given stretch of road at any POTENTIAL
one time). With the former, vehicles will be widely spaced, while vehicles
being obliged to travel at reduced speeds will result in higher traffic
densities. For shopping centre locations, the main consideration will be
current usage and the maximum capacity for traffic generated by any
new development, and the avoidance of any higher density roads.

Studies in America and Britain have shown that, at speeds of 35–40
mile/h, and uninterrupted flow, one lane of a multilane road will take 1,500
vehicles per hour, whether one of 2 or one of 4 lanes. At 45–50 mile/h,
this capacity is reduced to 1,000 vehicles per hour, while the outer lane
of English motorways (before restrictions) of 120 mile/h will taken only

120 vehicles per hour. From these figures, it can be seen that sites of greatest potential are not necessarily located on motoways, or at motorway intersections, but on roads of excess capacity and with average speeds between 30–40 mile/h, at which speeds ramps at junctions need not slow other traffic.

CAR OWNERSHIP Total car ownership within the trade area must be ascertained, with an emphasis placed on two car families, and on those families where the car is available and regularly used for shopping trips. The 1966 Sample Census of Greater London showed that 42 per cent of households owned one car, while 6 per cent possessed two or more.[47] In the absence of other detailed regional statistics, sample or complete surveys of owners or private garages should be undertaken, especially in those areas beyond the normal walking distance of the proposed centre.

Bearing this in mind, the future car ownership may be projected from population estimates and national car ownership expectations. For example, in 1964 about 33 per cent of the population had exclusive use of a car, and 8 per cent of two cars, while 24·3 million cars are anticipated by the year 2000, or 0·39 cars per person.[48]

PUBLIC TRANSPORT It is likely that public transport will prove more important to British out-of-town centres than is the case in America, since car ownership is lower than America, where public transport has suffered a steady decline, especially in the lower density suburbs. 'Bus transport places some limitations on the amount of bulk purchases that customers can carry on each shopping trip, but will be more important for serving the shopping centre staff. The main factors to be considered for public transport serving the subject location are as follows:

1 *Type of service* The number of trips per hour, the operator, capacity, cost of fare and return.
2 *Potential service* The number of trips and actual rerouting the operator would be prepared to offer if servicing facilities were supplied at the centre.
3 *Service area* The scope of the services to all areas, whether urban, surburban or rural, together with connecting services.
4 *Travel times* These should be plotted as for driving times, using 10, 15 and 20 minute rides without change of 'bus.[49]

CORRELATION OF PRIVATE AND PUBLIC TRANSPORT Where both cars and public transport are anticipated, accessibility can be measured in terms of the average time taken to reach the centre, depending on the level of car ownership and differing journey times. As an example, the West Midland Study quotes a village being 20 minutes travelling time from the nearest town by 'bus and 10 minutes by car, and that 60 per cent

of households own cars. In this case, it was stated that the average travel
time would be:

$$\frac{10 \times 60}{100} + \frac{20 \times 40}{100} = 14 \text{ minutes}$$

The influence of a centre would be considerably reduced if no public
transport existed. If 40 per cent of trade of a community having access to
public transport goes to a particular centre, a similar community with 50
per cent car ownership but no public transport would only have 20 per
cent dependence.[50]

Nelson gives the following reasons for an assessment of shopping habits **5.6 SHOPPING**
as part of an economic analysis: **HABITS**

1 They may assist in delineating the trade area.
2 They measure the effectiveness of existing competition.
3 They determine the residential areas from which competition draws
   most.
4 They may indicate any special or unusual circumstances affecting
   shopping patterns within the trade area.

Certain general characteristics of consumer response should be recognized,
all other things being equal:

1 Shoppers will move towards the dominant trading centre.
2 Shoppers will not go through one trade area to reach another having
   equal facilities.
3 Shoppers will patronize the closest centre with equal facilities.
4 Shoppers will tend to follow traditional circulation patterns.[51]

Two major factors influence shopping habits: wide selection and convenience of shopping facilities, particularly the point of travel time. Indeed
travel time and the range of facilities appear to be more decisive than
parking.

Over 80 per cent of all shopping is done by women, to whom the old SOCIAL FUNCTION
retail pattern served both an economic and a social function. With the
advent of self-service and supermarkets, the two have become less compatible; the retailer, either independent or multiple, wishes to utilize the
most modern methods available, and may use other means to fulfil any
social function. Gruen has stated that shoppers will travel greater distances
to reach a centre with outstanding characteristics and a greater number of
comparison shopping facilities than they will to one with a limited range
of facilities and poor design.[52] This, in fact, has been the deliberate
policy adopted in the development of out-of-town centres in America,

though Table 5.17 indicates that, at the survey date of 1953, variety and price still favoured central areas, and may be compared with Table 2.3.

Table 5.17   MOTIVES FOR SHOPPING PREFERENCE U.S.A.[53]

	Against central area, percentage of customers	Against shopping centres, percentage of customers
Difficulty in getting to store	47	11
Treatment by sales people	43	11
Handling adjustments	21	11
Shopping discomfort	33	8
Choice of merchandise	6	35
Prices	14	38
Deliveries	10	26
Range of sizes/colours	8	32

SHOPPING HOURS Restricted shopping hours prevailing in many instances prevent the family car being available for shopping trips, and the Kent County Council survey showed that one third of all car owners did not use their cars for shopping even when it was available, owing to congestion and parking problems, and the availability of good public transport.[54]

It was assumed at Haydock that the difficulties of shopping hours would be overcome by adjusting the hours of business to permit evening and week-end shopping on the American pattern, and this has already been carried out (see Table 5.18) at two out-of-town centres now in operation in Britain, the Breda Centre, Belfast and the Gem Centre, Nottingham. At the Belfast Centre, for example, up to 1,200 people pass through the checkouts in less than 1 hour on a Friday evening.[55]

Table 5.18   SHOPPING HOURS, BREDA AND GEM CENTRES

	Breda centre	Gem centre
Monday	Closed	Closed
Tuesday	9.30–5.30	10.00–6.00
Wednesday	9.30–5.30	10.00–8.00
Thursday	9.30–5.30	10.00–8.00
Friday	9.30–9.00	10.00–9.00
Saturday	9.30–6.00	9.00–6.00
Total trading hours	44	48
Total trading hours after 5.30 p.m.	4	$9\frac{1}{2}$

In America, the preference for evening shopping hours is emphasized by the duration of the stay, which is an average of 51 minutes compared with 29 minutes during the day; 31 per cent of all trips are made after 6 p.m. In community centres, up to 60 per cent of all trade is done after 6 p.m., and up to 40 per cent in regional centres.[56]

THE SHOPPING TRIP The continuing reduction in the number of shopping trips made each week has been brought about by the following factors, which should be considered in the trade area analysis:

1 The growth of car ownership, as previously described.
2 The development of larger stores and supermarkets, where customers may obtain a wider range of goods.
3 The 'one stop' attitude engendered by the opportunities for bulk buying.
4 The increasing ownership of refrigerators, to store perishable goods.

The percentage of trade done on each day of the week will be used to indicate the peak number of parking spaces required, any day to be preferred for early closing and the likely demands for staff. The percentage varies considerably from day to day and also between regions, as indicated in Table 5.19.

FREQUENCY OF SHOPPING TRIPS

Table 5.19   PERCENTAGE OF TRADE BY REGIONS 1966[57]

	Monday	Tuesday	Wednesday	Thursday	Friday	Saturday
South	8·9	11·0	7·1	14·3	30·7	26·0
West	7·4	9·7	5·5	16·5	34·5	26·5
Midlands	6·3	10·9	8·5	13·8	33·8	26·8
North West	8·4	12·5	9·7	13·5	31·7	24·3
North East	6·3	8·4	6·5	15·7	36·8	26·8
Scotland	11·8	9·3	8·2	15·7	26·8	28·3
National average	8·6	10·9	7·7	14·0	31·5	25·7

In Table 5.19, the national average was calculated from individual questionnaires, not from the regional averages, and indicates the importance of Friday as the major shopping day.

While the ownership of refrigerators should not be overemphasized in a temperate climate, recent surveys do indicate the general reduction in the number of shopping trips for food, as shown in Table 5.20.

Table 5.20   FREQUENCY OF SHOPPING TRIPS FOR FOOD[58]

	Refrigerator owners (%)	Non-owners (%)
Every day	41	60
Every 2–3 days	40	31
Every 4–5 days	9	6
Once a week	10	3

The survey carried out in central Manchester in connection with the Haydock Report showed that one third of all shopping trips began from work, though expenditure during these trips was 50 per cent of the normal amount, while one fifth of all home based trips were multipurpose with spending 20 per cent less than the normal figure.[59]

METHODS OF These are dependent on the type of location and centre, and on the extent
TRANSPORT USED of car ownership and public transport services. Approximately 60 per cent
of customers at the Gem Centre, Nottingham now travel by car, but in
1965 a free 'bus service was provided to and from the city centre. This
service has now been rerouted to serve a neighbouring residential district,
rather than connecting two shopping areas. Similarly, a free half hourly
'bus service was provided by Gem on their takeover of the Fame discount
store in Preston. The Kent Survey showed that, in that area, 59 per cent
of all luxury shopping trips and 42 per cent of all weekly shopping trips to
all centres were made by car, whereas the Leicester Survey indicated that
57 per cent of all trips into the cordon area were by car, and 34 per cent by
'bus, for shopping purposes.[60] These figures stress the importance of the
motor car for 'regional' shopping trips, especially when compared to the
following three 'suburban' centres, Cowley (Oxford), Drumchapel
(Glasgow) and Ormesby (Middlesbrough).

Table 5.21   METHODS OF TRANSPORT USED TO COWLEY,
DRUMCHAPEL AND ORMESBY CENTRES 1965-66[61]

	Percentage of customers		
	Cowley centre (%)	Drumchapel centre (%)	Ormesby centre (%)
By car	8·8	31·0	35·2
By 'bus	18·6	16·0	11·6
By bicycle	—	13·0	—
On foot	72·6	40·0	53·2
	100·0	100·0	100·0

5.7 COMPETITIVE Major competitive facilities to a projected centre will have been analysed
FACILITIES in the preliminary assessment of the trade area. If, as a result of the analysis
of population and potential spending power, the subject location is
considered feasible, account must be taken of existing smaller competitors
within the trade area:

1 For projected convenience goods centres, all shops within 1 mile
radius should be analysed in terms of square footage, sales area,
quality and volume of business.
2 For projected larger centres, two concentric trade zones should be
ascertained (possibly coinciding with the zones suggested in Section
5.2).

The first zone is for convenience goods without any extra facilities within
the centre, but all competition for convenience goods sales is measured
as in (1). This is necessary because, in a large centre a supermarket, for
example, will draw from approximately the same area even if other facilities
are provided, but will secure some additional business from incidental
shopping for groceries by people living beyond this inner zone, whose
main purpose was to visit the larger stores. The second zone extends to the

boundary of the whole trade area, in which all major competitors should be analysed on the basis of parking, accessibility, attractiveness, price/quality/choice of merchandise, sales turnover, selling ability and amenities.[62] In the economic analysis, most miscalculations occur in estimating competition. A recent survey in America indicated that only 9 per cent of new supermarkets did as predicted, 52 per cent were doing 10 per cent or more below estimated performance, and 39 per cent were doing 10 per cent or more above predictions (though this may be considered dangerous since it may encourage competitors to move into the area).[63] L. Smith & Company consider that approximately 70 per cent of their estimates are within 10 per cent accuracy, and 85 per cent within 15 per cent accuracy.[64]

The approximate trade area applicable to each major competitor is best determined by surveys at the competitive centre; this will also give further information on shopping habits. The following should be ascertained by the survey:

EFFECTIVENESS OF COMPETITIVE FACILITIES

1 Place of residence.
2 Purpose of visit, i.e. convenience and/or durable goods.
3 Single or multipurpose trip, and trip frequency.
4 Method of transport, and route adopted.
5 Number of shoppers per car, if applicable.
6 Reasons for choice of particular centre.

Once competitive facilities have been plotted and tabulated, subjective judgements must be made on 'trade interception potential', the power of the project centre to intercept some measure of business normally given to other centres. The assessment of the degree of interception should be based on factors outlined, especially the characteristics that shoppers will not go through one trade area to reach another having equal facilities, and will patronize the nearest centre having equal facilities. Greatest interception will occur on customers to other centres whose normal route passes the subject location, and the extent of this potential may be gauged from the results of the survey outlined above.[65]

BUSINESS INTERCEPTION

In America, the proliferation of competitive centres within the same trade area has resulted in the failure of several, especially among older centres. Evidence of the overprovision of city centre and suburban shops is apparent in this country. For the development of successful stores or centres, Nelson advocates a 'competitive hazard survey' in three parts:

COMPETITIVE HAZARD SURVEY

1 A survey of all non-intercepting competitors within 1–5 miles, depending on the type of centre proposed, to indicate the potential of the competitors to upgrade their accommodation and services to interception capability.

2 A survey of all vacant sites, or potential sites, including area, topography, restrictions, rental/sale price, accessibility, etc.

3 A survey of all sites on which planning permission has been granted
for retail facilities but on which work has not yet commenced.[66]

5.8 OTHER FACTORS

DEVELOPMENT PLAN

For almost all out-of-town centre sites, the consent of planning permission
would represent a departure from the provisions of the Development
Plan or Town Map, and this, together with traffic considerations, has
resulted in the majority of previous applications being refused. Even if
planning permission is granted, the conditions imposed may be such as to
make the site an uneconomic proposition for the developer. In addition,
any application may cause opposition among local traders who could be
potential tenants if the centre were built.

In the case of the Haydock proposal, the Minister of Housing and Local
Government, following an appeal, refused the application on the grounds
of the potential harm to urban renewal in neighbouring towns, rather than
as being a departure from the Development Plan, or being likely to cause
traffic congestion. In some cases, the Local Authority may be prepared to
give consent provided that any facilities lost by the development of the new
centre are replaced elsewhere in the area, at the developers' expense.

RETAIL DISTRIBU-TION

The retail distribution facilities within and around the trade area should be
considered, including the central warehousing provisions. The existing
transport network, including trucking, rail freight yards and goods delivery
services should be analysed, and the growth potential assessed, especially
in terms of 24 hour service and maintenance.

ADVERTISING MEDIA

The range of distribution of daily and evening papers gives a further guide
to the trade areas of existing major centres, and indicates the extent of
effective advertising media within the area. Other media, such as magazines,
trade journals, poster facilities and local television and radio channels
should also be assessed in terms of effectiveness and coverage.

REFERENCES

1 R. Nelson, *Selection of Retail Locations*, p. 44–45.
2 V. Gruen and L. Smith, *Shopping Towns U.S.A.*, p. 278.
3 R. Nelson, op. cit. p.183 and 189.
4 W. J. Reilly, *The Law of Retail Gravitation*.
5 R. Nelson, op. cit. p. 150–151.
6 R. J. Green and R. M. Beaumont, 'The size of shopping centres' *T.P.I. Journal*, Dec. 1962, p. 311–314.
7 Manchester University, *Haydock Report*, Fig. B18.
8 Manchester University, op. cit., p. 207–208.
9 Manchester University, op. cit., p. 27–28 and 207.
10 R. Nelson, op. cit., p. 188–195.
11 H. Hoyt, *Shopping Centres —Design and Operation*, p. 18.
12 L. Smith, 'The assessment of shopping needs', *Chartered Surveyor*, Jan. 1964, p. 325.
13 Manchester University, op. cit., p. 114 and 208
14 Manchester University, op. cit., p. 116 and 120.
15 Manchester University, op. cit., p. 140–141.
16 Manchester University, op. cit., p. 116.
17 Manchester University, op. cit., p. 117 and 118.

18 Manchester University, op. cit., p. 122–123.
19 Manchester University, op. cit., p. 167–168.
20 W. L. Waide, 'Changing shopping habits and their impact on town planning', *T.P.I. Journal*, Sept/Oct. 1963, p. 264.
21 H. Bliss, 'Local changes in shopping potential', *T.P.I. Journal*, Sept./Oct. 1965, p. 337.
22 Manchester University, op. cit., p. 169–170.
23 Manchester University, op. cit., p. 169.
24 H. Bliss, op. cit., p. 337.
25 C. Clarke, 'Shopping centres', *Chartered Surveyor*, April 1965, p. 532–533.
26 C. A. Orndahl, 'Choosing a shopping development', *Stores and Shops Journal*, Sept. 1965, p. 66.
27 Manchester University, op. cit., p. 37.
28 Stores and Shops Journal, Dec. 1965, p. 17.
29 Manchester University, op. cit., p. 188–189.
30 Manchester University, op. cit., p. 194–195.
31 Manchester University, op. cit., p. 44–45.
32 G. Baker and B. Funaro, *Shopping Centres —Design and Operation*, p. 196.
33 H. Bliss, op. cit., p. 335, for Tables 5.10 and 5.11.
34 C. A. Orndahl, op. cit., p. 70.
    W. K. Smigielski, *Traffice Plan for Leicester*, p. 9 and 20.
35 Cumbernauld Development Corporation, *Revision of Retail Requirements*, p. 3.
    R. K. Cox, *Retail Site Assessment*, p. 49.
    C. Clarke, op. cit., p. 532–533.
    National Cash Register Co. Ltd., *Thoughts on Future Shopping Requirements*, p. 8.
    E. L. Cripps, *Retail Turnover and Floorspace*, (Paper).
36 R. N. Percival, 'Shopping centres in Britain', *T.P.I. Journal*, Oct. 1965, p. 329–333.
37 W. L. Waide, op. cit., p. 258–259.
38 H. Bliss, op. cit., p. 335.
39 *T.P.I. Journal*, 'West Midlands shopping study (review)', April 1966, p. 149.
40 *Self-Service and Supermarket Journal*, June 1966, p. 19.
41 T. Rhodes and R. Whitaker, 'Forecasting shopping demand', *T.P.I. Journal*, May 1967, p. 188–192. and Nov. 1967, p. 414–416.
42 W. L. Garrison *et al.*, *Studies in Highway Development and Geographic Change*, p. 57.
43 L. Smith, op. cit., p. 324–325.
    Urban Land Institute, *Shopping Centres Re-studied*, Vol. 1, p. 19.
    A survey (1966) for a major centre in Adelaide, Australia, indicated the following distances travelled by customers:

    14%   from up to ½ mile from centre
    22%   from up to 1   mile from centre (36%)
    17%   from up to 1½ mile from centre (53%)
    14·5%   from up to 2   mile from centre (67·5%)
     9%   from up to 2½ mile from centre (76·5%)
     6%   from up to 3   mile from centre (86·5%)
    13·5%   from up to 4   mile and over (100%)

44 Manchester University, op. cit., p. 36–37.
45 R. Nelson, op. cit., p. 209–211.
46 R. Nelson, op. cit., p. 328–350.
47 H.M.S.O., *Sample Census of Greater London*, 1966.
48 Ministry of Transport, *National Travel Survey*, 1964 (Preliminary Report 1967).
    J. C. Tanner, *Roads and Construction*, Sept. 1962, p. 263–274.
49 R. Nelson, op. cit., p. 328–350.
50 West Midlands Shopping Research Group, *Predicting Shopping Requirements*, p. 14 and *T.P.I. Journal*, April, 1966, p. 146.
51 R. Nelson, op. cit., p. 185 and 208.
52 V. Gruen and L. Smith, op. cit., p. 33. For an opposite view, see C. Darlow in *Estates Gazette*, Dec. 17, 1966, p. 1031.
53 J. P. Alevizos and A. E. Beckwith, 'Shopping habits', *Business Week*, 24 Oct. 1953, quoting survey 'Downtown and Surburban Shopping Study of Greater Boston' by Boston University College of Business Administration.
54 Kent County Council, *The Influence of Car Ownership on Shopping Habits*.
55 National Cash Register Co., *Supermac Notes* 1 and 2.
    Self-Service and Supermarket Journal, July 1965, p. 77.
56 Urban Land Institute, *Operation Shopping Centres*, p. 6 and 188.
57 *Self-Service and Supermarket Journal*, Jan. 1967, p. 30.
58 Birds Eye Foods Ltd., *What's in Store?* p. 4.
59 H. R. Cole, 'Shopping assessments at Haydock and elsewhere', *Urban Studies* June 1966, p. 153.
60 Kent County Council, op. cit.
    W. K. Smigielski, op. cit.
61 Arndale Developments Ltd., *Drumchapel Survey*, 1965.
    J. Hinton, *Ormesby Survey*, 1966.
    B. J. Wratten, 'Cowley centre', *Chartered Surveyor*, Sept. 1965. Similar surveys for a major centre in Adelaide, Australia, showed the following methods of transport used:

	Percentage of customers	
	1964	1966
By car	61%	67·0 %
By 'bus	12	11·0
By bicycle	10	6·5
On foot	17	15·5

62 R. Nelson, op. cit. 211–212.
63 R. W. Stephenson, *Self-Service and Supermarket Journal,* March 1966, p. 76.
64 L. Smith, op. cit., p. 328.
65 V. Gruen and L. Smith, op. cit., p. 35.
    R. Nelson, op. cit., p. 349–350.
66 R. Nelson, op. cit., p. 211–213.

methods of assessing locational potential

The general factors considered in Chapter 5 constitute the bulk of research necessary to calculate the potential of a subject site. These factors are used in various ways in the different methods which will be considered below. It is not intended that the analysis in this chapter should provide the complete formulae and actual calculations required in each method, but is designed to enumerate their separate stages and consider the merits and disadvantages of each system.

6.1 THE CUMBERNAULD METHOD[1]

The first Cumbernauld Report sought to estimate the shopping needs of the New Town, based on a population of 70,000. A comparative technique was evolved, which analysed 100 other towns having a similar relationship to that of Cumbernauld, and all being within 20 miles of one of Britain's nine largest cities, these being (excluding London) Newcastle, Leeds, Sheffield, Edinburgh, Bristol, Glasgow, Birmingham, Manchester and Liverpool. The retail trading structure of the sample was carried out on the basis of the 1950 Census of Distribution, to assess the degree of correlation between sales and population for each town. This involved the calculation of the coefficient of correlation for each trade in each town. It was considered that, when the correlation coefficient reached a unity, a perfect correlation existed. The Report then drew up a graph of these results, which showed a correlation coefficient of 0·84, (compared with 0·98 for retail sales and town plus hinterland population). The actual expenditure of a population, based on 1959 sales, was then calculated for a town of 70,000 and this was converted to floor area, using the conversion factor for each trade. (See Fig. 6.1).

DISADVANTAGES

While this method represented a considerable advance in analysis techniques, its results and its suitability for use on out-of-town projects may be questioned. The average population of all the sample towns was in

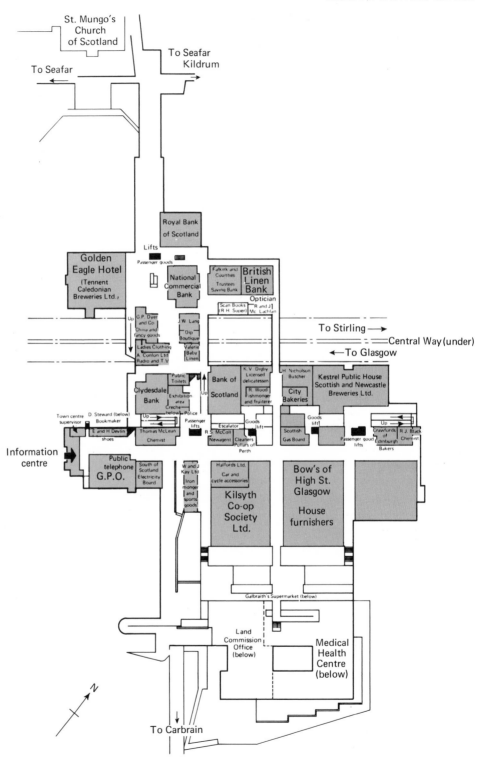

Fig. 6.1 CUMBERNAULD TOWN CENTRE showing the retail layout on the main shopping level, in the first phase.

fact only 48,400, and subsequent calculations for particular categories of trade were based on this average. It has been shown by Lomas that town size must be taken into account when assessing sales potential, and this was recognized in the 1964 revision to the report, in which a second survey was undertaken of 74 towns between 50,000 and 90,000 population. The average population of the 74 towns was 64,773. The second report also states that some turnover factors were underestimated, especially for the motor vehicles group, which rose from £12 per square foot per annum to £20 per square foot per annum.[2] Similarly, it was estimated that the maximum hinterland population would be about 35,000, but no extra retail or service areas were provided for this demand. The Report states that 'it would not be wise at the outset to provide for the hard-core of 20,000 potential regional shoppers but rather to regard them as an insurance policy which will help the town's shopping to get started and provide a little extra turnover for the traders'.[3] It is for this reason that the use of this method for large out-of-town centres may be suspect, since such centres are especially reliant on sales of durable goods over a wide hinterland area, but the method, since it is 'comparative', involves fewer projections than others. It is also important that comparative centres with similar characteristics are selected for analysis, since trading patterns will vary considerably with local circumstances.

The King's Lynn Study (1962), supposedly derived from the Cumbernauld method, was in fact based on 'straight line' projections of trends occurring between 1950 and 1961, the stages in the analysis being as follows:

6.2 THE KING'S LYNN METHOD[4]

TECHNIQUE

1 *Calculate population and trade area* This was based on the function and effectiveness of attraction of five categories of shop, all assessed by survey. The population contained within the zone of influence was projected on the basis of 1951–1961 trends, making allowance for the increasing industrial employment and for the contraction of agricultural employment.

2 *Calculate retail floor space* For 1961, a survey was carried out of all selling areas. To ascertain the areas in use in 1950, previous planning permissions were examined and local knowledge used. The two figures were then compared on a percentage change basis, which indicated a 6 per cent total change in 10 years.

3 *Sales turnover* Since no information was available later than 1954, it was assumed that changes in turnover between 1950 and 1961 followed the national pattern. The 1950 Census of Distribution figures were adjusted to 1954 base value of the £, and national changes in expenditure, 1950–61, were applied to these figures. The results showed an 80 per cent increase in sales between 1950 and 1961.

4 *Sales per head of population* The ratio of sales per head of population was calculated for 1950 and 1961 for each of the 13 retail groups, as well as the ratio of sales to floor space. This indicated a 4·63 per cent increase each year in the value of sales per head, and a 0·9 per cent increase each year in the value of sales per square foot of the floor space.

5 *Projections* It was assumed that these percentage increases would continue at the same rate as for 1950–61. The floor area required for each trade at 1981 was assessed on the formula previously noted, i.e.

$$\text{Floor area 1981} = \frac{\text{Sales per head 1981} \times \text{Total population 1981} \quad \pounds(1954 \text{ value})}{\text{Sales per square foot 1981} \quad \pounds(1954 \text{ value})}$$

The projections showed an overall increase of 109 per cent in the value of sales, at the 1954 value of the £, but an increase of only 24 per cent in the floor space in the 20 years up to 1981.

DISADVANTAGES The retail floor area of King's Lynn amounted to 4·5 square feet per person, when applied to the trade area population, but the calculations suggest that only 4·7 square feet per person would be required by 1981. This is considerably lower than other estimates. Percival, for example, suggests 13 square feet per person in the central areas and 6 square feet per person in the suburbs, while Clarke, quoting American experience, used 8 square feet per person. His national estimate for Britain, based on the 1961 Census of Distribution, was 7·89 square feet per person.[5] There are three main disadvantages of this method as described:

1 The 'straight line' projection method assumes a constant growth rate, which has to be proportional in each case. Little account could be taken of the possibilities of large overspill schemes now being planned in the area.

2 It was thought necessary to establish the relative efficiency and attraction of each shop by survey methods. This technique, even if on a sample basis, is lengthy, and depends on effective interviewing and data processing.

3 No account is taken of increased car ownership, or of different expenditure and changing shopping habits in the various income groups.

The number of assumptions made places the validity of the results of this particular study in doubt, and also emphasizes the necessity of obtaining accurate data from census material, rather than forward and backward projections from a fixed intercensal date.

EXAMPLE OF PROJECTION FIGURES An example of the projection technique, using up-to-date expenditure and sales conversion factors, is given in Appendix C.

The vacuum or residual method calculates the potential trade available to a new centre after allowing for prior claims on total consumer expenditure of other shopping facilities, both in and out of the area. Nelson states that this technique is the more usual for out-of-town centres, but considers that future predictions are hazardous, at least in America.[6] The technique advocated by Nelson for the market share method (considered in the following section), is similar to that of Development Analysts in this country for the vacuum method, at least in the early stages. For this reason, the method suggested by the latter is considered below, since it relates directly to English conditions.[7] (This synopsis of the method assumes that the relevant factors given in Chapter 5 will be included under the appropriate sections of the analysis.)

6.3 VACUUM OR RESIDUAL METHOD

TECHNIQUE

1 Determine trade area. Locate and classify shopping facilities covering a fairly wide area around the subject location; examine relative accessibility to all shopping centres in this area; establish the actual trade area of the centre in relation to accessibility.

2 Determine population within trade area. From Census and Local Authority sources, using Census districts.

3 Calculate total expenditure by category of goods. Spending per head should be calculated by socio-economic groups. and results multiplied by population to give total expenditure in each Census district.

4 The division of total spending. Prior claim on spending by more convenient local shops or town centre shops. This can be calculated from shopper questionnaires, the Census of Distribution and surveys of selling areas in retail outlets. This is not to assess actual turnover of shops, but what their effective turnover would be under an equilibrium distribution of shopping facilities.

5 Estimate potential trade available to centre. Potential trade available to centre is calculated by subtracting central area and suburban sales from the total expenditure in each good.

6 Allowance for local traders. From the results of (5), deduct effective sales of existing traders in the immediate vicinity. Where the remainder is positive, this potential turnover is available to the new centre; where it is negative, too much shopping capacity already exists in the area.

7 Reassessment of future potential. Future potential at a target date may be established by the same stages of analysis, assuming that spending per head will increase at a constant rate, and that existing traders will tend to increase their sales per square foot through improved methods, shop layout, etc.

8 The analysis of these figures will give the total expenditure available in the trade area at the target date after the 'draw off' by existing establishments. Depending on the breakdown in stage (3), this total expenditure can either be in terms solely of convenience and durable goods sales, or the summation of the extra expenditure available for each good. The latter will, of course, give a better indication of the floor area supportable for each tenant type, though this assumes that the type of business can be fixed before the centre is opened, which is not always the case.

ADVANTAGES AND DISADVANTAGES

The main advantage of this method is the limited number of assumptions required. As described above, this method assumes that the whole of the extra expenditure available at the target date will go to the new centre. Both Nelson and L. Smith recommend that this expenditure should be subdivided within the primary and secondary zones, and assume that a lesser percentage will go to the new centre.[8] This arbitrary percentage assignation, which is a compromise with the market share method, is difficult to estimate, particularly for a large regional centre, where over 80 per cent of sales may be in durable goods sold to customers from virtually the whole of the trade area.

6.4 MARKET SHARE METHOD

This method is based on the assumption that a particular tenant of any particular type is likely to be capable of achieving a certain share of the market in his own business classification, almost regardless of competition. This share varies from store to store, and even for the same type of store in different trade areas. The method considered below is that advocated by Nelson for a projected centre with unknown tenants; in stages 1 to 7, the relevant factors given in Chapter 5 should be included in the appropriate sections.[9]

TECHNIQUE

1 Define trade area.
2 Subdivide trade area in census districts or octant-segments.
3 Enumerate population in the trade area and in each subdivision.
4 Tabulate earnings and family size for each subdivision.
5 Analyse existing shopping habits.
6 Carry out accessibility studies.
7 Assess competitive facilities.
8 Calculate total gross income. Multiply average family income by the number of families in each area.
9 Percentage assignment. Making subjective judgements, give an arbitrary assignment of percentage factors, which represent the total volume of trade in each area that will go to the projected centre. For the purposes of accuracy, two percentage factors are applied to each subdivision within (say) 3 miles radius, one for convenience goods, the other for durables.

10 Calculate total income of prospective customers by the application of the percentage factors to the total gross incomes of all residents in each area. The summation of these results gives the total volume to be spent in the centre, on convenience and durable goods.

11 Retail expenditure factors. These are calculated for convenience, primary, secondary and general goods, as the percentage of the gross income expended by the average family in each area on each separate good.

12 Franchise area calculations (for convenience goods sales). The total income of prospective customers living within (say) 2 miles radius who will make convenience goods purchases at the centre is calculated; the same calculation is made for those living outside this area, to which the second percentage factor is applied. The personal expenditure factors calculated in stage 11 are then applied for each convenience good.

13 Outside area calculations (for convenience goods sales). Subjective judgements are used to assess a percentage figure, being the portion of the total convenience purchases of the prospective customers which will actually be made at the subject centre, normally 10–15 per cent. The results of stages 12 and 13 are then added.

14 Durable goods expectancy. The retail expenditure factors calculated in stage 11 are applied to the total income of prospective customers for each category of primary, secondary and general purchases.

15 Add up volume expectancy figures for convenience, primary, secondary and general goods to obtain the totals for the centre.

16 Sales per net square foot. These are assessed from local practice comparisons, for each category listed in stage 15.

17 Required net sales area. Divide the expected annual volume of sales by sales per square foot. This will not include storage or utility areas.

18 Volume expectancy and net sales area. Allowance should be made for 'crossed lines' of several tenants (see also Table 8.1).

19 Personal consumption expenditures. The percentage of total income spent by each family in selected income groups on retail purchases is calculated, and applied to the total gross income of each area, and personal expenditures at the subject centre are calculated for convenience and durable goods.

20 Estimate total business at other business districts. Subtract personal expenditure in stage 19 from the total expenditure.

21 Calculation check. Expenditure at the subject centre plus that in stage 20 must equal total expenditure in the whole trade area.

This technique involves a multiplicity of separate judgements, thus ADVANTAGES reducing the potential for cumulative error. The depth of the preliminary research gives useful information which can be used in the design of the shopping centre and in its promotional techniques. Nelson suggests that a conservative attitude should be adopted with regard to future volume of trade, and that leases will only be signed if the present volume indicates a considerable underprovision of retail facilities.[10]

DISADVANTAGES The length of time necessary to undertake any research of this type is its main disadvantage, especially where competition for sites and potential markets is high. Similarly, it involves considerable field surveys and consumer research studies, which are expensive and rely on experienced interviewers, particularly in the assessment of shopping habits and preferences.

The main disadvantage, however, is the calculation of the correct percentage factors in stages 9 and 13. Although these are based on local and national circumstances, they are still arbitrary and subjective judgements.

COMPARISON OF VACUUM AND MARKET SHARE METHODS The vacuum method tends to produce a more conservative estimate than the market share method, which generally gives an optimistic assessment of turnover potential. The following example set out in Table 6.1 gives the comparative results when each method is applied to the same subject location for a small scale redevelopment project.[11]

Data A suburban area with 70–80 shops, 2–3 miles from the city centre, with grocery selling space of 8,000–9,000 square feet. A local cinema would convert into a supermarket of 5,000 square feet (equivalent to 60 per cent increase in floor space).

Problem Is the project viable?

Table 6.1   CALCULATIONS FOR VACUUM AND MARKET SHARE METHODS

Trade area	Population	Grocery spending head/week	Vacuum potential (£)	Market share potential (£)
Ward A	10,000	11 *s*	5,500	5,500
Ward B	15,000	12 *s*	9,000	9,000
Total potential spending			14,500	14,500
Spending in town centre (25%)			3,625	
			10,875	
Local shop sales			2,875	
Potential available to centre			8,000	16%
Existing shops in centre			6,100	
Available to new store			1,900	2,300
Total sales of new store (grocery × 2)			£3,800	£4,600

(In this example, only groceries have been taken into account.)

The Haydock Report, commissioned by the Metropolitan Railway Surplus Lands Company as proposers of the development, represents the most comprehensive attempt yet made to assess a particular out-of-town shopping centre site. At the same time, the Report attempted to measure the likely effects of such a centre on the trade in existing neighbouring towns. The method used was the variation of Reilly's Law, as discussed in Chapter 5, and the market share system; the estimated trade capture was deducted from the projected sales in the neighbouring towns. In view of Nelson's reservations on projections, it is significant that the Report only considers development up to 1971, i.e. 7 years after its publication, and 10 years since the previous major Census. The Report noted that the main variable which cannot be projected beyond 1971 is regional planning policy and its effect on the distribution of population and employment. For comparative purposes, the main stages of the analysis are given below.

TECHNIQUE

1 Analysis of retail sales in 1961. The modified version of Reilly's Law was used to define a system of hinterlands, with the grades of centre as previously described. The analysis was undertaken for convenience and durable goods sales for each type of centre, and the expenditure generated by each hinterland calculated.

2 Population and employment 1961–1971. The 1961 population of the region was analysed in terms of households, age/sex structure, and incomes and employment according to social status classifications of the Family Expenditure Survey. Future changes up to 1971 were based on probable changes in the employment structure, changes owing to trends in natural increase or voluntary migration of population, the growth of incomes and expenditure, and public policy on housing and planning generally. To meet the large number of variants in these considerations, the three different projections listed in Chapter 5 were used.

3 Changes in the hierarchy, 1971. These were evaluated on the basis of competitive facilities, future redevelopment proposals, the redistribution of population and accessibility. The three different projections noted above were applied to these factors.

4 Projection of results. Using these different postulations, regional sales at 1971 were calculated on the basis of the new hierarchy, new hinterlands being drawn for Grade 1 and Grade 2 centres in the region. As a result of this reassessment, three possible situations were analysed:

a With a Grade 1 centre at Haydock. The potential hinterland is very extensive, the further reaches being more than 60 minutes driving time away. (See Fig. 5.2.)

b With a Grade IIA centre at Haydock, virtually all of the hinterland is within 30 minutes driving time.

c If no centre was built at Haydock, the likely increase of 33 per cent in retail sales by 1971 would be expended in the region generally.

5 The effects of development at Haydock. As a result, the percentage of trade lost in 1971 by established centres would be 12 per cent each for Liverpool, Manchester and Bolton, 16 per cent for Preston and Crewe, 34 per cent for St. Helen's, 41 per cent for Wigan and 46 per cent for Warrington. The total impact in 1971 on neighbouring towns in terms of turnover is given in Table 6.2.[13]

Table 6.2   IMPACT OF HAYDOCK CENTRE IN TERMS OF 1971 TURNOVER (1961 = 100)

	Without centre at Haydock	With centre at Haydock
Liverpool	136	120
Manchester	127	113
Blackburn	161	155
Blackpool	185	184
Bolton	125	112
Chester	153	146
Hanley	147	141
Preston	164	136
Southport	156	146
Warrington	278	148
Wigan	136	89
Crewe	161	135
St. Helen's	98	70

With a minimum situation, sales at Haydock would be approximately £10 million per annum. In this case, only Warrington, Wigan and St. Helen's would suffer any loss, of between 5 per cent and 10 per cent of sales in 1971. Naturally, the maximum situation would only be attained if a sufficiently wide range and choice of shops were provided, but the Report states that sales of about £50 million per annum might be needed to make the venture commercially viable.

CRITICISM OF THE REPORT One criticism of the Report noted the apparent failure to allow for the increasing efficiency in the use of shopping floor space, in terms of sales per square foot.[14] Professor Kantorowich later stated that this index could not be considered as a reliable measure of efficiency, since it ignored the total costs of achieving this increase in sales, and would not be a decisive factor in measuring the capacity of existing centres to accommodate future increases in shopping.[15]

The Report also notes the necessity for some form of cost-benefit analysis to be undertaken, to evaluate advantages of the centralization of major retail and social facilities. Unfortunately, such an analysis, which would have proved most valuable for future studies, was not carried out. It was also unfortunate that the survey of the shopping habits and characteristics of Manchester, given in Appendix C of the Report, should have proved inadequate for any assessment to be made of likely sales to workers, particularly as the survey was especially commissioned for this purpose.

Similarly, no satisfactory explanation was given of how trade of shops in rural areas has been apportioned between the various hinterlands which cut across them, although this was done for incomes and the generation of spending power.[16]

Apart from the necessary assumption of the 'maximum' and 'minimum' situations used in assessing future trade volume, the major assumption in the Report was that the projected centre would be patronized by every car owning family in its hinterland. Consequently the use of public transport was not considered for this centre. Again, it was assumed that difficulties concerning the use of private cars for shopping trips would be overcome by adjusting shopping hours and providing extensive free parking, and that accessibility would be no problem. In fact, the Minister's decision letter refusing the application stated that excessive growth of traffic would develop on the neighbouring East Lancashire Road, despite an improved junction with the M.6 motorway. (This, however, was not the main grounds for refusal.)

Despite these reservations, on the details of technique, this Report is the most comprehensive analysis of the future trade potential available to an out-of-town centre, in addition to assessing the likely impact of such a development on existing towns.

In December 1966, Manchester University Department of Town and Country Planning published a second volume to their original Report, based on the mathematical model published in America in 1965 by Lakshmanan and Hansen,[18] and using the University's Atlas computer. While the original Report was based on the identification and assessment of the various centres and their hinterlands, the mathematical model assumes that retail expenditure is 'drawn from all parts of the region to each and every centre: the region is not sub-divided into hinterlands but treated as one economic space differentiated by zones of spending power, centres of shopping attraction and the "friction" involved in overcoming the distances between them'.[19] The model does not accept the rigidity of trade area boundaries, but rather 'describes a situation of overlapping competition between shopping centres and develops a mathematical framework for measuring it.'[20]

THE HAYDOCK REPORT PART TWO: A RETAIL SHOPPING MODEL[17]

Using the extensive data already collected for the Haydock Report, the Manchester University team calibrated the model for 1961 and prepared the 1971 imput data, before carrying out predictive runs, which were tabulated as follows:

APPLICATION AT HAYDOCK

1 The model for 1971, assuming no development at Haydock, which was compared with the results obtained in the original Study.

2 A similar comparison for 1971, assuming both the 'maximum' and 'minimum' centre at Haydock.

3 A similar comparison of the amount of sales captured from existing towns by a centre at Haydock in 1971.

Because of a lack of accurate floor space figures, which are used in the American example as the measure of the attractive power of shopping centres, the University team developed the individual indices for each of the 47 centres which had been used in the original study, classified as 'F' values, which varied between 10 and 45 or 50, depending on the extent of the facilities provided. Using 'F' values, alternative sites for a new centre were tested along the M.6; the probable sales at these locations are indicated in Table 6.3.[21]

Table 6.3   PROBABLE SALES FOR ALTERNATIVE LOCATIONS OF HAYDOCK CENTRE

Size (F)	Sales (£ m)							
	10	15	20	25	30	35	40	45
New centre at:								
M.6 Haydock	2·7	5·8	9·9	15·2	21·7	29·3	38·0	47·5
M.6 Risley New Town	1·9	4·8	8·8	14·1	20·6	28·2	36·9	46·3
M.6 Knutsford	1·2	3·3	6·6	11·1	16·7	23·4	30·8	39·0
M.6 Leyland	2·4	4·5	7·7	11·9	17·0	22·9	29·6	36·8
M.6 Audley	1·1	3·1	6·0	9·5	13·5	18·0	23·0	28·4
Preston	—	—	—	18·4	22·2	26·5	31·2	36·3
Wigan	—	—	—	16·8	22·2	28·3	35·1	42·5
Warrington	—	—	13·1	17·9	23·6	30·1	37·5	45·5
Crewe	—	—	6·9	9·2	12·0	15·2	18·9	22·9

As the group states, sales of over £40 million could be expected from centres developed at Haydock, Risley, Warrington and Wigan, while nearly comparable results might be obtained at Knutsford, Leyland and Preston. It was also possible to estimate the impact of the development of a scheme comparable to the Haydock maximum being located at each of the nine sites considered in Table 6.3. The results of this assessment are given in Table 6.4, in terms of the ratio of 1971 sales to 1961 sales, and assuming that the loss due to the introduction of the centre exceeds 5 per cent and that the resulting growth between 1961 and 1971 is less than 25 per cent.[22]

ADVANTAGES As the study concludes, this technique, because of its simplicity and time saving, could be most beneficial to regional and local planning offices in the assessment of present and future retail requirements. Results can be obtained with relatively low outlays of money and manpower, provided that there is access to a computer, which unfortunately is not always the case for smaller authorities or independent

Table 6.4 EFFECTS ON OTHER CENTRES OF ALTERNATIVE LOCATIONS FOR HAYDOCK CENTRE: SALES IN 1971 (1961 = 1·00)

With New or Expanded Centre. F = 45

	Without Haydock	Preston	Leyland	Wigan	Haydock	Risley	Warrington	Knutsford	Crewe	Audley
Lancaster	1·36	1·20	1·18							
Preston	1·68	—	1·01							
Blackburn	1·48	1·23	1·16							
Darwen	1·07	0·90	0·80	0·99	0·98	1·01				
Wigan	1·68	0·71	1·22	—	0·88	1·15				
Chorley	1·27		0·71	1·06	1·08	1·15	1·18	1·19		
St. Helen's	1·31		1·18	1·10	0·87	1·08	1·08	1·11		
Leigh	1·25		1·17	1·04	0·94	1·06	1·11	1·14		
Manchester	1·38				1·24	1·20	—	1·23		
Warrington	1·78				1·14	0·95	—	—		
Widnes	1·57				—	1·19	0·81	—		
Northwich	1·60				1·20	0·92	1·05	0·49		1·15
Hanley	1·39					1·20		1·13	1·04	0·80
Longton	1·32					—		1·22	1·18	0·96
Stoke	1·09					1·03		1·00	0·96	0·78
Newcastle	1·43								1·17	0·86
Crewe	1·53									0·89

researchers. It is not apparent from the study how much of the data required for the computer input was in fact collected for the first Report, and how much further research was necessary. Nevertheless, the power and flexibility of the technique is impressive, and the group suggests that intelligence units should be set up to exploit the potential, possibly subscribed to by central, regional and local government, universities and independent organizations.

Further work using the mathematical model has been undertaken by Rhodes and Whitaker[23] in an analysis of south London shopping centres, and the results, produced by an IBM 7094 computer, have again been compared with the actual retail sales in 1961, and expressed as a percentage. In addition, further research was carried out on existing and new shopping floor space requirements for central areas in selected centres throughout Great Britain, the results of which were given in Table 5.16.

OTHER REFERENCES

The Research Group of the West Midlands Branch of the Town Planning Institute states two main topics for examination:

6.6 THE WEST MIDLANDS STUDY[24]

1 The distribution of expenditure among competing centres.
2 The conversion of this distribution into floor space requirements.

The report, *Predicting Shopping Requirements*, deals only with the first item and reviews techniques employed in previous surveys by F. H. W. Green and H. W. E. Davies, and especially that by G. M. Lomas in his original analysis of the Midlands.[25] From these studies, two factors were isolated for detailed consideration and measurement:

1 Accessibility, defined as the ease with which a centre can be reached.
2 Attraction, being a measure of the qualities that draw shoppers to a centre.

In assessing accessibility, the report emphasizes several of the factors already outlined in Chapter 5, especially with reference to journey times according to the various modes of transport. Accessibility parameters are produced for different journey times, related to the number of visits per week to any centre. For the measurement of attraction, two possible systems were considered:

1 The use of indices, as employed in the Haydock Report, according to the range of retail and other facilities in a particular centre.
2 Central area durable sales.

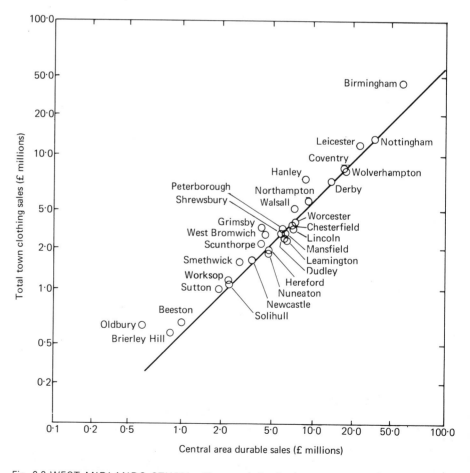

Fig. 6.2 WEST MIDLANDS STUDY.   The correlation between clothing sales and durable sales in selected Midland towns.

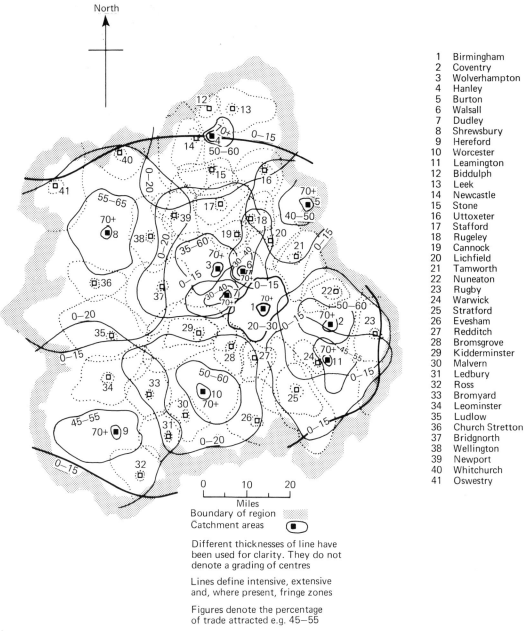

Fig. 6.3 WEST MIDLANDS STUDY.   Regional catchment areas.

The latter was considered more reliable than indices, and a good correlation was noted between central area durable sales and a town's clothing sales. (See Fig. 6.2.) It was suggested, therefore, that where total central area sales figures were not available, clothing sales turnover could also be used to gauge relative attraction.

TECHNIQUE[26] The technique is concerned with the analysis of turnover in existing shopping centres, and the definition of trade areas. Nevertheless, its use may be especially beneficial in the assessment of one particular location being considered for a regional or subregional centre, since the existing retail structure may be compared easily with the trade area calculated for such a centre. In the Study, each stage of the analysis can be related to a flow diagram for calculating shopping turnover and floor space, and is used as input data for a computer program. The detailed information required for each stage, together with the layout of the diagram, is given in full in Appendix C.

ADVANTAGES To test the technique, the model was applied to the West Midlands Region for 1961 (see Fig. 6.3), and the percentage variation was calculated between the published Census turnover (corrected for non-response), and the estimated turnover for all major centres. Although individual results vary, the correlation between published and estimated turnover was as high as 0·99, which indicates the accuracy and validity of the technique, especially with such anomalies as occur in Census data and in expenditure patterns. For smaller areas, the technique has the further advantage of manual application in a series of clearly tabulated stages. For both computer and manual applications, the Research Group is investigating the conversion of total expenditure into floor space requirements.

REFERENCES
1 Cumbernauld Development Corporation, *Retail Trade Provision Report* 1960; *Revision,* Sept. 1964.
G. Copcutt, 'Shopping facilities at Cumbernauld', *Architects' Journal,* 5 Dec. 1962 p. 783–789.
G. M. Lomas, 'Retail trading centres in the Midlands', *T.P.I. Journal,* March 1964, p. 104–119.
2 Cumbernauld Development Corporation, 1964 *Revision,* p. 5–6.
3 Cumbernauld Development Corporation, 1961 *Report,* p. 49.
4 R. J. Green and R. M. Beaumont, 'The size of shopping centres', *T.P.I. Journal,* Dec. 1962, p. 311–314 and March 1963, p. 80–81.
5 C. Clarke, 'Assessment of floor space', *Chartered Surveyor,* April 1965, p. 532–533.
R. N. Percival, *Assessment of Shopping Needs,* T.P.I. Summer School Report 1965, p. 107–109.
Shopping Centres in Britain, *T.P.I. Journal,* Sept./Oct. 1965, p. 329–333.
6 R. Nelson, *Selection of Retail Locations,* p. 230.
7 T. Rhodes, 'Techniques of site evaluation', *Self-Service and Supermarket Journal,* March 1966, p. 79.
8 R. Nelson, op. cit., p. 151.
L. Smith, 'The assessment of shopping needs', *Chartered Surveyor,* Jan. 1964, p. 325.
9 R. Nelson, op. cit., p. 188–195, 216 *et seq.*
10 R. Nelson, op. cit., p. 230.
11 T. Rhodes, op. cit., p. 79–80.
12 Manchester University, *Haydock Report,* 1964.
13 H. R. Cole, 'Shopping assessments at Haydock and elsewhere', *Urban Studies,* June 1966, p. 153.
14 J. A. Noble, 'Planning in the North-West (review)', *Architects' Journal,* 17 Feb. 1965, p. 387.
15 R. H. Kantorowich, Letter to *Architects' Journal,* 10 March 1965, p. 568.
16 H. R. Cole, op. cit., p. 151.
17 Manchester University, *Haydock Report* Part Two: A Retail Shopping Model 1966.
18 T. R. Lakshmanan and W. G. Hansen, 'A retail market potential model', *Journal of the American Institute of Planners,* May 1965.
19 Manchester University, *Haydock Report* Part Two, p. 10–11.
20 Manchester University, op. cit., Part Two, p. 11.
21 Manchester University, op. cit., Part Two, p. 36.
22 Manchester University, op. cit., Part Two, p. 38.
23 T. Rhodes and R. Whitaker, 'Forecasting shopping demand', *T.P.I. Journal,* May 1967, p. 188–192.
24 West Midlands Shopping Research Group, 'Predicting shopping requirements', Aug. 1967. See also Interim Report, *T.P.I. Journal,* April 1966, p. 146–149 and *T.P.I. Journal,* Feb. 1968, p. 96–97.
25 G. M. Lomas, 'Retail trading centres in the Midlands', *T.P.I. Journal,* March 1964, p. 104–109.
26 West Midlands Shopping Research Group, op. cit., p. 43–44.

finance and management

7

site economics and finance

Shopping centre finances depend on the rental return compared with the cost of the site, its development and building construction costs. Therefore, even if the site is already owned by the potential developer, the economic analysis should contain a realistic assessment of the likely site costs and other implications of the development, especially the following factors:

1 The site should be located so as to maximize on the potential expenditure from the whole of the trade area.

2 Preferably, possession of the site should already be in the hands of the developer, or under negotiation, and its development must be feasible. This consideration applies particularly in Britain, where suitable sites with good access are at a premium. In most cases, the site will have been purchased or options taken prior to the economic survey. This purchase may have required the acquisition of several separate parcels of land, and multiple ownership of a potential location often results in considerable delays. The piecemeal method of purchase may result in what is termed 'hold-outs', owners of desired land who are unwilling to sell on any basis, or who hope to increase the value of their property. Again, the extra cost involved must be equated against the anticipated returns without that parcel being included in the site.

3 The cost of the land must be in keeping with the overall economic consideration. The need to minimize acquisition costs, coupled with the desirability of obtaining as much property in order to accommodate fringe property and to provide for future growth of the centre itself, frequently necessitates a compromise as far as location is concerned. Because the principal controlling factor for site acquisition is business potential, compromises regarding location should be made only if it

can be established with absolute certainty that the economic potential of the centre will not suffer. Virtually all sizes and types of shopping centres are faced with approximately the same acreage/cost limitations in site acquisitions. L. Smith considers that the initial land value is a critical factor, though not necessarily the most important, and that, in suburban centres in America, the cost of building and the efficiency of the design may be more important. But when land costs exceed £2 per square foot of usable area, the entire economic equation should be re-examined.[1] In fact, building costs must be regarded as the prime variable which need careful control.

Good locations, even with high land costs, are likely to produce successful projects, whereas similar developments in poor locations, with low land costs, may result in failure, both in merchandising and as ventures. In most cases, the developer will compare sites by the application of a percentage factor, being the maximum potential (100 per cent) less the probable loss of trade owing to poor location, access, site topography, etc. In the case of the Gem site at Nottingham, limitations resulted in a '60 per cent potential' classification.[2]

7.2 EXISTING SITE USE

The desirability of purchasing relatively inexpensive sites generally results in the acquisition of vacant land, or that containing obsolete or derelict properties. In the case of the latter, the costs of demolition, clearance, stopping up of highways and discontinuance of utilities must be added to the site costs. Even where the land is 'undeveloped', the existing use must be considered, since objections may be raised purely for agricultural reasons, as in the case of Haydock. Thus, lower quality agricultural land should be selected where possible, preferably in large single units to avoid disruption of other uses. Occasionally, unusual sites have been investigated by developers, such as unsightly refuse tips owned by local authorities, as at the Gem Centre, Nottingham. In these cases considerable benefit may accrue to the Local Authority, but the cheapness of the site must be equated against the extra costs of foundation works, and the limitations on development owing to poor load bearing capabilities.

NEIGHBOURING USES

Objections to out-of-town or suburban centres have been raised by neighbouring property owners, on the grounds of competition or amenity, based on the theories of unfair trading and loss of residential property values.

In the case of neighbouring retailers, it has been established that trade will in fact increase in these outlets, primarily by reason of the centre's traffic generating capacity, both vehicular and pedestrian.[3]

In many cases, the service trades may prosper considerably, especially banks and public houses, as is the case at the Gem Centre, Nottingham. At the Ormesby Centre, Middlesbrough, the developer negotiated with an adjoining public house to amalgamate their respective car parks for their mutual benefit.[4] This combination of car parks, or of other facilities within or adjacent to the shopping centre, may be considered controversial. Nelson states that any facilities with large evening patronage should be avoided, as well as the dual use of parking, since successful neighbours may require too much valuable parking space.[5] The types of facilities which may be incorporated within the centre are considered further in Part Four.

In America, it has been necessary for the developer to control the neighbouring areas, especially those on the opposite side of access roads, to eliminate the possibility of competitive outlets being opened. These 'pirate' enterprises make use of the shopping centre's car parking areas. In Britain, such competition is unlikely to develop against genuine out-of-town centres, but cut price or discount stores may attempt to undersell the suburban centres.

While it may be preferable for the surrounding areas to be undeveloped, in most cases the neighbouring districts will be residential, whose 'amenity' should be protected. This is normally done by providing 'buffer' zones between the car parking areas and adjacent properties, and by the careful location of access points on the road network, to prevent disturbance and kerbside parking in residential streets. Where land is available, the buffer zones may be donated as public open space and provided with recreational facilities, though such layouts are more easily achieved if the centre is part of a new 'planned' community development.

7.3 FINANCE

The stages of site assessment prior to financing are:

1 to consider potential sites available.
2 to take options.
3 to make an economic survey, possibly including outline planning permission.
4 to prepare proposals for tenants.
5 to secure lease agreements.
6 to borrow money.[6]

Because of the severe requirements of mortgagees regarding minimum guarantees, in addition to a well presented economic survey, the financing of new centres has been difficult. The amount obtained will depend on the following:

1 *Location* The quality of the location and the nature of any competition.

2 *Tenants and rents* The availability of suitable tenants to pay satis-factory rents, preferably supported by 'offers to lease' or 'letters of intent'.

3 *Economic value* The economics of the project in terms of capital costs, returns, operation costs and expenses.

4 *The developer's investment* Where factors (1), (2) and (3) are favourable, it is possible that 80–100 per cent of the cost will be obtained (generally excluding the land costs). Where some of the former conditions are less favourable, possibly only 55–65 per cent can be obtained, the developer being expected to make a substantial cash equity investment in addition to the ownership of the site as a condition of first mortgage financing. This also ensures that the project will have a strong and interested management.[7]

SOURCES OF FINANCE The developer may be able to obtain the necessary finance from various sources, such as insurance companies, savings banks, loan associations, national or merchant banks, investment trusts or pension funds. It has also become customary to launch out-of-town schemes in this country under the aegis of subsidiaries of parent companies, often with American backing. For example, the parent company holds 52·7 per cent of the equity of Woolworths, of which the Woolco stores are an offshoot. Similarly, the American GEM International held 65 per cent interest in the original GEM Supercentres, with the remaining 35 per cent held by merchant bankers and their clients.[8]

In addition to these various sources, Gruen and Smith give certain techniques which have been developed in America to finance larger centres:

1 Split mortgages, by which mortgagees may loan on portions of the project, rather than on the whole project, though this may involve ease-ments with respect to parking, delivery facilities and other common areas.

2 Participation in a single 'blanket' mortgage by more than one mortgagee, to cover the whole project rather than a portion, as in (1).

3 Sale and lease-back, by which the property may be sold to a prospective investor and leased back to the developer, who will guarantee a certain return on the capital investment in the project, and may possibly agree to divide the surplus earnings with the investor.

4 Sale or ground-lease of the land upon which the department store or any other principal tenant is located to such a tenant. Also the con-struction of the building or buildings for the use of such principal tenant, by the tenant himself rather than by the developer. This has the effect

of reducing the total investment made by the developer and reduces the developer's portion of the construction work.

5 Ground-leases, by which owners of property lease it to a developer on conditions which may permit the subordination of the ownership in the land to the mortgagees.[9]

Valid consultations with finance organizations will not be possible until PLANNING the market study, preliminary drawings and contacts with potential PROGRAMME tenants have all been undertaken. Only at this stage will it be possible to ascertain likely costs and returns. However, assessment of the financial requirements and likely sources should be made before detailed architectural drawings are prepared, after which the precise amount of equity can be ascertained. The extent to which the leasing programme can be carried forward before permanent financing can be negotiated will depend on the source of finance, but signed agreements from key tenants are essential at this stage.[10]

In America, 'high land cost cannot be considered for any centre except CAPITAL COSTS one which would have a high concentration of pedestrian traffic, in addition to the anticipated automobile shoppers.'[11] Unfortunately, no comparative figures are available for actual site costs in this country, apart from those at Cowley given below, but higher land costs should not necessarily preclude the selection of a particular site. Hoyt quotes an American example of a large regional centre, where construction costs would be about £2,300,000. The 40 acres required could cost £640 an acre on the periphery or £3,300 an acre for a vacant tract surrounded by development. By taking the closer in location, the total cost would rise from £2,326,000 to £2,432,000, an increase of only 5 per cent, whereas the higher priced location might well produce 50 per cent more sales and net income.[12]

It is also important to look at cost figures per square foot in relation to the gross building area, since the latter includes all construction and maintenance costs. Square foot figures are derived by dividing the gross construction costs, including the parking area and site improvements, by the total square footage in the gross building area.

High capital costs are not necessarily an extravagance in shopping centre **7.4 CONSTRUC-** construction. They may be a sound investment if they result in lower **TION COSTS** operating costs and higher rentals, which can be based on pulling higher volumes and better quality trade. This is especially relevant to large regional centres which rely on the sale of durable goods to a higher class of patrons. Similarly, lower capital costs can be an extravagance if they result in exorbitant maintenance costs and too low rental income. The latter 'guaranteed' rentals should always be designed to cover such expenses, as well as to give a return on the investment. Meyers and Kaylin quote a cash return of 12·5 per cent of the owner's equity for an average American example.[13] The distribution of capital expenditure on construction for the Southdale Centre, Minneapolis, was as follows:[14]

Rental space	51%	
Public services	9%	
Fees/insurance	13%	Paid from rentals
Site costs	9%	
Off-site costs	2%	
Off-site costs	2%	Paid from separate charges
Utilities	14%	on tenants as 'services'

Available figures for the Cowley Centre, Oxford show the following breakdown:[15]

Acquisition of land and property	£118,000	(6·0%)
Roads, sewers and other site costs	£133,000	(6·8%)
Commercial and residential buildings	£1,359,000	(69·7%)
Multistorey car parks	£343,000	(17·5%)
Total cost	£1,953,000	(100·0%)

At Cowley, the full rental for the first year was £122,000, a return of 7 per cent after all outgoings (the Centre also produced additional rateable value of between £80,000 and £90,000). In the future, the high percentage taken by construction costs may be reduced by 'package deals' between the developer and the contractor, though this will depend on the nature of the development. A relatively simple structure, such as that used at the Gem Centre, Nottingham, though not a package contract, cost under £3 per square foot for over 80,000 square feet of building area.

REFERENCES   1 L. Smith, 'Assessment of shopping needs', *Chartered Surveyor*, Jan 1964, p. 329.
2 *Architects Journal*, 5 May 1965, p. 1074.
3 V. Gruen and L. Smith, *Shopping Towns U.S.A.*, p. 39.
   Urban Land Institute, *Shopping Centres Re-studied*, vol. 1, p. 27.
4 *Self-Service and Supermarket Journal*, 'American shopping, Ormesby style', March 1965, p. 44–46.
5 R. Nelson, *Selection of Retail Locations*, p. 41.
6 National Cash Register Co.
7 V. Gruen and L. Smith, op. cit., p. 57.
   R. Nelson, op. cit., p. 274.
8 *Self-Service and Supermarket Journal*, Sept. 1964, p. 17.
9 A. E. Goodens, 'Profits from sale and leaseback', *Shop Property*, Oct. 1967, p. 3.
   V. Gruen and L. Smith, op. cit., p. 58.
10 V. Gruen and L. Smith, op. cit., p. 58.
11 G. Baker and B. Funaro, *Shopping Centres —Design and Operation*, p. 24.

12 G. Baker and B. Funaro, op. cit., p. 24.
13 P. Meyers and S. O. Kaylin, 'Planning Shopping Centre Profits', *Shopping Centre Age* (n.d.).
14 *Architectural Forum,* March 1963, p. 132.
15 Oxford C.B., *Cowley Centre,* (Brochure).
    B. J. Wratten, 'Cowley centre', *Chartered Surveyor,* Sept. 1965, p. 131.

8

tenants and leases

8.1 TENANTS Shopping centre tenants may be classified in two categories, depending on their size and function:

1 Major key tenants, such as department stores or supermarkets, which act as 'magnets' to generate pedestrian movement through the centre.
2 Other lesser units and service trades benefiting from this pedestrian movement, and which normally pay higher rental charges than the key tenants.

As Gruen states, 'The character of a shopping centre determines, in large measure, the character of the tenants it will attract. By the same token, the type and character of the shopping centre will usually reflect the kind of tenants available to it'.[1] In assessing potential tenants, the following considerations should be borne in mind:

1 *Key tenants* These have been listed previously according to the size of centres, but in each case, the key tenant is 'signed up' as early as possible at the planning stage and before negotiations are entered into with other potential tenants. To attract a key tenant, it may be necessary for the developer to offer unusually favourable rental and leasing arrangements, especially if the subject site is not in a prime location in relation to its trade area, or if no suitable alternative tenants are available. In all cases, tenants will require evidence of the viability of the project, which will itself be related closely to the size and reputation of the key tenant, whether it is a department store or a supermarket. Considerable difficulty may be encountered in attracting a local department store as a key tenant, since its trade at the central store may be expected to decline. But most major centres in Britain have obtained a major or a branch

department store as the key tenant—two such stores were envisaged at the original Brent Cross Centre.

2 *National chains and independent traders* The allocation of space between national chains and independents will depend on the class of centre, and the interest shown by each type of retailer. National chains will attract greater patronage, but may at the same time have other branches in competitive centres, while the independent traders may possibly pay higher rentals. In America, the Urban Land Institute recommends that not more than 50 per cent of the leasable area should be allocated to national chains, and states that the independent local trader is important, especially in neighbourhood centres.[2] For the smaller retailer, an economic rent will be dependent on the total expenditure necessary to generate the minimum volume of trade, including any expense incurred on advertising. In this respect, rent and advertising are reciprocals, in that the more spent on advertising, the less can or need be spent on rent, and vice versa.[3]

In Britain, however, multiple chains may be reluctant to enter many smaller suburban centres, and agreement to lease by one such chain store will often preclude other competitors from the centre though, in major centres, department stores and multiples can be regarded as joint key tenants.

3 *Supermarkets* The role of supermarkets varies according to the size of centre. While in the neighbourhood centre the supermarket will be the prime tenant, in the larger centre it is doubtful whether it will achieve even as great an impact on the normal trade area of a supermarket as it would in a smaller project in the same location. Conversely, it would also draw trade from a wider area beyond the immediate catchment zone, from those shoppers attracted to the shopping centre for other goods. There is some doubt as to whether two supermarkets are justifiable in a regional centre—the benefit accruing from the competitive influence must be compared with the possible congestion in the adjacent parking areas, thus increasing the customers' walking distances to the centre, and the extra space required for the greater number of delivery vehicles. Further extentions of supermarket space increase the potential for multiple trading or 'crossed lines' as indicated in Table 8.1.

The net profits of American supermarkets as a percentage of turnover is about 2 per cent of sales, though margins on non-grocery types as listed above are an average of 29 per cent.

Table 8.1   INCIDENCE OF NON-FOOD LINES
IN U.S. SUPERMARKETS 1964[a]

Category	Percentage of supermarkets carrying
Health and beauty aids	100
Stationery	91
Baby needs	91
Housewares	87
Vitamins	75
Children's books	72
Magazines	71
Soft goods	66

8.2 TYPES OF TENANT Apart from the key tenants, the type and required area of each tenant will be directly related to:

1   The amount of trade done in any particular good by the key tenant.
2   The estimated total turnover or floor space as calculated in the economic survey.

In general, the smaller retailer should offer a range of goods of a more expensive or specialist nature. The sports or photographic goods store for example, may obtain a large sector of the market, and thus be an important operator in the centre, or provide a service closer to the main catchment area than stores operating in the town centre, i.e. 'business interception'. While the above may be the American practice, and desirable in most locations, the caution of smaller retailers in Britain has limited the measure of choice offered to developers, who have been obliged for financial reasons to accept virtually any offer of tenancy, in order to promote the growth of the subject centre so as to retain those traders already in operation. On the other hand, the advantages of the inclusion of any locally accepted retailer must be weighed against any possible loss in trade to other shops in the area and under the same ownership, especially if the loss occurs among the higher income and account customers on which the genuine out-of-town centre depends.

LOCATION OF TENANTS   The precise location of individual stores within the contemplated project, as well as the location of the project itself and its estimated potential turnover, is based on the assumption that the detailed planning and architectural design will maximize the locational potential resulting from the relationship and juxtaposition of different tenant types. The principles of store location are considered in Chapter 11.

SELECTION OF TENANTS   The types of tenant planned or incorporated into the shopping centre will depend on five major factors:

1   The type of centre.
2   The estimated turnover or square footage required.
3   Local consumer habits.
4   Competitive facilities.
5   The availability of suitable tenants.

Owing to the variable nature of these factors, no definite rules on tenant selection can be formulated, though British practice would not seem to differ radically from that in America, where the order of most popular tenant types are: chemist/drug store, food market, variety store, bakery, dry cleaner, beauty parlour, women's wear, shoes, gift and book shops, children's clothes, jewellery, barber, men's wear, sweet shop and shoe repairs.[5]

The actual average number of tenants for each type of centre has been listed in Part Two.

The inclusion of such institutional tenants as post offices, banks, insurance offices and statutory undertakers' offices is generally recommended, for the following reasons:

INSTITUTIONAL TENANTS

1 They are 'secure' tenants who pay fairly high fixed rentals.
2 They may attract potential customers who do not visit the centre primarily for shopping purposes.
3 They require relatively less storage space and warehousing facilities.

The location of these tenants and other facilities within the centre are considered in Chapter 11.

A list of types of tenants suitable for regional centres, together with their occurrence in certain British centres, is given in Appendix D.

CHECK LIST OF TENANT TYPES

In most centres it has been the practice, once the key tenant is agreed, to proceed with leasing arrangements with other willing tenants, but it is preferable for 10–20 per cent of the rental area to be unleased at the commencement of trading, so that immediate future demands may be met from traders and customers. In the assessment of any lease, Nelson lists the following five important variables:

8.3 LEASING

1 The amount of business which the tenant can produce per square foot (used to assess the rental).
2 The degree to which the retailer rather than the location can generate business.
3 The amount of mark-up on goods to be sold.
4 The tenant's ability to retain the sales volume.
5 The detailed lease terms, particularly the clauses relating to maintenance charges.[6]

In Great Britain, two types of lease are used as the basis of rent payment, though the conditions of each are similar. In type (1) the 'fixed rent', tenants pay a fixed exclusive rent, plus the cost of rates, lighting, heating and shop fronts, together with a contribution towards the maintenance of the common ways, parking areas, and the cost of promotions. This

TYPES OF LEASE

type of lease is the more usual in Britain up to the present; the rental in this case may be paid weekly, monthly or annually.

In type (2) the 'percentage rent', tenants pay as rent a stipulated percentage of their gross volume of sales of merchandising and services. In most cases, the tenant agrees to pay a specified minimum of rent, even if the rent payable on the percentage factor would produce a lesser amount. These specified minimum rents are designed to cover the developer's fixed expenses, such as interest, taxes, insurance and upkeep, to which the added percentage will give the profit return.

ADVANTAGES OF THE PERCENTAGE LEASE

The percentage lease became necessary in America because tenants were sceptical of results, and were reluctant to invest considerable capital; the same conditions now apply to a large extent in Britain. Discussing this form of lease, L. Smith has stated that 'percentage rents are probably proportionately better for the developer than for the trader, although in current practice they permit the fixing of a rent at the beginning of a substantial lease period at a figure which provides the trader with a moderate rent as a guaranteed factor, and still allows the owner a basis for developing an adequate return on the enhancement of land value, by relating it to the annual sales as they increase. In many cases of new shopping centres, sales will increase 10 or 15 per cent a year for a period of five years or more—in other words, the initial volume may be only half that produced at the end of six years. A combination of minimum and percentage rents allows the tenant to operate in the early years at a lower rent than would otherwise be possible, but it provides the developer with a return for competent planning and development activity to the extent that the quality of his location justifies.'[7]

EXAMPLES OF RENTALS

1 Comparative fixed rentals are not available for all centres, but at the Ormesby Centre, Middlesbrough, concessionaires pay between 22s and 30s per square foot per year, including rates, underfloor heating and lighting,[8] while Table 8.2 gives the annual exclusive rentals at the Yate and Elephant and Castle centres.

2 Table 8.3 gives the average percentage rates applicable in America in 1962; the lowest rates are of course paid by the most profitable stores.[9]

At the Gem Centre, Nottingham, the percentage rental is about 10–12 per cent, irrespective of department, plus the contributions towards promotions, heating, lighting and rates, and a proportion of the cost of any storage space required.

CHARACTERISTICS OF RENTALS

A survey carried out by the Urban Land Institute showed marked trends in shopping centre results. The minimum rentals in community centres

Table 8.2 ASKING FIXED RENTALS AT YATE AND ELEPHANT AND CASTLE CENTRES, 1967

	Yate Centre		Elephant and Castle centre		
	Area (ft²)	Rental (ft²)	Area (ft²)	Rental (ft²)	Service charge (£)
Betting office	905	22s 1d	1,000	25s 6d	300
Café/coffee bar	905	22s 1d	1,248	46s 9d	375
Kitchen equipment/D.I.Y.	1,910	26s 2d	1,045	44s 0d	315
Jeweller	905	22s 1d	1,350	44s 5d	410
Greengrocer	1,120	22s 4d	880	44s 3d	265
Men's wear	3,460	15s 10d	1,100	43s 7d	330
Ladies' wear	1,010	25s 8d	930	44s 1d	280
Furniture/furnishings	2,500	24s 0d	2,074	46s 3d	660
Launderette	905	22s 1d	848	42s 6d	250
Hairdresser	905	22s 1d	384	47s 11d	116
Tobacco/newsagent	905	22s 1d	960	45s 10d	315
Bank/shoes/carpets/electrical	905	22s 1d			
Cleaners/baker/hardware	1,120	22s 4d			
Grocer/cycles/paints–decorators	1,640	18s 3d			
Multiple chemist	4,170	14s 5d			
Chemist	1,915	23s 6d			
Off-licence	3,000	16s 8d			
Estate agent	1,620	14s 9d			
Insurance office			990	25s 3d	300
Bingo hall			1,000	25s 6d	330
Travel agent			384	47s 11d	116
Restaurant			1,200	45s 10d	380

Table 8.3 PERCENTAGE RENTALS 1962

	Percentage of sales
Supermarkets	1·0
Department stores	2·5
S.S. drugs	3·0
Men's clothing	4·0
Variety	5·0
Women's clothing	5·0
Service drugs	5·0
Hardware	5·0
Bars	8·0

operating for one or two years were substantially higher than in older centres. On the other hand, percentage rents tended to increase steadily with the number of years of operation of the centre, and similar trends were apparent in regional centres.[10] Expenses also tend to increase according to the age of the centre, especially local taxes and maintenance charges, and the majority of leases ensure that these increases are met by the tenant.

For major tenants, a 21–30 year lease is usual, though this will depend on the nature of the site ownership. Arndale Developments, for example, arrange all leases to terminate on the same date as the ground lease from

DURATION OF LEASES

the Local Authority, and are shortly to introduce 15 year leases, reviewed every 5 years, rather than the 21 year lease reviewed every 7 years.

In certain supercentre types, between 50 per cent and 100 per cent of the space is let to concessionaires on 90-day leases, with 1 month's notice; this enables 'non-conforming' tenants to be changed. In other centres, possibly 5–10 per cent of the smaller units will be let on similar short leases, especially those located adjacent to major tenants who may wish for further space for expansion.

LEASE CONDITIONS In addition to the normal leasing and service charge arrangements, two major conditions are frequently imposed in new centres, concerning the following:

1 *Merchants' Associations* Although the tenants may be in some competition, the centre may be run co-operatively by a jointly elected committee, the Association paying jointly for advertisements, promotions, office maintenance, common areas, communication systems, janitors and legal costs. While this system has not yet developed in Britain to a great extent, it would seem a logical progression for independent traders with common aims. Recent information suggests that these associations will become more prevalent with the growth of more complicated enclosed centres, and that the landlord will generally contribute between 20 and 25 per cent of the budget. As a guide, therefore, Table 8.4 gives the formulae used in the assessment of the trader's contribution to the Merchants' Associations operating in American centres.

Table 8.4   ASSESSMENT FORMULAE FOR MERCHANTS' ASSOCIATION
            CONTRIBUTIONS U.S.A.

Store category	Proportion of turnover	Maximum per square foot
Stores paying less than 3 per cent rent	1/20 of 1 per cent	up to 10 cents
Stores paying 3–6 per cent rent	1/4 of 1 per cent	up to 20 cents
Service stores paying over 6 per cent rent	1/2 of 1 per cent	(see text)

For the service trades, the maximum is 15 cents per square foot for areas of 10,000 square feet or more, 20 cents for areas between 5,000 and 10,000 square feet, and 40 cents for areas between 2,500 and 5,000 square feet. There is generally no maximum on stores with areas less than 2,500 square feet, while the landlord will normally give 25 per cent of the total in all cases, having a 25 per cent voting power.[11]

2 *Shop hours* Generally, all stores agree to keep the same hours, which are normally those of the key tenant, except for banks and possibly off licenses. This condition may be to the advantage of

the trader, since trade potential would otherwise be reduced by closing on different days or different hours. Any such conditions may be affected by the Shops Act (1950), though this allows a retailer to stay open until 8 p.m. on four nights and 9 p.m. on one night and also by a recent High Court ruling that 'the Local Authority cannot apply closing hour restrictions under the Shops Act to a store carrying on a multiplicity of trades and businesses'.[12]

REFERENCES

1 V. Gruen and L. Smith, *Shopping Towns U.S.A.*, p. 52.
2 Urban Land Institute, *Shopping Centres Re-studied*, p. 29.
3 R. Nelson, *Selection of Retail Locations*, p. 46.
4 N. Berry, 'U.S. food retailing', *Self-Service and Supermarket Journal*, June 1966, p. 44.
5 K. Welch, *Design for Modern Merchandising*, p. 152.
6 R. Nelson, op. cit., p. 292.
7 L. Smith, 'Assessment of shopping needs', *Chartered Surveyor*, Jan. 1964, p. 327–328.
8 *Self-Service and Supermarket Journal*, March 1964, p. 44.
9 National Cash Register Co.
10 Urban Land Institute, *The Dollars and Cents of Shopping Centres.*
11 Urban Land Institute, *Operation Shopping Centres*, p. 161.
12 *Stores and Shops Journal*, March 1965, p. 22.

site planning and design

9

site size and topography

The site should be at least the minimum acreage set up by the preliminary estimate in the economic analysis, together with the estimated area required for parking, as considered in Chapter 13. It has been shown in the United States that a centre of about 500,000 square feet of rental area can be accommodated on sites ranging from about 15 to 70 acres, but greater limitations are encountered in this country, where land is scarce and relatively expensive. The greatest limitations occur in smaller neighbourhood centres, which generally require single level plans, in contrast to regional centres, where several levels may be employed.

Wherever possible, the size of the site should allow for potential growth within the centre. The actual area should also be related to the likely maximum walking distances from the extremities of the parking zones, as discussed in Chapter 13. If the site area is too great, other uses may be introduced, such as residential accommodation, offices, motel or similar facilities.

As a general formula to gauge site adequacy, an acre of ground can be counted as providing 10,000 square feet of building coverage and 30,000 square feet of parking space. This presupposes that this ratio is a typical or acceptable allocation of space for each use. Table 9.1 gives an indication of the application of this 'rule' to various centre types.[1]

Table 9.1 APPROXIMATE SITE AREA
FOR SHOPPING CENTRES U.S.A.

Type	Building area (ft²)	Site area (acres)
Neighbourhood	50,000	5
Community	150,000	15
Regional	400,000	40

SITE SHAPE The site must be in one piece, and uninterrupted by roads, except if there is grade separation between the shopping and road levels. A regularly shaped property without acute angles, odd projections or indentations is desirable, to eliminate dead areas, though such faults can be corrected with ingenuity. Even with sites of sufficient area, major irregularities in shape may make them unsuitable since their full utilization is not feasible. Conversely, such sites may give rise to imaginative solutions and successful operation.[2] Site feasibility may rely on the frontage available, though total frontage is less vital than easy access, in terms of transfer of vehicles from the surrounding road system.[3] Frontage may be considered more important for the supercentre type, which preferably is developed with the longer side parallel to the main access road, the length of this side varying between 250 and 400 feet.

9.2 TOPOGRAPHY The topography of the site and the surrounding area may be a decisive factor in site assessment and viability. Extensive site works and extra construction costs necessitated by unfavourable topography must be added to the site development costs, though unusual site characteristics may result in lower initial purchase costs. The shortage of suitable sites places almost any site of sufficient area at a premium, and the growth of two-level shopping means that sites previously considered as un-economic can be investigated; the topography can in fact be used to the centre's advantage, to distribute the flow of customers more con-sistently on different levels. No definite rules can be given for the accept-able degree of slope, though it has been suggested that it should not exceed 10 or 12 feet. A steep slope will automatically determine the direction of the parking lanes, in order to park cars across the prevailing slope rather than parallel to it, and customers may be obliged to walk up such inclines. The use of sloping sites may also facilitate the construc-tion of basement sales or storage space, and the grade separation of public and goods vehicles.

OTHER PHYSICAL CHARACTERISTICS Any other features, such as rights of way, easements in respect of overhead or underground services and drainage patterns should be considered; the possible effects on the latter should be noted where extensive earth-works and regrading might affect the drainage of adjoining properties. Similarly existing utilities must be assessed in terms of surplus capacities. The landscape features, such as trees and bushes, may also limit site development, especially where their retention is required by the Local Authority. Soil characteristics and bearing capacity tests must also be carried out in the site survey, preferably prior to purchase, to indicate any limitations on development and any extra construction costs.

VISIBILITY Visibility of the site and the centre from the surrounding road network is generally considered important, especially in smaller centres which are less likely to advertise or to sponsor promotions. The main views of any centre should be from the main level of that centre. A high viewpoint will overemphasize the roof areas, and below grade roads may be obscured by embankments. (See Plate 9.1.) Similarly, trees on the site or bordering the frontage will limit visibility. Here, the potential developer must equate the desire for maximum visibility with the added attractiveness created by established landscape features, as in the case of the Woolco centre at Oadby.

Plate 9.1 BREDA CENTRE, BELFAST.   Emphasis is placed on the availability of ample free parking, rather than on an imposing building complex.

Though the economic and social analyses may make a particular site a SUMMARY desirable location, the size, shape or topography may make it uneconomic. Only rarely will an investigated site fulfil all requirements; in most cases, advantages will have to be balanced against shortcomings. However, owing to the scarcity of sites which meet adequately any of the requirements or have planning permission, a greater potential danger exists in this country for developers to build centres in poor locations or on un-satisfactory sites. In many cases, the site has already been purchased before the economic survey is completed, representing a considerable capital investment, and the subsequent centre may become a compromise of planning and architectural principles, merely as a result of poor site selection.

REFERENCES 1 Urban Land Institute, *Shopping Centres Re-studied*, Vol. 1, p. 25.
2 V. Gruen and L. Smith, *Shopping Towns U.S.A.*, p. 41.
3 G. Baker and B. Funaro, *Shopping Centres —Design and Operation*, p. 29.

10

basic shopping centre types

The basic types of centre, developed with growing expertise in America to suit various site and retailing conditions, are characterized by their plan forms, and the location of the key tenants. These plan forms are designed to attract the greatest number of customers to the centre, and to channel them through it, to create the maximum of pedestrian traffic and interstore shopping opportunities.

By placing the key tenants in locations where they act as attractors, patrons are drawn through the shopping areas, possibly from one key tenant to another, and so past the smaller units, who thus rely on this movement for their trade. This 'pull' principle can be applied to each of the categories of centre considered below, this pull acting in three possible ways. The single pull plan is employed in centres requiring only one key tenant, the double pull plan where two major tenants are required, and the triple pull form of layout, which is especially useful in centres developed in phases, when the plan form expands from the single or double pull types with each successive stage. (See Fig. 10.1.) The following summary describes the main characteristics of the various types of centre and the location of the key tenants; the location of other tenants is considered in Chapter 11.[1]

The most usual form of this type is the straight row of units, similar to **10.1 THE STRIP CENTRE** a traditional parade development, except that site planning and parking are controlled and co-ordinated. The length of the strip should be limited to 400–600 feet, to reduce walking distances, and should be placed parallel to the main access road. Public parking should always be in front of the shops and not at the rear, where deliveries and servicing

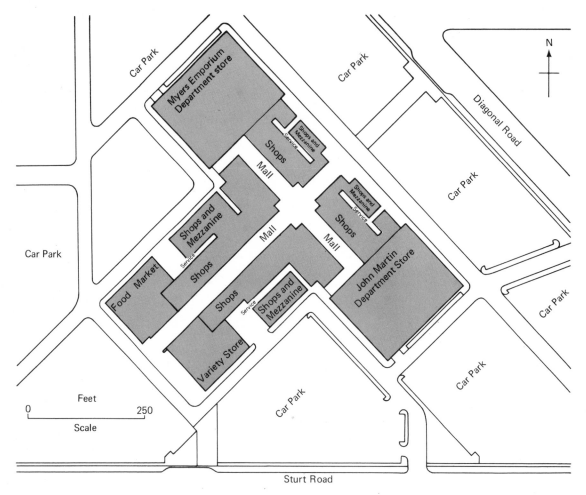

Fig. 10.1 MARION CENTRE, ADELAIDE, AUSTRALIA.   The 'triple-pull' plan, with four major tenants and 300,000 square feet of retail space on a 28 acre site 7 miles from the city.

usually take place. Rear parking space should only be provided for employees' cars, or for the public, where the depth of the front parking area from the road exceeds 600 feet. Despite visual considerations, it is vital that the public parking area is easily seen from the access roads, rather than the shops themselves. The key tenant, such as a branch department store, is usually placed in the middle of the strip, with super-markets at one or both ends.

On deep sites at right angles to the road, the strip should be placed against one side of the site, with sufficient space for rear servicing, usually 40–60 feet. The store fronts should face the direction from which the greatest trade is expected, but the set-back from the road should be

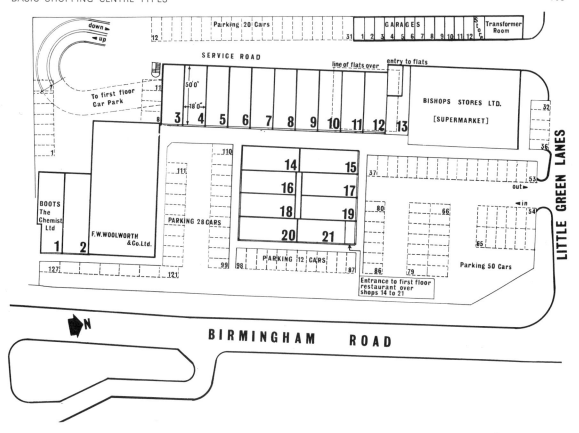

Fig. 10.2 TERMINUS CENTRE, WYLDE GREEN, SUTTON COLDFIELD. A typical 'strip' type plan, with two major tenants and car parking for 175 cars; the estimated catchment population is 75,000, and total cost is about £250,000.

less than for parallel development. The supermarket is usually placed nearest to the access road, and the department store at the further end. In both types of layout, any excessive length or over-long walking distances will encourage the shopper to use the car to travel along the strip from store to store.[2] (See Fig. 10.2).

Both L- and U-shaped centres are variations of the strip type, and are used to reduce the overall frontage length or to meet special site conditions. Two strips are placed close to the inner site boundaries, with the key tenant located at their junction, and projecting behind the rear of these strips. As in the previous type, the set-back from the road boundary should not exceed 600 feet. The main advantages of this system are the reduction in the department store frontage, with the corresponding reduction in the overall frontage length, and that the centre faces two roads rather than one.

10.2 L- AND U-SHAPED CENTRES

The U-shaped centre is more suitable for square or rectangular sites with single road frontages, with key store locations at each end or in the middle. Again, the total frontage length should not exceed 600 feet, with servicing confined to the rear of the units.[3]

10.3 MALL CENTRE In mall layouts, two 'strips' are planned opposite to each other, with a pedestrian mall in between, thus corresponding to a traditional street without vehicular traffic. Normally, two key tenants are located at opposite ends of the mall to generate customer movements. The placing of only one key tenant in the middle of one side of the mall or at one end has not proved successful, since less interchange of shoppers occurs. For example, in a centre with only one department store, 92 per cent of customers were at one time or another in the store, but of this percentage, 31 per cent were found to have entered and left directly from the parking area.[4]

Because two major tenants are preferable, the mall form is more suitable for large centres of regional class, where this plan form has considerable advantages—a traffic free concourse, opportunities for landscaping and display and a consistent pattern of good store locations. It is also more convenient to provide a completely enclosed mall area, giving all-weather protection.

The main problems of the mall type are that the units are orientated inwards, which may not offer an attractive prospect when seen from the access roads or parking area, and customers are obliged to pass between units to reach the central mall, unless double fronted shops are planned. Where this is done, servicing of these units may be complicated unless basement warehousing facilities are provided, together with a goods vehicle access tunnel. This is often considered essential in current practice.[5] A variation of the straight mall is the T-plan, where the mall is T-shaped to cater for three major tenants, on the triple pull principle.

10.4 CLUSTER OR HUB CENTRE The cluster centre is designed to place one major tenant in the prime location, being surrounded by the other units, from which it is separated by pedestrian walks. (See Plate 10.1.) This introverted type will reduce the overall length of the building area as found in strip or mall centres, and the enclosing smaller units prevent customers entering and leaving directly from the parking area. Customers are obliged to enter the pedestrian areas via controlled entrances, and screened service courts are provided at the rear of the units. Difficulty may arise in servicing the key tenant, and the use of basement warehousing is advocated in major centres.[6]

Plate 10.1 NORTHLAND CENTRE, DETROIT, U.S.A. The 'cluster' plan is adopted in one of America's largest centres, which has over 1,300,000 square feet of floor space and parking for over 10,500 cars. A special 'bus station is located in front of main store, while goods vehicles enter and leave the centre via a separate tunnel access road. The water tower is designed as a symbol for the whole centre.

SUMMARY OF   Table 10.1 indicates the incidence of the different types of centre, as
PREVIOUS TYPES   revealed in a survey carried out in America.[7]

Table 10.1   BUILDING PATTERNS FOR SHOPPPING
CENTRES U.S.A.

Pattern	Number of centres	Percentage
Strip	68	41·7
L-shaped	38	23·3
U-shaped	14	8·6
Mall	33	20·2
T-shaped	2	1·2
Court/cluster	8	5·0
	163	100·0

10.5 TYPES OF CENTRE IN BRITAIN   Early out-of-town centres in Britain were based on traditional town centre squares, and on New Town precinct plans. Generally, the form was U-shaped, but the enclosed area between the wings of the building group was left open and paved, rather than being used for car parking as in American examples. This intervening area was too wide to permit cross shopping, and totally inappropriate for normal climatic conditions, especially in the North and in Scotland. (See Plate 10.2.)

Plate 10.2 DRUMCHAPEL CENTRE, GLASGOW.   The broad precinct plan was used in many earlier British projects.

More recent developments have adopted a variety of layouts (see Plate 10.3 and Fig. 10.3), some schemes even employing a combination

Plate 10.3 YATE CENTRE, GLOUCESTERSHIRE.   This is a mall type centre, with a series of linked squares and canopies.

of plan forms, as in the Stillorgan Centre, Dublin. This absence of ideal layouts stems from the lack of viable sites in isolated locations, and results in the development of irregular and often unsuitable 'backland'

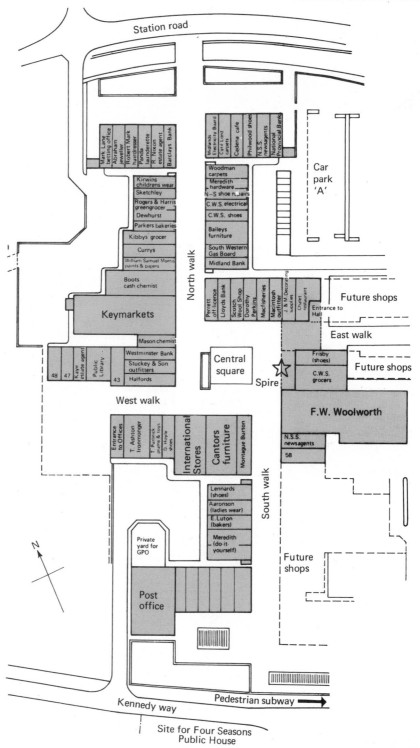

Fig. 10.3 YATE CENTRE, GLOUCESTERSHIRE.   The first two phases of the mall-type centre, with pedestrian routes radiating from the central square to the Civic Square, bus station and residential areas.

areas with restricted access points and surrounded by existing suburban housing. Only with the development of the supercentres by Gem and Woolco has a recognizable form of centre emerged, although this is primarily a building type rather than an overall site plan. Apart from these centres, only the 'off centre' schemes at the Elephant and Castle, the Bull Ring, Birmingham and Cross Gates, Leeds have attempted to realize the potential and attraction inherent in fully enclosed and air conditioned shopping areas, and no category of centre has yet attempted to provide completely covered car parks (as at Macy's Centre, Queens, New York), or even canopies to walkways in the parking areas.

REFERENCES

1 V. Gruen and L. Smith, *Shopping Towns U.S.A.*, p. 132–133.
2 V. Gruen and L. Smith, op. cit., p. 75–76.
  R. Nelson, *Selection of Retail Locations*, p. 235.
  Urban Land Institute, *Shopping Centres Re-studied*, Vol. 1, p. 28.
3 R. Nelson, op. cit., p. 238–239.
  Urban Land Institute, op. cit., p. 28.
4 R. Nelson, op. cit., p. 239.
5 V. Gruen and L. Smith, op. cit., p. 76.
  R. Nelson, op. cit., p. 239–240.
  Urban Land Institute, op. cit., p. 28.
6 V. Gruen and L. Smith, op. cit., p. 78.
  R. Nelson, op. cit., p. 240.
  Urban Land Institute, op. cit., p. 28.
7 Urban Land Institute, op. cit., Vol. 2, p. 9.

11

the retailing plan

In major centres, the primary attractors, such as the department stores, are first located within the overall plan form, as discussed in the previous chapter. Similarly, some other units may exercise a primary function and must be planned accordingly. This applies especially to multiple stores and supermarkets, whose importance varies from centre to centre.

SECONDARY ATTRACTORS Again, the size and type of secondary attractor will depend on the class of centre, but in each case its purpose is to draw customers through the shopping areas, even though it will be subsidiary to the key tenant or tenants. Consequently, secondary attractors are often those types of tenant who may expect to obtain trade whatever their locations, such as groups of clothing shops, or service trades, such as post offices, banks and repair shops, and these units can often be placed on side malls, thus preventing 'dead ends' in the retailing plan. Similarly, shoppers can be induced to cross malls or squares to store locations not directly on the main routes generated by the key tenants.

OTHER TENANTS The smaller units in major centres usually offer a wide range of specialist goods, and thus contribute to the overall attraction of the centre. Since they do not themselves generate customer movement, but rely on passing trade, they must be allocated prime positions on the main pedestrian routes, and are normally required to pay higher rentals.[1]

11.2 TENANT
GROUPING The location of stores is determined to some degree by the principle of grouping stores selling similar goods, in type, quality and price. (See Fig. 11.1.) Experience has shown that this general arrangement tends

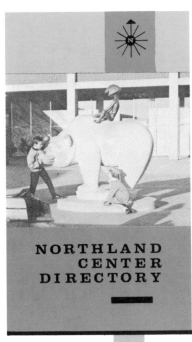

NORTHLAND CENTER DIRECTORY

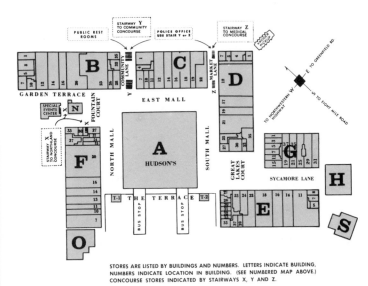

Directory of NORTHLAND STORES and BUILDING LOCATIONS

STORES ARE LISTED BY BUILDINGS AND NUMBERS. LETTERS INDICATE BUILDING, NUMBERS INDICATE LOCATION IN BUILDING. (SEE NUMBERED MAP ABOVE.) CONCOURSE STORES INDICATED BY STAIRWAYS X, Y AND Z.

The Abbey Lounge Cocktails
  and Restaurant B-3
Albert's, Ladies & Junior Apparel...C-18
Alexander & Hornung, Meats.........D-5
Appearance Shop,
  Northland Concourse ....X stairs
Artiste Beauty Salon.................F-37
Auditorium,
  Community Concourse ....Y stairs
Awrey Bakeries D-7
Bache & Co., Inc., Stockbrokers.....B-7
Baker's Shoes D-19
Barber Shop (Hamby's)
  Community Concourse ....Y stairs
Barna-Bee Children's Shop F-11
Barricini Candies G-7
A. S. Beck Shoes F-14
Bernard's Beauty Salon.............G-35
Bessenger's, Window Shades........E-5
Best & Co., Women's & Children's
  Fashion Apparel ....H-Bldg.
Better Made Potato Chips,
  Community Concourse ....Z stairs
Big Boy Restaurant E-29
Brennan's Millinery E-37
Brother's Restaurant &
  Delicatessen C-1
Chandler's Shoes E-22
Community Key Shop,
  Community Concourse ....Y stairs
Coney Island Lunch Bar,
  Northland Concourse ....X stairs
Corey's Jewelry, Inc...............E-30
Coronet Cards T-1
Cunningham's Drugs F-7
Dairy & Nut House
  Community Concourse ....Y stairs
Dairy & Nut House T-2
The Detroit Bank & Trust Co. E-16
  Annex B-1
The Detroit Edison Co. B-10
Morris Disner & Son, Men's Clothier .E-25
Dunham's Inc., Sporting Goods B-12
Dunn's Camera & Art Supplies C-4

Elliott Travel Service,
  Northland Concourse............X stairs
Englander Furniture Shops D-35
Face Place, The
  Northland Concourse ....X stairs
Fanny Farmer Candy...............F-25
Father & Son Shoes C-11
Fischer Gift Shop G-3
Flagg Bros. Shoes F-27
Flowers by Maskell D-1
Franklin Simon, Women's Apparel...E-18
Harry Garden, Jewelry Repairs &
  Sales—Northland Concourse ...X stairs
Max Green's Men's Wear, Inc......F-23
L. G. Haig Peacock Room Shoes....F-13
Harty, Austin & Jones, (Attorneys)
  Northland Concourse ....X stairs
Himelhoch's, Women's Children's
  Specialty Shop E-11
Hot 'N' Kold Shops................B-16
Hudson's ....A
Hudson's Car Care Center
  Northland Drive and Greenfield
Hudson's Garden Center............O
Hudson's Pantry Shop ....O
Hudson's Pick-up-Station,
  Lower Level, Below the Terrace ...A
Hughes, Hatcher, Suffrin..........B-23
Kay Corsetiere D-32
Kelly Girl Service, Inc.
  Northland Concourse ....X stairs
G. R. Kinney Shoes................C-14
Kresge F-20
Kroger D-12
Lady Orva Hosiery
  Community Concourse ....Z stairs
Lane Bryant, Women's Clothing B-14
Thom McAn Shoes B-26
McBryde Boot Shop G-15
Macauley's, Stationery B-32
Maple House Restaurant...........N

Marianne, Ladies Apparel..........F-16
Maternity Modes E-31
Marwil Book Co.,
  Community Concourse ....Y stairs
Dr. Sherman A. Mendelsohn, Foot
  Specialist, Community Concourse ...Y stairs
Meyer Jewelry Co..................C-10
Miami Bake Shoppe G-5
Modern Stamp & Coin Shop,
  Northland Concourse ....X stairs
Jerry Morse—
  Gentlemen's Attire G-29
Nadon's, Junior Sportswear, et cetera E-24
Northland Center Offices,
  Community Concourse ....Y stairs
Northland Drug Co. C-22
Northland Duplicate Bridge,
  Northland Concourse ....X stairs
Northland Theatre
  Joseph L. Hudson Drive
Northland Tobacco Shop,
  Community Concourse ....Y stairs
Northland Underwriters, Inc.,
  Northland Concourse ....X stairs
Northland Watch & Clock Service ...E-33
Optometrist, Stein, Dr. Benj. H.,
  Northland Concourse ....X stairs
Palmer's Sandwich Shop D-4
Peck & Peck G-31
Peter's Small Size Ladies Wear......E-39
Phillips Florsheim Shoes G-19
Phillips Shoes B-28
Dr. Edward C. Pintzuk, Foot
  Specialist, Community Concourse ...Y stairs
Police Office,
  Community Concourse ....Y stairs
  Community Concourse ....Z stairs
Post Office,
  Northland Concourse..........X stairs
Mary Radcliffe Employment Agency
  Northland Concourse ....X stairs
Raimi's Curtains C-16

Reid & Cool, Consulting Engineers
  Community Concourse ....Z stairs
Rest Rooms,
  Community Concourse ....Y stairs
Richman Bros., Men's Clothing C-12
Robinson Furniture B-20
Rose Jewelers F-33
Ross Music Co....................E-32
Sallan Jewelers D-27
Salt Cellar — Community Concourse ...Z stairs
Sanders D-30
Schiller Millinery E-27
Sero's Restaurant G-37
Shoe Tree, Inc. E-8
Shopping Center Inc. Offices,
  Community Concourse ......Y and Z stairs
Singer Sewing Center.............B-35
Singer Sewing Room
  Northland Concourse ....X stairs
Special Events Center...... Garden Terrace
Spencer Shoes E-35
Stevens, Women's Sportswear D-25
Dorothy Stofer,
  Community Concourse ....Y stairs
Stouffer's Restaurant ....S-Bldg.
Surwin's — Women's Specialty Shop ...G-25
Susan Ives — Up's 'N' Down's
  Women's Sportswear G-21
Suzy Hats F-24
Tall-Eez Shoe Co. G-1
Tall Girls Shop E-7
Teen Man Store for Boys G-11
Tie Rak F-30
Todd's, Hollywood Clothes F-10
United Shirt Distributors C-7
Van Horn's, Men's Wear C-19
Winkelman's Ladies Wear D-21
Wright Kay, Jewelers E-14
WWJ Radio,
  Community Concourse ....Z stairs
Zuieback's, Suburban, Ladies Wear D-17

Fig. 11.1 NORTHLAND CENTRE, DETROIT, U.S.A. This shows the free directory of tenant locations issued to customers and illustrates the careful arrangement of compatible types.

to increase the productivity of each member of a group, while the group itself will benefit from what is termed 'cumulative attraction'.

THEORY OF RETAIL COMPATIBILITY
Nelson propounds a formula for the measure of compatability between different store types, where a greater volume of trade is done by each

Plate 11.1 YATE CENTRE, GLOUCESTERSHIRE.   The compatible grouping of similar tenant types for their mutual benefit, and individual pictorial signs suspended from the canopy are here illustrated.

tenant as a result of their adjacency than would be done otherwise, as expressed in the following:

> Two compatible businesses located in close proximity will show an increase in business volume directly proportionate to the incidence of total customer interchange between them, inversely proportionate to the ratio of the business volume of the larger store to that of the smaller store, and directly proportionate to the ratios of purposeful purchasing to the total purchasing in each of the two stores.

A purposeful purchase is defined as one made where the shopper visits the store as the major purpose of the trip, and total purchases include all incidental and impulse purchases. Nelson states that high compatibility exists where 10–20 per cent of shoppers visit both stores; moderate compatibility exists where 5–10 per cent visit both; slight compatibility exists where 1–5 per cent visit both, and that where interchange is negligible the stores may be considered as incompatible or even deleterious.[2]

The following tenant types are considered compatible:

COMPATIBLE GROUPS

1 *Men's stores* Clothing, shoes, haberdashery and sports goods.

2 *Women's stores* Similar types as men's stores, together with millinery, children's clothes and toys.

3 *Food stores* Small specialized food shops, such as health foods, delicatessen, confectionery and fish shops are best located close to the supermarket.

4 *Hardware stores* Hardware, appliances, radio and television, records and musical instruments.

The following principles should be considered when assessing tenant locations:

OTHER LOCATIONAL PRINCIPLES

1 The supermarket should be at one end of the centre, so that the adjacent parking spaces are not taken by others doing long term shopping.

2 Chemists should be located close to good parking space, preferably near the access road.

3 Clothing, shoe and related stores should be near a major generator, preferably the department store.

4 The department store should be near the supermarket but if the store has no restaurant, one should be located nearby.

5 Service shops should not be placed so as to monopolize the best parking spaces, nor should they interrupt the continuity of shop frontages.[3]

Naturally, no definite rules can be given for the total rental area, or for each trade, since each will depend on the economic analysis and local circumstances, but certain basic principles can be applied to each project, both for overall layout and for individual units.

11.3 PLANNING DIMENSIONS

To allow for impulse shopping, a mall should be narrow, possibly 25 feet wide to be most effective, but this would destroy amenity and cause congestion, for which 80 feet might be a desirable width. For these reasons, a compromise width of between 40 and 60 feet has been adopted in America. In Britain, similar widths have been used in most centres,

MALLS

both in out-of-town locations and in New Towns, such as Stevenage, where the North–South mall is 50 feet wide, and the two East–West malls are each 40 feet wide. In most cases, it is preferable that needless set-backs or projections or breaks in continuity should be eliminated, except at entrance points, though this should not be allowed to produce a stereotyped design. The same limitations apply to mall lengths as to strip centres, in that 600 feet is considered a maximum. The orientation of the mall is not critical, and will be affected chiefly by overall site requirements. Where some flexibility exists, a north–south orientation may be preferable to allow an even distribution of sunlight, though this will require shop blinds where canopies are not provided. Where an east–west orientation is employed, the height of the units or first floors on the south side should be reduced where possible.

SIZE OF UNITS The buildings containing individual tenant stores are, in most cases, planned for multiple tenancy. Only in some categories, such as department stores, supermarkets or restaurants, will special or free standing structures be required. The multiple-tenant block must allow for considerable internal flexibility, which must be related to the most economic grid layout and overall heights. For example, while internal heights of 10 or 11 feet are usually sufficient for single storey units, an additional 4 or 5 feet provided in the initial stages would allow for later expansion, in the form of mezzanine levels. The depth of units will be dependent on the method of storage and servicing, and would be reduced where these services are on a different level. Unit widths are best fixed on a module within the overall structural column spacing, with tenants leasing the frontage they require for their particular trades.[4]

1 *Department stores* The department store is generally of multilevel construction, the actual number of storeys being determined by the merchandising policy and site conditions. In terms of area, the average department store in major American centres occupies about 45 per cent of the gross rentable floor area, with variations in smaller centres from 30 per cent to 60 per cent.[5] In the British centres listed in Appendix A and possessing genuine department stores, the average size is about 17,000 square feet, occupying between 9 per cent and 23 per cent of the gross rentable area. Not included in these figures are the Breda centre, which is a self-service store of 31,000 square feet (70 per cent), or the Gem and Woolco supercentres.

2 *Variety stores* In America, a central location is considered preferable for variety or multiple stores, the sizes ranging from 23,000 to 39,000 square feet for major centres, though this represents only 3·5 per cent to 10 per cent of the total area. The average size of the variety

stores in British out-of-town centres is about 15,000 square feet, ranging from 11,000 to 18,000 square feet, or 7 per cent to 12·5 per cent of the total rentable area, excluding the Woolco stores.

3 *Supermarkets* Modern grocery retailing requires much greater flexibility in store layout than formerly, and supermarkets are normally provided with large single storey selling areas within a column free space. No one size or type will prove more efficient for all types of centre. In major centres in the United States, super-markets occupy between 3·5 per cent and 11 per cent of the total area in major centres, and between 5·5 per cent and 22 per cent in smaller regional centres.[6] In the British centres, the square footage allocated to supermarkets varies between 7,000 and 24,000 with an average of 8,500 square feet, which represents between 5 per cent and 11 per cent of the total rentable area. The result of a survey undertaken in 1963 indicated an average frontage of central area supermarkets of between 30 and 50 feet, with an average depth of 100 feet, plus an area half this size at the rear or over the shop for storage and preparation. Recent trends indicate that 60 feet should be the minimum frontage width, to allow for a greater number and flexibility in checkouts. The percentage of sales area to storage space has already been given in Tables 5.15 and 5.16.

4 *Other units* Most of the smaller units in British out-of-town centres have retained the traditional shop widths and overall layouts found

Table 11.1   RECOMMENDED DIMENSIONS FOR DIFFERENT TENANT UNITS 1963[7]

Unit type	Frontage (feet)	Depth (feet)	Remarks
Traditional food shop	25 min.	80	
Off-licence	15–20	100	On main routes
	15–20	40	On secondary routes
	18–20	20–30	Plus additional storage
Shoe shops	18	70	For population under 25,000 plus first floor storage space
	22	100	For population over 25,000
	33	100	On main routes
	20	80	Plus first floor storage space
Shoe repairs	13–18	24	Plus same area for stock and workrooms
Men's wear	18–20	60–80	
	20	80	Plus first floor
Women's wear, woollens and accessories	18	50	
	18	30–35	Plus first floor
	20	80	
	20	40–60	Plus first floor
Newsagents, booksellers	25	60–70	Plus first floor storage
Chemist, hardware	18	50	For smaller tenants
	40	100	For major tenants
Furniture	40	100	For ground floor, plus 8,000–10,000 on floors

in central areas, often with marked inflexibility, owing to inappropriate building techniques, based on load bearing walls rather than frame construction. While the average sizes may in fact be suitable, any design must allow for a variety of tenants and tenant requirements, which can be achieved best with standard modular layouts. Table 11.1 gives the average dimensions of different types of shops in central areas in 1963, as supplied by the Multiple Shops Federation. The different dimensions quoted indicate the preferred proportions of the various units, the actual size selected being dependent on the analysis of trade potential in the specific area. The dimensions given correspond closely with units being built today, both in central areas and in out-of-town centres.

USE OF DIFFERENT LEVELS   Considerable variation exists in the use of multilevel shopping facilities, though site costs prevalent in Britain often require such layouts to achieve an economic return. (See Plate 11.2.) Certain developers, such as super-centres and supermarkets, never provide more than one retailing floor,

Plate 11.2 THORNABY-ON-TEES CENTRE with the two level shopping area and integrated landscaping.

but the Elephant and Castle has three levels, and the Bull Ring, Birmingham, five levels; both have experienced considerable difficulty in leasing and selling. The former, opened in June 1965, has tenants for only half the units. (See Plate 11.3.) American experience shows that more

Plate 11.3 ELEPHANT AND CASTLE CENTRE, LONDON.   The prospect of the upper shopping level is bleak and unattractive, owing to the difficulty in attracting suitable tenants and the complicated circulation required to reach the centre on foot.

than two levels are rarely provided, except in department stores or where basements are partly used for selling space, as indicated in Table 11.2.[8]

Table 11.2   USE OF DIFFERENT LEVELS IN AMERICAN SHOPPING CENTRES

	Percentage with basement	Percentage with basement used for selling	Percentage with first floor used for selling
Neighbourhood centres	20	—	1
Community centres	40	20	20
Regional centres	70	55	50

Apart from department stores and those centres noted above, out-of-town centres in Britain have not provided more than two shopping levels, and even in these cases, public ramps, escalators and lifts have sometimes been omitted.

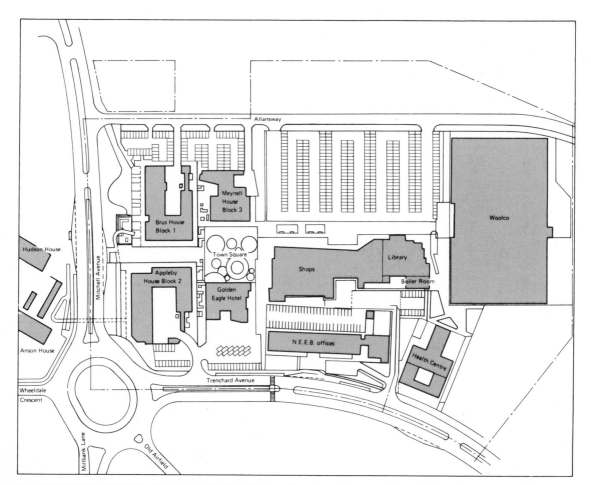

Fig. 11.2 TOWN CENTRE, THORNABY-ON-TEES.   Site plan of the new Central Area, incorporating a Woolco store and designed to serve a population of 35,000, while also serving as an out-of-town centre for Middlesbrough and Teesside.

Reference has already been made in previous sections to the provision of various other facilities, whether social, service or entertainment, in conjunction with shopping centres. Certain types, such as children's nurseries or playgrounds are designed to attract customers to the centre, while others such as hotels, light industry or offices, while contributing to the rental income of the centre, are independent of its operation. Often many facilities are provided to develop the centre as the main social and entertainment attraction in the area, with great patronage after shop hours and on Sundays.

11.4 OTHER FACILITIES WITHIN THE CENTRE

While any extra facilities may be beneficial to the centre, their site location should be considered carefully; offices for example, should not be provided directly over shops, and should in all cases have special parking areas; doctors' clinics will require one-storey buildings or lifts, and preferably should be located across the parking area; space over shops is best let to tenants who require no display area, such as studios or teaching facilities, and staff flats should be in a separate building with its own access, private play space and parking area. Similarly, entertainment facilities should not be located so that their patrons will occupy prime parking spaces for long periods.

REFERENCES

1 V. Gruen and L. Smith, *Shopping Towns U.S.A.*, p. 132, 134 and 137.
2 R. Nelson, *Selection of Retail Locations*, p. 66–67. Compatibility tables are given for a rural centre, a neighbourhood centre, a large regional centre and a central business district.
3 V. Gruen and L. Smith, op. cit., p. 136–137.
  R. Nelson, op. cit., p. 103 and 244.
  Urban Land Institute, *Shopping Centres Re-studied*, Vol. 1, p. 44.
4 V. Gruen and L. Smith, op. cit., p. 141–142.
  Multiple Shops Federation, *The Planning of Shopping Centres*, p. 11.
5 Urban Land Institute, op. cit., Vol. 2, p. 35.
6 Urban Land Institute, op. cit., Vol. 2, p. 39–40.
7 Multiple Shops Federation.
8 Urban Land Institute, op. cit., Vol. 2, p. 9.

12

servicing and utilities

Goods deliveries to all stores within the centre can be by one of the following methods. The actual systems selected will depend on the size and type of centre, and on site conditions:

1 *Direct rear service* Each unit is served from a rear access road; as would be expected, this system predominates in strip and strip variation centres in America where over 75 per cent use rear delivery, and 8 per cent use it in conjunction with front servicing, though this may be considered poor practice.[1] Direct rear servicing has been adopted widely in British centres, sometimes in conjunction with service courts, and is also used in the supercentre type.

2 *Service courts* Each unit is served from a common service court, which preferably should be screened from public areas; those units requiring the most service, such as supermarkets, should be located at the ends of the block or court.

3 *Basement service* The figures given previously in Table 11.2 indicate the extent of basement storage in American centres. This system, which is the most productive, is generally the most expensive to construct, and is used mainly in the larger centres, or where site conditions are particularly favourable. The highest total revenue per square foot has been produced by projects with the largest amount of basement area coupled with underground delivery.[2] This system requires early consideration in site planning and circulation, since the service tunnel will be excavated first, but has the added advantage that basement storage areas can be converted into sales space if the turnover justifies. Of the British centres listed

in Appendix A, only the Elephant and Castle and Tivoli centres have basement servicing.

4 *Overhead service* Where soil conditions are unfavourable, or site levels suitable, storage areas may be placed over units, with direct access from a service road at the higher level. In both (3) and (4) vertical service cores are required, and some retailers estimate a 20 per cent loss in efficiency with storage on different levels, and sales turnover on basement or first floors only 15–30 per cent of that achieved on ground floors.[3]

Because of the financial ramifications, grade separated servicing is often impossible, but separation of customers and goods deliveries by time is rarely successful, unless a 24-hour delivery service is undertaken.[4] This type of service is possible where underground storage areas are controlled by a continuously manned control office, and has proved most successful. The recent experimental operation on out-of-hours deliveries to central area shops showed that travel speeds increased by nearly 20 per cent, off-loading times were reduced by 30 per cent, and the incidence of vehicles returning to depots without completing the drops because of non-acceptance was cut to negligible proportions.[5] Similarly, bulk deliveries are increasing, especially the use of standard cartons in bulk containers suitable for both rail and road transport.

GOODS DELIVERIES

Availability of utilities at or close to the subject site is a positive factor in site assessment and planning. Long runs to reach available utility connections should be avoided, especially extra off-site requirements. On-site works are part of the development costs, but the reduction of utility services should not be to an extent which places limitations on the flexibility of tenant types or requirements.

12.2 SERVICES AND UTILITIES

1 *Drainage* Building and land drainage should be considered in relation to the maximum capacity of the sewers, especially for surface water, since large areas of paving or parking require drainage. Individual units are usually provided with drainage connections only.

2 *Water supply* The adequacy of any existing supply on-site must be related to likely demands by the centre, especially where sprinkler systems or water cooled plant are installed. In certain cases, a water tower may be required, and possibly incorporated into a 'symbol' for the centre.

3 *Electricity* In most centres, an electricity substation will be required within the site, or within the centre itself, together with an emergency supply. Individual tenants are normally responsible for all installations within the units, though in some cases a service charge may be

made by the landlord for such supplies according to the square footage.

4 *Gas service* A gas supply may be required, for heating or process machinery, or for gas fired incinerators.

5 *Heating* Normally, tenants are responsible for the heating of each unit, though in some major centres, both heating and hot water are supplied from a central boiler house. Heating for common areas is provided by the landlord, and a service charge made on individual tenants.

6 *Refuse collection* Lease stipulations usually give the requirements for the storage and collection of refuse. Any spaces allocated for this must be in closed areas, and a dumper service is now generally adopted. In large centres incinerators and crushing and baling plant may be provided or refuse disposed of in the central boiler plant.

AIR CONDITIONING About 80 per cent of American shopping centres have air conditioning, and 12 per cent partial air conditioning, while 90 per cent also have canopies and covered walks. The air conditioning has been confined to individual stores in 84 per cent of the centres, the remaining 16 per

Plate 12.1 ELEPHANT AND CASTLE CENTRE, LONDON.   The external ramps provide split level access from the main pavement, and encourage customers to enter the upper shopping concourse.

cent being supplied from a central plant.[6] Of British centres listed in Appendix A, only the Elephant and Castle and Cross Gates are fully air conditioned, and all other examples employ only covered walks or canopies, with a limited number of schemes having enclosed malls. No doubt a great potential exists in Britain for the fully enclosed centre, possibly with a retractable roof, as at the Elephant and Castle; or with removable arcade glazing units, as at Shoppers' World, Framingham, Massachusetts. In such cases, the heating, temperature and humidity are controlled from the central plant and the cost apportioned between tenants. Further expense may be incurred in extra insulation costs, and in the control and management of access points.

Customer facilities, such as lifts, escalators, moving pavements and ramps, are added attractions to shoppers, and may be considered essential where different levels are used. Public escalators are provided at the Elephant and Castle, and should be considered as essential in any multi-level scheme. (See Plate 12.1.)

12.3 MECHANICAL INSTALLATIONS

The American 'Speedwalk', a moving ramp system, was provided at the Merrion Centre, Leeds, which opened in March 1964. (See Plate 12.2.) The ramp rises at 15 degrees, is 3 feet 6 inches wide, and can carry a maximum of 7,200 persons per hour, at a speed of 140 feet per minute. For window shopping, continuous horizontal belts set in the paving can have static side entry at speeds up to 50 feet per minute, the recommended width being 6 feet.[7]

SPEEDWALK SYSTEM AND PEDESTRIAN CONVEYORS

Mechanical or roller conveyors are normally incorporated in basement storage areas, and may be used to transport goods in tunnels to pickup stations close to exit points in the parking areas, where customers may collect selected items on leaving the centre. The location of pickup stations should be carefully considered in relation to the main traffic flows, so as to avoid any congestion, and may with advantage be combined with a petrol filling station or car-wash booths. Where these pickup facilities are not provided, the major tenants may offer porterage services between the shops and the car parks; this service is undertaken at the Woolco store at Oadby. In some centres, wheeled trolleys are provided for transporting purchases to the car park, and in this case care must be taken to avoid steps and kerbs which would cause inconvenience. At the same time, it may also be more difficult to control traffic with road markings only and without conventional kerbs and pavements.

GOODS CONVEYORS

While trade may be increased by such conveniences, the extra costs for maintenance and management must be added to the rental charges;

CHARGES FOR SERVICES

Plate 12.2 MERRION CENTRE, LEEDS.   The 'Speedramp' connects different shopping levels, and is of a type being employed more frequently in new British Schemes.

these costs may be considerable in large centres. At the Bull Ring, Birmingham, for example, the morning opening requires the unlocking of 96 separate sets of doors, and the operation and testing of 19 escalators and 40 lifts.[8] The extent of extra facilities is reflected in the service charges imposed on tenants and, as such, may represent a deterrent in the attraction of prospective occupants.

REFERENCES   1 Urban Land Institute, *Shopping Centres Re-studied*, Vol. 2, p. 9.
             2 V. Gruen and L. Smith, 'How to plan successful shopping centres', *Architectural Forum*, March 1954, p. 144–147.
             3 Urban Land Institute, op. cit., Vol. 1, p. 56.
             4 G. Baker and B. Funaro, *Shopping Centres —Design and Operation*, p. 51.
             5 N.E.D.O., Newsletter, 5 July 1967, Press Notice, 13 Dec. 1967.
                Self-Service and Supermarket Journal, Nov. 1966, p. 91; Jan. 4, 1968, p. 16–17; Jan. 11, 1968, p. 8–9.

6 Urban Land Institute, op. cit., Vol. 2.
7 J. P. McElroy, 'Pedestrian conveyors', *T.P. Review*, July 1961, p. 125–140.
   Self-Service and Supermarket Journal, April 1964, p. 75.
8 J. A. Hepburn, 'Bull Ring, Birmingham', *Chartered Surveyor*, April 1965, p. 530.

13

site access, circulation and parking

13.1 ACCESS Reference has already been made to the necessity for spare capacity in the access roads surrounding or serving the centre, but easy access from this network is equally vital for the success of the project. It is obvious that vehicles cannot be driven directly into the parking area, and slip roads or lanes are recommended at site entry and exit points. The latter should not be within 400, and preferably 600 feet, of major intersections. Greater emphasis should be placed on exit points, since greater congestion is liable to occur than with entrance traffic, especially with evening closing time, when employees are also leaving. Where peak hour exit traffic might be excessive, closing hours may be staggered, as is often done for restaurants and food shops, but this must be related to the overall merchandising policy of the centre.[1]

In major centres, access may be by underpasses, but where this is not possible, a central waiting lane should be provided for right turning traffic wishing to enter the site, possibly with signal systems. In all cases, consultations are necessary with local highways authority and/or the Ministry of Transport, both to achieve the successful transfer of traffic to and from the site, and also because difficulties in this respect have been one of the main reasons for the rejection of out-of-town centres in Britain.

In most cases, goods vehicles and 'buses will use the same access as private cars, but many authorities and developers require separate access to be made for pedestrian shoppers, which will affect overall site circulation. No definite rules are applicable in this case. At the Gem Centre, Nottingham (see Plate 13.1), the Local Authority required a pedestrian walkway but this was not required for the Oadby Centre. The Safeway Food Stores Limited, a subsidiary of Safeway Stores Inc. of California,

Plate 13.1 GEM CENTRE, NOTTINGHAM.   The flat site required by supercentres is here provided by part of a refuse tip. Because of the unfavourable shape of the site, the building is placed end-on to the road. Private and goods vehicles circulate between the car parks and the store entrances, while the cut-price filling station is in direct competition with the garage and showroom almost adjacent.

who are now developing large suburban supermarkets, rely largely but not solely upon car borne patronage and pedestrian access is considered necessary. (See Plate 13.3.) In many smaller centres, traffic free pedestrian access may be linked directly to neighbouring residential areas.

13.2 SITE CIRCULATION

The customer must be given the choice of selecting any parking zone, so that he or she may park close to any particular store, such as the supermarket or chemist. Such a choice will facilitate the overall circulation within the centre if it also eases access and egress for the short term parker. Secondary circulation will also develop when customers wish to collect large packages, either from individual stores or from a pickup

Plate 13.2 HAMPSHIRE CENTRE, BOURNEMOUTH.   The Woolco store and food hall are linked by twelve smaller units in a traditional 'strip' layout, with the main access road separating the shops and car park.

station, or visit other buildings located elsewhere on the site, such as filling stations or car-wash booths.

In large centres, a considerable amount of circulating traffic may develop, and is best catered for with separate roads placed around the perimeter of the site, though removed far enough from the site boundary to permit easy access and egress from the public roads, the intervening area being landscaped. Again, in major schemes, the larger parking zones are often separated into inner and outer areas by secondary circulation routes around the centre. Similarly, some centres have also located important circulatory routes immediately surrounding the building core itself, but this road would have to be crossed by all pedestrians moving to the centre from the parking area. (See Fig. 13.2.) All circulatory roads may be for one or two way traffic. In deciding between the two systems, the readiness of shoppers to follow traffic directions must be taken into account, and also the detailed layout of the parking spaces.[2]

Ideally, goods vehicles should be entirely separated from customer circulation. Where service tunnels are provided, this is more easily achieved, but where this is not possible, service roads should branch off the outer circulatory roads, as one way routes. Gruen and Smith list the following requirements for these delivery areas:

1 The minimum of interference by service vehicles with customers' vehicles and pedestrian movement.
2 Delivery spaces out of sight of normal customer areas.
3 Sufficient space for the manoeuvre of large vehicles, both in height and turning circle.
4 Properly marked service roads to prevent the entrance of other vehicles.

Public transport vehicles, such as 'buses and taxis, should be directed to stands adjoining the main shopping area, and not on the site boundary,

Plate 13.3 SAFEWAY STORE, MUIREND, GLASGOW.   A suburban food store of 24,000 square feet is typical of many being developed in Britain, with free parking and convenient pedestrian access from surrounding residential districts.

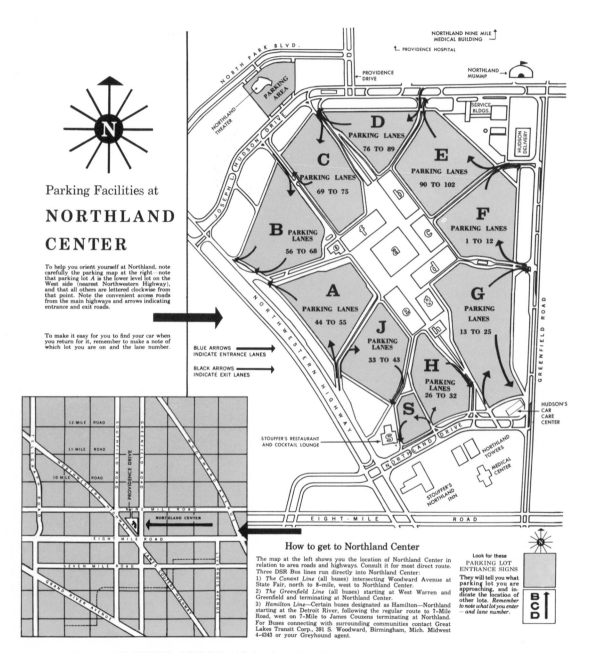

Parking Facilities at

NORTHLAND
CENTER

To help you orient yourself at Northland, note carefully the parking map at the right—note that parking lot A is the lower level lot on the West side (nearest Northwestern Highway), and that all others are lettered clockwise from that point. Note the convenient access roads from the main highways and arrows indicating entrance and exit roads.

To make it easy for you to find your car when you return for it, remember to make a note of which lot you are on and the lane number.

BLUE ARROWS INDICATE ENTRANCE LANES

BLACK ARROWS INDICATE EXIT LANES

How to get to Northland Center

The map at the left shows you the location of Northland Center in relation to area roads and highways. Consult it for most direct route. Three DSR Bus lines run directly into Northland Center:
1) *The Conant Line* (all buses) intersecting Woodward Avenue at State Fair, north to 8-mile, west to Northland Center.
2) *The Greenfield Line* (all buses) starting at West Warren and Greenfield and terminating at Northland Center.
3) *Hamilton Line*—Certain buses designated as Hamilton—Northland starting at the Detroit River, following the regular route to 7-Mile Road, west on 7-Mile to James Couzens terminating at Northland.
For Buses connecting with surrounding communities contact Great Lakes Transit Corp., 391 S. Woodward, Birmingham, Mich. Midwest 4-4343 or your Greyhound agent.

Look for these
PARKING LOT
ENTRANCE SIGNS

They will tell you what parking lot you are approaching, and indicate the location of other lots. *Remember to note what lot you enter — and lane number.*

Fig. 13.1 NORTHLAND CENTRE, DETROIT, U.S.A.   Location plan and diagram illustrating site circulation, parking area and other facilities provided by the developer within the site.

where pedestrian walking distances may be over-long. Storage spaces for such vehicles should be provided on or adjacent to the centre, so that transport may be available to meet peak loads, especially at closing hours.[3]

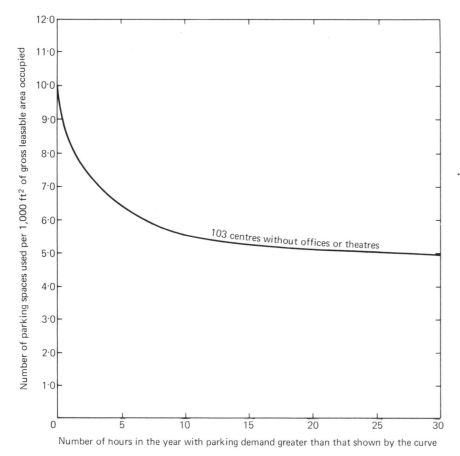

Fig. 13.2 Hourly parking requirements assessed in a recent survey of shopping centres in America.

The amount of parking required in any centre depends on a number of variable factors which Nelson lists as follows:

13.3 CALCULATION OF PARKING REQUIREMENTS

1 The amount of business from car borne shoppers, as opposed to customers on foot, those arriving by public transport, or 'let-outs', being those dropped and collected at the centre in private cars. The last may vary between 5 and 10 per cent of customers.
2 The number of shoppers per car.
3 The rate of turnover in parking spaces, being the number of cars in each space per day.
4 The type of stores provided.
5 The incidence and amplitude of 'peaks'.[4] (See Figs. 13.2 and 13.3.)

METHODS OF
CALCULATING
NUMBER OF CAR
SPACES

There are two basic ways of assessing the number of car spaces required for any particular centre:

Method 1: Area Ratio Method

This system relates the gross parking area to that of the building area, translated into a ratio of the number of cars per thousand square feet of gross floor area. This ratio will vary according to the size of each car space. For example, assuming an acre to be approximately 40,000 square feet, a 3 to 1 ratio would be 30,000 square feet of parking to 10,000 square feet of gross floor area, To calculate the number of cars that can be accommodated in this area, the 30,000 square feet is divided by the area allocated for each space. This area should include allowances for access aisles, waiting spaces and incidental landscape areas within the parking zones. If the car space was 300 square feet, then 100 cars could be parked per acre, or a 3:1 ratio equivalent to 10 cars per 1,000 square feet; or a 2:1 ratio translates into 6·7 cars per 1,000 square feet of building area. Quoting American experience, the Urban Land Institute stated in 1957 that a 2:1 ratio should be considered as an absolute minimum, but recent research indicated that 5·5 spaces per thousand square feet has in fact proved adequate to meet all demands, except for the highest 10-hour peak in any year.[5]

This method is more useful in preliminary site planning, but may be difficult to apply unless the approximate building area is known. This area should include all basements and upper floors, but exclude separate service facilities outside these stores, such as boiler houses. Some authorities recommend that the ratio should be related to selling floor space only, though this is even more difficult to estimate at the early stages.

Method 2: Unit Sales Method

This system relates the number of parking spaces required to the estimated sales volume, as set up by the economic analysis. To employ this method, four variables must first be ascertained:

1 The minimum turnover per space per day.
2 The number of customers per car.
3 The percentage of customers arriving by car.
4 The average sales per unit.

For example, if (1) was 3·0, (2) was 1·5, (3) was 50 per cent and (4) was £4, then the minimum sales per space per day are (1) multiplied by (2) multiplied by (4) = £18. But since only 50 per cent arrive by car, this minimum should be £36 per day, and assuming 300 shopping days each year, each space would bring in £10,800. If the economic analysis indicated annual sales of £21,600,000, then the number of spaces required would be 2,000. Since this is based on minimum turnover, extra spaces should be allowed for seasonal peaks.

This method may involve too many assumptions, such as the number of customers per car or the number arriving by other means which may vary in different areas and at different seasons, but it does not attempt to equate the sales required for economic success to the number of spaces provided.[6] (See Fig. 13.3.)

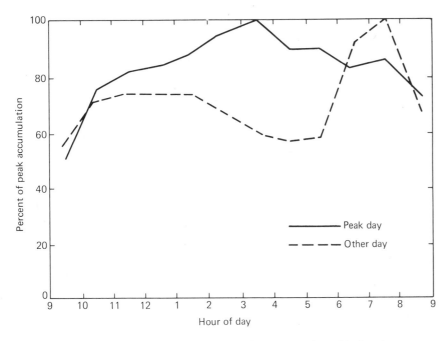

Fig. 13.3 Accumulation pattern on peak and other days, as experienced in American centres.

Certain other factors will cause the revision of the estimated numbers of spaces calculated by either of the foregoing methods:

FACTORS AFFECTING SPACE REQUIREMENTS

1 *Parking turnover* This may vary from only one per day for branch department stores to over 10 per day for supermarkets, but it does not follow that proportionally less spaces should be provided near the department store, since customers to the latter may be expected to spend longer on each trip. It seems that marked variations occur in turnover, depending on the type of centre and its relationship with its catchment area, and consequently is most accurately assessed by local surveys of potential customers.

2 *Peak loads* The accepted principle in American centres has been to allocate sufficient parking spaces to provide for the estimated average weekly peak load, without catering for any excessive seasonal demand except where land is cheap. In fact, any excessive allocation may look unattractive, and encourage customers to shop elsewhere.

3 *Walking distances* The distances from the farthest parking bay to the nearest store should not exceed 600 feet, and preferably 400 feet as a maximum. Both these figures may be excessive in British climatic conditions, except where covered walks are provided. In most cases, such walkways are not provided, because they are too expensive in land and money. The Urban Land Institute states that shoppers prefer to walk in wider access roads, and that 400 feet is the most acceptable distance, depending on the parking layout and site topography.[7] This distance may be used to establish the approximate area suitable for parking where the site is sufficiently large.

13.4 PARKING PATTERNS The parking zone should be planned to ensure the maximum turnover of cars per space in any specified period, rather than the provision of the estimated maximum number of spaces possible. (See Plate 13.4 and

Plate 13.4 BREDA CENTRE, BELFAST demonstrates conventional marking of parking spaces, with a form of covered link to the main store being provided by the canopy to the single storey shops. This emphasizes the horizontal nature of the buildings as in many other centres of this type.

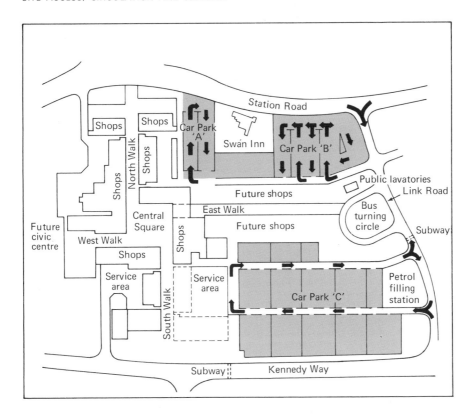

Fig. 13.4 YATE CENTRE, GLOUCESTERSHIRE, showing the distribution of car parks and traffic flow together with the areas to be developed in later phases.

Fig. 13.4.) With an ample number of bays of generous proportions, the exact angle of laying out the spaces is of secondary importance, provided that access and egress are convenient and quick. Various authorities recommend 90 degree or angled parking layouts. Table 13.1 shows the results of a survey of parking patterns in American centres.

Table 13.1   PARKING PATTERNS IN AMERICAN CENTRES[8]

Pattern	Number reported	Percentage
90 degrees	53	32·5
Diagonal	102	62·5
Not reported	8	5·0
	163	100·0
60 degrees	39	38·2
45 degrees	35	34·2
Other angles	14	13·7
Combination	8	8·4
Not reported	6	5·4
	102	100·0

ADVANTAGES OF The 90 degree pattern allows for more cars linearly, but parking is more
DIFFERENT ANGLES difficult and greater aisle widths are required. This greater width required
for turning does permit two way circulation without special traffic
directions, and reduces travelling distances within the parking area.

With diagonal parking, entrance and egress are more convenient and
accurate, and therefore the parking bay size may be reduced slightly.
One way circulation is generally necessary, though this itself will reduce
the possibility of accidents with pedestrians using the aisles to reach the
centre, and also with other vehicles negotiating into spaces. Where the
dimensions of the parking area are restricted, diagonal systems may not
provide the required number of spaces, but will ease access and egress.

PARKING BAYS The minimum size of bays should be 18 feet by 8 feet, though widths
of 8 feet 6 inches or even 9 feet are more convenient for 90 degree parking,
especially where customers have large parcels.

Using the standard 18 feet × 8 feet bay size, Table 13.2 indicates the
overall bin widths, being the width of one aisle and two adjoining parking
bays, and also the approximate number of car spaces per acre, including
aisles but excluding circulatory roads.

Table 13.2   OVERALL BIN WIDTHS AND CARS PER ACRE FOR DIFFERENT
PARKING PATTERNS

Pattern	Circulation system	Bay depth at right angles to aisle	Bay width parallel to aisle	Aisle width recommended	Overall bin width	Cars per acre (approx.)
90 degree	Two way	18 ft 0 in	8 ft 0 in	24 ft 0 in	60 ft 0 in	180
60 degree	One way	19 ft 6 in	9 ft 3 in	18 ft 0 in	57 ft 0 in	170
45 degree	One way	18 ft 6 in	11 ft 3 in	11 ft 0 in	48 ft 0 in	150
30 degree	One way	16 ft 6 in	16 ft 0 in	10 ft 0 in	43 ft 0 in	130

LAYOUT OF BAYS The following principles should be adopted in the detailed layout of bays:

1   Large parking areas should be subdivided by walkways or landscaping.
2   Parking aisles should always be set at right angles to the store
group, except where separate pedestrian walkways are provided.
3   Double marking lines of hairpin pattern should separate individual
bays; this will increase parking accuracy and reduce straddling of
bays.
4   Kerbs or buffer strips may be used to separate stalls opposite to each
other in herringbone pattern, but these may be inconvenient for
drainage and for customers. Metal or concrete bollards are also
effective, but are unsightly in empty parks.

In some cases, it may not be practical to extend ground level self-parking ATTENDANT PARKING space to meet the estimated demand, and attendants may be employed to park customers' cars. In this case, the saving in space may be as much as 30 per cent, but self-parking is usually smoother, involving no waiting, and therefore is essential where a high turnover is anticipated.

Parking space for employees should be separated from public areas, EMPLOYEES' PARKING or confined to the outermost spaces. In no case should employees be permitted to use spaces near the building core from which valuable revenue may be expected. The actual number of spaces required will depend on the number of staff and the extent of public transport, but where special areas are provided, individual spaces may be smaller than those for public use. The previous methods of calculation do not allow for employees' cars, and Nelson recommends that between 4 per cent and 10 per cent should be added to the total number calculated for the public.[9] More recent research by the Urban Land Institute suggests that, if up to 20 per cent of the retail area is office space, the total parking requirements may be calculated solely on gross leasable area devoted to retailing. Where more than 20 per cent is in office use, the generally accepted standard of 2·5 spaces per thousand square feet of offices should be allowed.[10] Table 13.3 indicates the number of spaces which have been provided in various types of American centres.

Table 13.3   EMPLOYEES' PARKING ALLOCATIONS[11]

	Gross floor area (GFA)	Number of spaces	Alternative formula
Neighbourhood centre	30–60,000	50	
	60–100,000	85	One space per 900 square foot GFA
Community centre	Less than 75,000	86	
	75–150,000	178	
	150–200,000	250	One space per 800 square foot GFA
Regional centre	Less than 200,000	212	
	200–400,000	235	
	Over 400,000	510	One space per 1,500 square foot GFA

In most British centres, apart from the Hampshire Centre, no specific provision has been made for employees' parking. In the case of the Gem Centre, Nottingham, employees park in front of the store at slack times to encourage potential customers.[12]

Where the cost per square foot of additional land for surface parking is **13.5 MULTI-STOREY PARKING** excessive, or where the area is restricted, multistorey parking may be considered; the actual point where such structures become economic will, of course, relate to the site costs and the type of construction adopted.

Because of expense and delays at peak periods, mechanical systems involving lifts or conveyors can rarely be considered for out-of-town centres. Similarly, self-parking is to be preferred to attendant parking, despite the proportional reduction in bay sizes with the latter system.

The use of multistorey garages may be appropriate in British centres, especially where deck levels can be directly connected to different shopping floors, with weather protection. The logical conclusion of this principle has now been built by Macy's at Queens, New York, where a circular store 426 feet in diameter, with three shopping levels, has been enclosed by five parking floors round its perimeter, 56 feet wide, to accommodate 1,500 cars, such that no parking space is further than 75 feet from a store entrance. Access to the parking floors is by separate ramps from exits, but traffic direction can be reversed to meet peak loads.

Plate 13.5 COWLEY CENTRE, OXFORD embodies the multistorey car park required to provide satisfactory parking for shoppers on a confined site.

At the Oadby centre, one parking deck is provided, while two multi-storey parks were provided at the Cowley Centre, Oxford, the second of which cost £400 per space. (See Plate 13.5). The semi-mechanical system used within the Bull Ring, Birmingham, has resulted in considerable congestion in the approach roads, owing to slow handling of vehicles without reservoir areas. Apart from this case, few centres have located public car parks over shop units, even where the levels on sloping sites would have permitted easy access. In the case of supercentres, it has been thought preferable to retain clear roof areas for air conditioning equipment. It seems probable that multistorey parks will be built in many future centres and Table 13.4 gives comparable data on those parks already built and in operation.

Table 13.4 COMPARATIVE ANALYSIS OF MULTISTOREY CAR PARKS[13]

	Type	Capacity	Number of floors	Floor area per car	Cost per car (£)
Coventry	Straight ramps split level	120	3 inc. roof	286	248
Canal Street, Nottingham	Level floor	152	4 inc. roof	250	310
Cole Bros. Sheffield	Straight ramps split level	400	6 inc. roof	240	—
Seacroft Centre, Leeds	One-level under shops	480	1	250	—
The Rows, Chester	Straight ramps split level	600	5 inc. roof	280	260
Cwmbran	Straight ramps split level	650	5 inc. roof	270	310

13.6 GROWTH AREAS

Any centre built in advance of its trade area's maturity must take future expansion into account. Planning for growth involves two factors:

1 The extension of the retail floor area at a future date must be considered at the initial planning stage, and also may require some capital investment, for basements and service connections. Similarly, the circulation patterns developed in the first stage should not be prejudiced by subsequent additions. Generally, any later additions will reduce the parking area adjacent to the centre, and place some parking spaces at further distances from some stores.

2 To cater for this loss of parking area, reserve space should be allowed beyond the first stage areas. This reserve space should be planned as previously stated, with special attention to walking distances. Further

parking could be given by multistorey structures, provided that pedestrian and vehicular access is equally convenient. An example of planned expansion is given in Appendix A, for the Northland Centre, Detroit, Michigan.

REFERENCES
1 V. Gruen and L. Smith, *Shopping Towns U.S.A.*, p. 123–124.
2 V. Gruen and L. Smith, op. cit., p. 124–125.
3 V. Gruen and L. Smith, op. cit., p. 129 and 131.
4 R. Nelson, *Selection of Retail Locations*, p. 249.
5 Urban Land Institute, *Shopping Centres Re-studied*, Vol. 1, p. 45–46.
  Parking Requirements for Shopping Centres, p. 5, et seq.
6 G. Baker and B. Funaro, *Shopping Centres —Design and Operation*, p. 36.
  Urban Land Institute, *Shopping Centres Re-studied*, Vol. 1, p. 47.
7 Urban Land Institute, *Shopping Centres Re-studied*, Vol. 1, p. 49.
8 Urban Land Institute, *Shopping Centres Re-studied*, Vol. 2, p. 13.
9 R. Nelson, op. cit., p. 256.
10 Urban Land Institute, *Parking Requirements for Shopping Centres*, p. 12.
11 Urban Land Institute, *Shopping Centres Re-studied*, Vol. 2, p. 13.
12 E. Beazley, 'Super-markets', *Architectural Review*, Nov. 1966, p. 333.
13 *Architects' Journal*, 6 July 1966, p. 59.

14
architectural design and landscaping

There are two main considerations concerning the three dimensional character of the shopping centre:

   1 That the centre should be attractive enough to draw and retain customers.

   2 That, once built, the centre should require the minimum of maintenance and overheads, both for the owner and for the tenants, so that competitive prices can be established. The architectural composition will develop concurrently with site planning, and consideration should be given to overall views of the centre from the surrounding areas as well as from within the centre itself.

The centre must present a stimulating and impressive appearance when seen from the surrounding roads, which may be at some distance, and the car scale must be considered. Difficulties may arise where many of the stores are only of one storey, except for the department store, and much of the view may be obscured by parked cars. (See Plate 9.1.) In these cases, the massing and silhouette should be considered, and designed to excite and to instil a sense of dependability. This may be done by creative handling of the many functional elements, such as water towers, tank or lift rooms, stacks and symbol signs. (See Plate 14.2.) Similarly, disturbing or unsightly elements, such as telephone or power cables should be placed underground, and a master television aerial incorporated for the use of all tenants. In all cases, the centre should be designed as a homogeneous group, not as a store surrounded by a huddle of small shops. OVERALL COMPOSITION

The first requirement in the detailed three dimensional design must be **14.2 DETAILED DESIGN**

L

Plate 14.1 HAMPSHIRE CENTRE, BOURNEMOUTH, showing the exterior of the Woolco store enclosing the single selling area on one level.

the successful transfer of customers from the transport scale of the parking areas to the entirely pedestrian scale of the shopping zones.

DEPARTMENT STORE Naturally, the department store is the most important element, becoming the prestige symbol for the whole development, and whose reputation should be a good advertisement in the region. Owing to marked variation in natural daylight, and the damage done by sunlight to goods on display, there are implied operating hazards in certain elevational treatments. Unfortunately, the glass wall is an enemy of merchandising, and imposes a costly maintenance factor. Therefore, large expanses of glazing are only used in display windows at pedestrian levels, or for restaurants and offices. Consequently, the large areas of blank wall must be carefully handled and moulded to provide interest and stimulation. They must be as much outward looking as inward: 'the shape must be simple, its surfacing such as to express prestige for the whole centre; its whole execution should be restrained, and not so rich and elegant that it makes the smaller elements appear insignificant'.[1] It should also be emphasized that the external aspect of the building is not sufficient to retain customers if the interior character and goods do not reach the required standard.

Plate 14.2 GEM CENTRE, NOTTINGHAM. The advertising sign in standard 'house' lettering is located adjacent to the main access road.

SUPERMARKET OR The supermarket relies very little on window shopping, and consequently
FOOD HALL has tended to become a rather bleak element externally. However, some
window space may be provided for special displays, preferably on the
north wall, as any direct sunlight must not be permitted to fall on goods
offered for sale. Maximum wall space is required up to 7 feet high, and
supermarkets are now generally lit by a high clerestory, shielded by a
large overhanging roof. The roof form can be more exciting than those
generally applied to urban stores, and barrel vaults and folded slabs have
been employed with advantage in some centres.

OTHER UNITS Any limitations on the handling of the smaller units should be designed
only for the benefit of the whole scheme, rather than to impose uniformity
for its own sake. Generally, the standard modular layout will provide the
basis of an overall design theme and pattern. As far as possible the
design of the shop fronts within the building framework should be left
to the individual trader, since the trader knows the particular requirements
of his specialist trading problems. Where restrictions are suggested regarding fascia heights and lettering, it is essential to take into account
the variety of frontages and shop types, so that a correct scale may be
adopted. In some cases, tenants may be given a choice of fascia and
lettering heights. Multiples who have built up particular house styles
will be reluctant to abandon them without good reason. Clashes between
different textures and colours can be minimized with the use of broad
separating panels dividing the various units, at the same time as providing
an additional modular feature which will contribute to the overall unity
of the whole centre. The overriding consideration is the necessity for
the whole grouping to possess the quality of a street, but that each unit
has a character of its own determined by the nature of its business and
by its style. And although it may be necessary to subordinate this to
achieve the successful character of the whole centre, the individual
trading character must not be lost completely.[2] (See Plates 14.3, 14.4
14.5 and 14.6.)

PEDESTRIAN AREAS The phrase 'Shopping should be fun' has often been applied to these
centres: 'the environment should be so attractive that customers will
enjoy shopping trips, will stay longer and return more often'.[3] Therefore,
the spaces in the centre should be more than narrow lanes between
stores, and have both open areas for cafes, markets and displays, and
opportunities for quiet and relaxation. Where fully enclosed malls are
provided, tenants should be encouraged to adopt completely open shop
fronts. Where this is not possible, projecting canopies should protect
both shoppers and displays in windows, and extra protection provided
in winter. Variety can be obtained by varying the height and depth of
overhang, and will also help to create focal points within the scheme.
Similarly, lighting should be varied but controlled, and special considera-

Plate 14.3 BREDA CENTRE, BELFAST, showing the main entrance to the department store.

tion given to the overall views of the centre at night when seen from the surrounding areas. This will also involve adequate and attractive lighting in the parking areas. (See Plates 14.6 and 14.7.)

The choice of materials will be related closely to the cost and location MATERIALS of the centre, but will also have a major effect on the total image of the centre. Coupled with this, maintenance will be a continuing expense, and therefore colourful, self-cleansing materials should be employed, such as marble, mosaic, hardwoods and glass. Decorated materials which require constant maintenance, such as painted brickwork, should be avoided.[4] Paving materials should be selected to give interest and variety, but also to wear consistently and be safe in wet weather.

Originally, the provision of all extra facilities, landscaping and sculpture AMENITIES met bitter opposition from tenants who were obliged to pay towards these amenities. (See Plate 14.8.) More recently complaints have been

Plate 14.4 ELEPHANT AND CASTLE CENTRE, LONDON.   As at the Breda Centre, entrances are often cluttered by prams and wire trolleys left by customers.

Plate 14.5 GEM CENTRE, NOTTINGHAM.   This incorporates a typical interior to be found in supercentres, with all departments on one level and contained within a completely enclosed, air-conditioned environment.

Plate 14.6 SHOPPING CENTRE, THE ROWS, CHESTER.   The covered mall principle employed in this central area project resulted in an attractive and successful development.

received from occupants of shops which do not have such amenities in the vicinity. (See Plate 14.9.) One American developer states that his trade increased 20 per cent with the provision of amenities. Thus, all forms of amenity may be beneficial to the environment and to the actual trade. The most usual facilities are landscaped areas, fountains, ponds, sculpture, advertisement kiosks, outdoor cafes, rest benches and telephone kiosks, all of which should be integrated into the overall plan and designed to complement the centre without interrupting its functional efficiency. In Britain, the provision of all-weather protection should not be regarded as an amenity, but as a necessity having great influence on the overall success of the project. (See Plate 14.10.)

Landscaping is an essential requirement in shopping centre design, especially in the open car park areas, but it should never take on the appearance of decoration limited to the addition of a few plants. Planting should be informal and natural as a contrast to the buildings, and existing

**14.3 LANDSCAP-
ING**

Plate 14.7 FROLUNDA TORG CENTRE, GOTHENBURG, SWEDEN. The main interior is attractively planned on three levels, two of which are directly connected to the car park and tramway. All floors are connected to one another by passenger conveyors, which also take shopping carts and invalid chairs.

Plate 14.8 WHITGIFT SQUARE, CROYDON is landscaped, and has a moving pavement integrated into the layout to facilitate pedestrian movement between the two shopping levels.

trees and other features on the site retained whenever possible. The appearance of the centre from the surrounding roads will be enhanced by landscaping, while careful planting can be used as wind or sound barriers. Trees can be used to modulate spaces or punctuate circulation

Plate 14.9 ELEPHANT AND CASTLE CENTRE, LONDON. Any landscaping within
enclosed centres must be integrated with the structure, and arrangements made for maintenance,
either by the landlord or by a tenants' organization.

Plate 14.10 ARNDALE CENTRE, DONCASTER. Attractive landscaping, sculpture and amenities will encourage shoppers to patronize this two level, covered mall centre.

paths. Where possible, trees and planting should be integrated into the structure, so as to eliminate unnecessary raised boxes, though this may be more difficult to achieve where decks are used.[5] In all cases, space should be allowed for roots, especially where the site is regraded, and trees carefully selected to avoid the damage done by the drip from some species.

Planting material should be indigenous to the area; not only will it look natural, but it will reduce maintenance requirements. Similarly, seasonal displays are an added attraction, but again budgeting and maintenance are necessary.

The main objective of the architect should be to ensure an overall unity SUMMARY and identity for the centre, at the same time allowing reasonable flexibility to suit individual requirements. Consequently, the architectural treatment must reflect the principles inherent in the total site layout, the vehicular and pedestrian circulation and in the trading policy. It must also be designed to promote an attractive traffic free shopping environment as well as profitable retail locations. Unfortunately, this has not always been realized by developers, who have only appointed architects after site and store layout have been planned. Indeed, the ability to provide pleasant shopping conditions is one major asset of out-of-town centres, which must be exploited to the maximum, so as to compete with the lower prices offered by cut price and discount stores in less favourable locations.

REFERENCES
1 V. Gruen and L. Smith, *Shopping Towns U.S.A.*, p. 160.
2 *R.I.B.A. Journal*, 'Shopping and the town centre', July 1963, p. 288–290.
3 V. Gruen and L. Smith, op. cit., p. 147.
4 J. S. Harris, 'The design of shopping centres', *T.P.I. Journal*, Sept./Oct. 1961, p. 250.
5 R. Zion, 'The landscape architect and the shopping centre', *I.L.A. Journal*, May 1961, p. 7–9.

15
out-of-town centres and the future

The foregoing chapters have considered the historical development of out-of-town and suburban centres, the factors to be analysed in the various methods of assessing potential location and the principles of site layout and design. Where possible, comparisons have been made between established American and current British practice, the latter being based on the relatively few out-of-town centres in operations or being planned in this country. This comparative analysis raises several major questions regarding existing and future centres.

The relevance of American practice to British conditions is often questioned by so-called experts in this country, though it would seem that the main differences concern socio-economic factors rather than site location and planning. For example, the previous dominance in Britain of the independent trader encouraged the traditional forms of daily local shopping, which only recently has begun to give way to the more modern techniques of supermarket retailing. Similarly, public transport, which does not foster one stop shopping, is considerably more important in this country than in America, where it has suffered a continual decline. It is probable that these and many other differences stem from the time lapse between the relative growth of retailing in each country, rather than from great variations in conditions. The length of this time lapse is being reduced rapidly with modern communications and by developments sponsored in this country by American organizations. It is significant that British developers, who are especially aware of the vagaries of local and regional circumstances have also financed visits by their architects and planners to America, to study current procedure and techniques. Similarly, American market research specialists have recently opened branch offices in Britain, **15.1 VALIDITY OF AMERICAN PRACTICE** and their more refined methods of site analysis should provide useful examples for future British practice, though it must be emphasized that all analyses will be affected radically by local circumstances; precedent should not replace examination of these local factors.

15.2 LOCATION AND SITING

In America, the abundance of land and capital, coupled with the 100 per cent increase in expenditure in the 20 years up to 1961, led to the over-provision of centres, and resulted in the failure of several of the earlier and less well endowed schemes. These failures were caused by poor location and management, and by the development of subsequent centres that were demanded by rising car ownership, increased spending power and the massive expansion of suburban residential areas. In Britain, however, suitable sites are relatively scarce, and planning and building requirements are considerable, stringent and occasionally misguided. Consequently, many centres have been developed on sites fortuitously acquired by property speculators, often for other uses. Emphasis has already been placed on the suburban nature of locations, rather than the genuine out-of-town situations occupied by many major regional centres in America, and on the important role played by highway construction in the promotion of new nodal points suitable for retail and social uses. Obvious examples of this factor are the site for the proposed Haydock Centre, and the increased trade experienced at the Yate Centre since the opening of the Severn Bridge.

15.3 LOCAL AND REGIONAL IMPLICATIONS

By far the most controversial aspect of out-of-town centres concerns their relationship with existing central areas, especially bearing in mind the failure of many new central redevelopment schemes to attract either tenants or customers. The reasons for the relative decline of existing central districts in America and Britain have been outlined and the present trends will be accentuated by the increasing use of private cars by house-wives, by the introduction of any form of road pricing and by the difficulties caused through congestion and lack of parking. In the case of the Hampshire Centre, Bournemouth, the Inspector's report, on the appeal against the original refusal of planning permission, stated that the development would help to ease future traffic congestion in the town centre. Further decline will be occasioned by the inability of existing traders to offer competitive prices and attractive shopping conditions in out-of-date and inappropriate units with difficulties in parking, servicing and mainten-ance, and also by the protracted negotiation and construction periods experienced in the redevelopment of most central areas.

The trend towards decentralization has been encouraged by the high cost of central area sites, and by the growth of many supermarkets and multiple chains of sufficient repute and resources to develop secondary sites away from the 'High Street', but with good servicing and parking facilities. Consequently, with the submission of an application for a major suburban or out-of-town centre, the Local Authority is usually faced with a dilemma. Should central area trading be protected, even if further congestion and damage to the environment results? Similarly, is it the planners' job to prevent competition between different shopping locations or between different traders, or merely to indicate the general direction for future commercial development? In fact, a new major centre might be beneficial if it served to stimulate improved facilities within its trade area. In the case of the Haydock proposal, it has been stated that the Minister considered that such a centre would prejudice the redevelopment of existing centres in the area. It is interesting to note that this restriction relates to a new location within the region and presumably does not apply to the undue expansion of one existing centre to the detriment of a neighbouring similar centre. It must be also be recognized that, in some cases, redevelopment will be lengthy, expensive and possibly undesirable. This applies particularly to historic town centres, such as Oxford, Cambridge or Canterbury, where suburban centres have been developed or are planned. In fact the Local Authority's responsibility with regard to out-of-town centres is apparent. Either proposals should be rejected and central area redevelopment undertaken before stagnation is complete, or possible sites should be allocated in accordance with the overall town or regional plans. The planning authority should not reject new shopping facilities solely because they might prejudice the trading position of existing facilities. Similarly, it is essential that new centres should be considered in the context of a regional plan, rather than within the confines of administrative boundaries. Great stress has already been placed on the absence of such statutory regional plans, which has only served to highlight the difficulties of those Local Authorities who have been required to consider applications for major schemes. These problems were emphasized by the Haydock Report, which concluded that only 12 centres of this type could be sited economically in this country, probably located in relation to the 12 existing major urban areas. Nevertheless, considerable scope exists for the development of smaller centres, possibly of similar size and status to the Woolco projects, and this type of scheme seems the most likely to succeed in the immediate future.

15.4 METHODOLOGY

Competition for the limited number of available central or suburban sites has previously resulted in only the most elementary economic analysis of market potential being carried out, often after the site has already been purchased. This same site shortage restricted the growth of professional knowledge and expertise in this type of development, and only recently have more reliable and comprehensive surveys been produced, often by American consultants.

Of the techniques previously considered, the projection method has been the most widely adopted in this country, owing to the availability of comparative data and the relative simplicity of its application. The accuracy of this technique will depend largely on the influence of local circumstances and on the target date selected. The more comprehensive and thorough analyses have employed the vacuum or market share techniques. For both these methods, the principal disadvantages are the length of time required and the difficulty experienced by private research teams in obtaining accurate and sometimes confidential material. Nevertheless, the market share technique, as employed in the Haydock Report, can be recommended as being particularly suitable for British conditions, provided that special attention is given to the influence of public transport. More recently, the American Retail Market Potential Model has introduced computer systems into this country and with it the possibility of detailed cost-benefit studies for different locations, together with a marked saving in time spent on research and analysis. Such cost benefit exercises will be advantageous to Local Authorities in the consideration of alternative out-of-town or suburban sites, and also for a comparison of the costs, both financial and social, with the expenditure necessary to renew or replace exisiting facilities, particularly in central areas.

With all the techniques, the choice of a target date is important. While projections are often made to 1981 or 1991, to suit Census material, it is preferable that a date is selected which is only 5 years in advance of the opening of the subject centre. In this respect, the new quinquennial Census may be informative, though taken only on a sample basis. In America, fewer target dates are fixed, since the estimated trade is expected to be available to the centre immediately after opening. This technique emphasizes the commercial aspects of store promotion. Therefore, it is especially unfortunate that several studies by Local Authorities of future shopping requirements have produced remarkably unrealistic and divergent assessments, even though the basic principles of data collection are now recognized and understood. Such miscalculations have resulted in the prevalent sight of bleak precincts in 'off-centre' locations surrounded by boarded shop fronts and deserted by customers and traders alike. Thus, the failure to analyse existing or future demands caused severe setbacks to developers and a serious loss of confidence among potential tenants of subsequent projects.

15.5 LAYOUT AND DESIGN There seems little doubt that Americal principles of layout and design are equally valid for most out-of-town centres in this country, with surprisingly few modifications except those of technical detail or adjustments for local conditions. The standards of development now reached in the United States and elsewhere in Europe embody a large volume of research and experience, but the few centres built in Britain have not utilized this expertise in full. There has been a marked tendency for the layout of suburban and out-of-town schemes to be a repetition of conventional central area shopping streets, with the motor car removed to further, and sometimes inconvenient locations. It has already been stressed that, in centres which rely upon car borne patrons, the aspect and accessibility of the shopping area from the car parks is vitally important. These features should not be sacrificed merely to provide the theoretical maximum number of parking spaces, nor should customers be confronted with goods service area and refuse stores at the rear of shop units. Too often, these service areas are insufficient, with goods vehicles becoming entangled with customers' and employees' cars. It is essential to the ultimate success of any centre that it is also convenient to the traders, especially those dependent on regular bulk deliveries of perishable goods. Consequently, goods vehicles should be provided with separate circulatory routes, particularly where customers are required to walk along the car park access roads, as occurs in almost every centre. Where these extra roads demand further site area, walking distances may be extended, and therefore the parking spaces on the extremities should be reserved for employees' cars, to prevent the latter occupying prime parking locations.

The detailed layout of the pedestrian areas and individual units, both in central and suburban locations, has also retained many of the characteristics of the conventional High Street shops. This transporting of standard layouts has resulted in proportionally smaller units than is prevalent in America, and in a marked inflexibility of unit size and type, all of which have a direct bearing on the profitability of the centre. To achieve the necessary degree of flexibility, it is essential that possible key tenants, such as department stores and multiples, are approached at the beginning of the design stage. Not only will this assist in planning the overall layout, but smaller tenants will also be able to state their space and location requirements in advance of construction. In this way, the floor layout can be prearranged to meet the demands of individual specialist traders. The apparent inability of developers to meet these demands has automatically precluded a certain percentage of potential tenants from many new centres. Similarly, this preplanning will indicate the likely tenants and areas which may require future expansion space, and which must be allowed for in the initial layout. The failure of some developers to recognize these factors and to establish a planned merchandising layout is reflected in the many unsuccessful schemes apparent in this country, in both central and suburban locations.

The prior selection of tenants requires the formulation of a definite retailing policy for a particular centre, to which these tenants will conform. For example, it may be assumed that differences between policy and some concessionaires resulted in the early failure of the first supercentres. Many nationally known chains experience wide regional variations in trade, and should be considered in relation to local circumstances. The new

M

Woolco stores, for example, offer higher quality goods than their parent company, while other more traditional outlets, such as the Co-operative are now adjusting their organization to meet modern demands, and are likely to provide greater competition in the future. All these factors only serve to emphasize the need for flexibility in layout, and for co-operation between planner, developer and trader.

Unfortunately, conventional and unimaginative layouts have been reflected in the three dimensional design, which has become stereotyped and boring, often being little more than the antiquated parade of shops with projecting canopies, claimed to provide 'all-weather protection'. While this may have been true of better climatic conditions in parts of America, it is a fallacy to believe that such 'amenities' provide little more than the minimal requirements for Britain. Both developers and local authorities should encourage completely enclosable shopping areas, at least during the winter months. Where this is done, careful handling of spaces and materials will avoid the claustrophobic and unreal atmosphere experienced in some centres. The covered walk principle can be extended into the parking areas, with canopies provided over pedestrian access routes, and with walking distances cut to a minimum.

As has already been mentioned, the provision of integrated amenities and landscaping is now regarded as essential in American centres, as a positive asset to business. In Britain, such amenities have often been considered by traders merely as a further service charge, and it is important therefore that their advantages should be realized and emphasized in future schemes.

Elevational design has varied from the complete freedom given to traders in some centres to the negative supercentre type of an introverted nature. With enclosed centres, the multiplicity of entrances will be reduced, to assist air conditioning and management, and tenants can be encouraged to dispense with conventional shop fronts, adopting a more progressive attitude towards design and supervision. The same requirements regarding flexibility apply also to elevational treatment, which must be capable of meeting changing demands and allow variety of types while maintaining an overall unity of the building group.

CONCLUSION It is obvious, of course, that the development of these centres in America resulted from the failure of the central area to meet many growing demands, and from the availability of cheap sites at suitable locations. Capital investment in commercial property within the central business districts was in no way comparable with that in the metropolitan suburbs, and many major outlets, notably department stores, were obliged to close. This situation does not exist at present in Britain, where central area redevelopment has been undertaken on a large scale, both by Local Authorities and by private concerns, and the growth of suburban and out-of-town centres has been correspondingly less than in the United States. However, the redevelopment is lengthy, and is unlikely to cater for the growing demands of the many motorized shoppers, who may soon expect to find special road pricing added to the other inconveniences of the central area. Consequently the growth of suburban centres will continue for several years and will stimulate an increasing demand for sites.

The foregoing chapters have emphasized the criteria to be considered in the assessment of any such sites, especially a good location based upon a comprehensive analysis of the potential market, prior selection and location of suitable tenants and careful site planning and design. It is interesting to observe that many of the basic principles already discussed are equally applicable to central area redevelopment. Indeed, Victor Gruen, the acknowledged American expert, giving an address in April 1968 to the Associated Merchandising Corporation of America, prophesied that within the next 15 to 20 years, many of the lessons learned during the growth of out-of-town projects would be used in the redevelopment of new multilevel city centres, with special importance placed on vertical integration.

The achievement of the main principles of satisfactory site selection and design will rest largely on the availability of suitably qualified planners, economists, engineers and architects, and on the willingness of developers and local authorities to co-operate, both in location assessment and in actual site planning. The shortage of suitable sites will be of fundamental importance in the future, and emphasizes the need for further research into this form of development and its repercussions. The lessons learned from American experience and practice should be used in conjunction with the planning administration and control to ensure the successful location and design of such centres as may be propsed in this country in the future.

Appendix A
comparative analysis of
shopping centres

Table A.1   COMPARATIVE ANALYSIS OF SHOPPING CENTRES

Name	Developer	Estimated trade area population	Distance from nearest centre	Plan type	Site area (acres)	Gross building area (ft²)	Gross retail area (ft²)
Breda	C. & A. Anderson	60,000 within 2 miles	2 miles Belfast	'L'	6	51,000	44,000
Cowley	Local authority	24,000 within 1 mile; 48,000 total	2 miles Oxford	Precinct and malls	23	265,000	97,000
Cross Gates	Arndale	119,000 within 3 miles	4 miles Leeds	Enclosed mall	9	193,000	158,000
Drumchapel	Arndale	40,000	7 miles Glasgow	Precinct	4·5	160,000	132,000
Elephant and Castle	Willett	1 million within 3 miles	2 miles central London	Enclosed malls on 3 floors	8	100,000	150,000
Gem	Gem Supercentres	250,000 within 15 minutes driving time	2 miles Nottingham	Single enclosed unit	14	84,000	84,000
Hampshire	Second Covent Garden	300,000	3 miles Bournemouth	Strip	20	140,000	130,000
Oadby	Woolco	24,000 by 1975	2 miles Leicester	Single enclosed unit	6	80,000	80,000
Stillorgan	M.E.P.C.	320,000 within 3 miles	5 miles Dublin	L-shaped mall	9	160,000	110,000
Tivoli	Murrayfield	140,000	4 miles Birmingham	L-shaped mall	5	128,000	107,000
Walkden	Arndale	74,000 within 2 miles	6 miles Manchester	Precinct	5	97,000	76,000
Yate	M.E.P.C.	28,000 by 1974	12 miles Bristol	Precinct and mall	9	218,000	163,000
Kilkenny	Arndale	200,000 within 4 miles	4 miles Adelaide	Enclosed mall	8	108,000	120,000
Northland	Hudson	800,000 within 10 miles	12 miles Detroit	Cluster	162	1,382,000	985,000

Major tenants Areas (ft²)	Number of Smaller units	Method of servicing	Other facilities	Number of car spaces	Car spaces per 1,000 ft² floor space	Approximate cost (£)
Department store (31,000)	10	Rear	Snack bar, motor showroom and filling station	320	7·3	250,000
Department store (11,000) Supermarkets (7,000)	75	Rear	Health centre, cinema, community centre, 110 flats	950	9·8	1,830,000
Department store (35,000) Variety store (18,000) Supermarket (13,000)	58	Rear	Offices (24,000)	400	2·5	Not available
Department store (16,000) Variety store (16,000) Supermarket (7,000)	47	Rear	Café, post office	300	2·3	Not available
Supermarket (8,400)	116	Basement	2 public houses, banqueting suite, offices	150 500 adjacent	1·0	2,000,000
Supermarket hall (9,000) Concessionaire lettings	None	Rear	Community room, filling station	1,000	12·0	284,000
Variety store (100,000) Food store (24,000)	14	Rear	Filling station	1,750	13·5	Not available
Variety/concessionaire lettings	6	Rear	Snack bar	700	8·7	400,000
Department store (16,000) Variety store (14,000) Supermarkets (10,000 & 8,500)	56	Rear and service courts	Restaurant	600	5·4	900,000
Variety (10,400) Supermarkets (6,600 & 5,500)	65	Basement	Bowling centre, filling station, offices 120 flats	480	4·5	1,250,000
Department store (11,300) Supermarkets (9,000 & 7,400)	52	Service courts	Bowling centre Market hall, Conference centre	400	5·2	Not available
Department store (18,000) Variety store (11,000) Supermarkets (9,600 & 7,500)	120	Service courts	Filling station, offices, bus station	1,500	9·2	2,000,000
Department store (60,000) Variety store (12,000)	31	Rear	Filling station	750	6·2	Not available
Department store (582,000) Variety store (34,000)	122	Basement	Theatre, zoo, pick-up station, rest rooms	10,500	10·6	10,000,000

Plate A1 Breda Centre, Belfast.

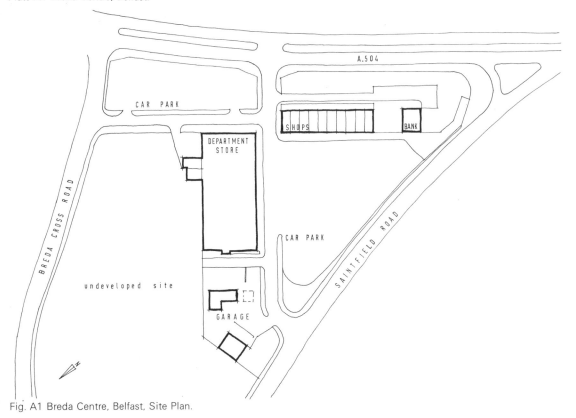

Fig. A1 Breda Centre, Belfast, Site Plan.

Plate A2 Cowley Centre, Oxford.

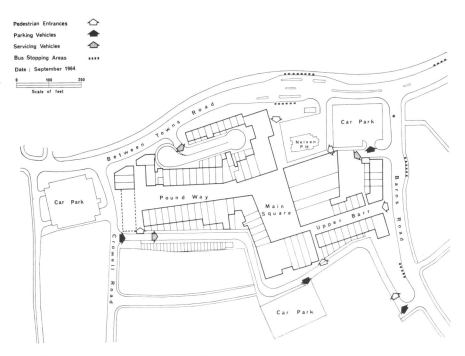

Fig. A2 Cowley Centre, Oxford, Layout Plan.

Plate A3 Cross Gates Centre, Leeds.

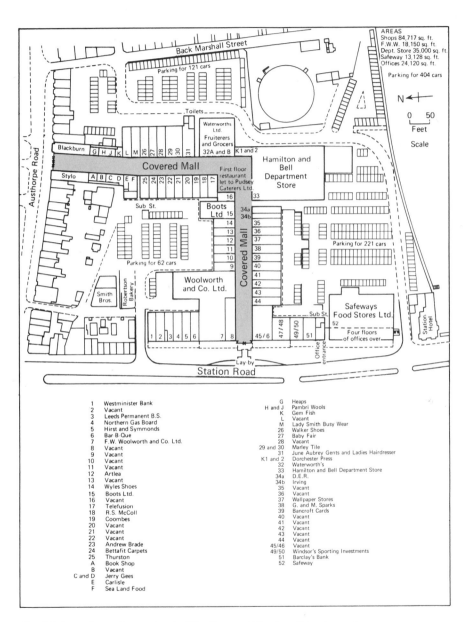

Fig. A3 Cross Gates Centre, Leeds, Site Plan and Merchandising Layout.

Plate A4 Drumchapel Centre, Glasgow.

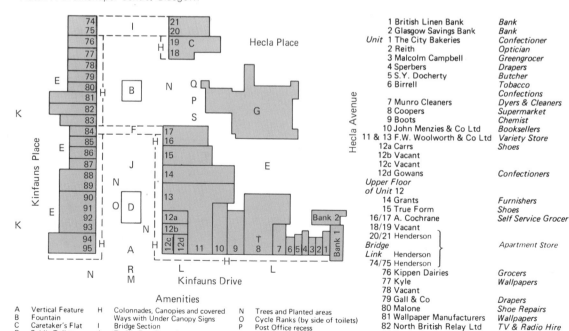

	1 British Linen Bank	*Bank*
	2 Glasgow Savings Bank	*Bank*
Unit 1	The City Bakeries	*Confectioner*
2	Reith	*Optician*
3	Malcolm Campbell	*Greengrocer*
4	Sperbers	*Drapers*
5	S.Y. Docherty	*Butcher*
6	Birrell	*Tobacco Confections*
7	Munro Cleaners	*Dyers & Cleaners*
8	Coopers	*Supermarket*
9	Boots	*Chemist*
10	John Menzies & Co Ltd	*Booksellers*
11 & 13	F.W. Woolworth & Co Ltd	*Variety Store*
12a	Carrs	*Shoes*
12b	Vacant	
12c	Vacant	
12d	Gowans	*Confectioners*
Upper Floor of Unit 12		
14	Grants	*Furnishers*
15	True Form	*Shoes*
16/17	A. Cochrane	*Self Service Grocer*
18/19	Vacant	
20/21	Henderson	
Bridge Link	Henderson	} *Apartment Store*
74/75	Henderson	
76	Kippen Dairies	*Grocers*
77	Kyle	*Wallpapers*
78	Vacant	
79	Gall & Co	*Drapers*
80	Malone	*Shoe Repairs*
81	Wallpaper Manufacturers	*Wallpapers*
82	North British Relay Ltd	*TV & Radio Hire*
83	Bowie-Castlebank	*Dry Cleaners*
84	Donald McKellar	*Butcher*
85	G. Boddie Ltd	*Chemist*
86/95	Clydebank Cooperative Society	*Co-op Store*

Amenities

A	Vertical Feature	H	Colonnades, Canopies and covered Ways with Under Canopy Signs	
B	Fountain			N Trees and Planted areas
C	Caretaker's Flat	I	Bridge Section	O Cycle Ranks (by side of toilets)
D	Public Toilets	J	Traffic-Free Shopping	P Post Office recess
E	Service Areas	K	Car Parks	Q Steps up to Post Office
F	Covered Way	L	Bus Lay-by and Car Lay-by	R Steps and Ramp up to precinct
G	Post Office	M	Bus Stop Route No 9	S Telephone Kiosks
				T Cafe (over Coopers)

Fig. A4 Drumchapel Centre, Glasgow, Site Plan.

Plate A5 Elephant and Castle Centre, London.

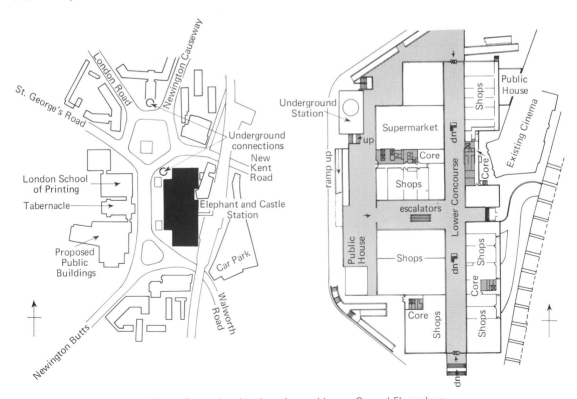

Fig. A5a and b Elephant and Castle Centre, London, Location and Lower Ground Floor plans.

Plate A6 Gem Supercentre, Nottingham.

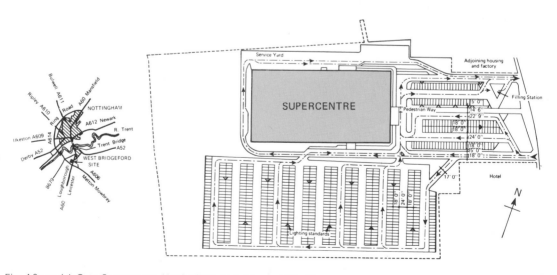

Fig. A6*a* and *b* Gem Supercentre, Nottingham, Location and Site Plans.

Plate A7 Hampshire Centre, Bournemouth.

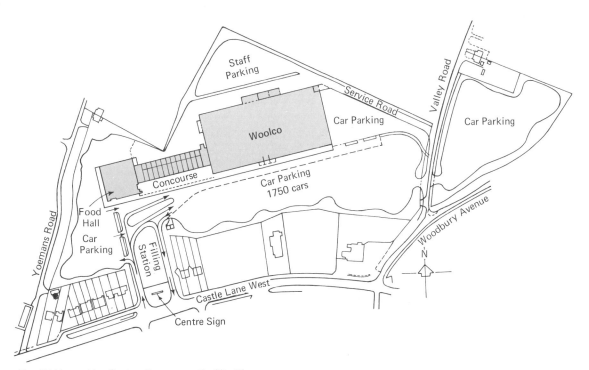

Fig. A7 Hampshire Centre, Bournemouth, Site Plan.

Plate A8 Woolco Store, Oadby, Leicester.

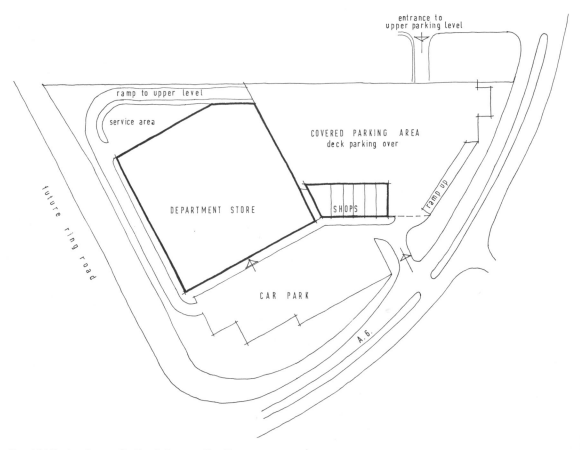

Fig. A8 Woolco Centre, Oadby, Leicester, Site Plan.

Plate A9 Stillorgan Centre, Dublin.

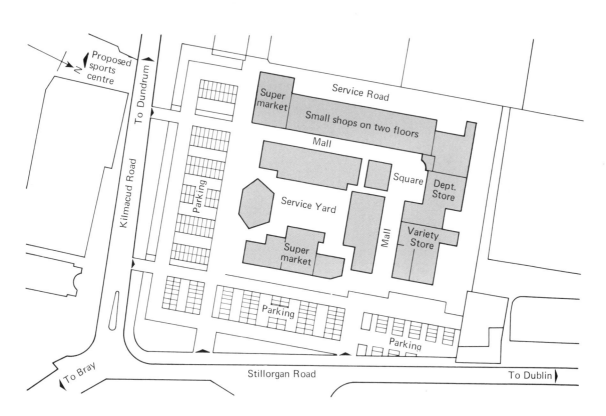

Fig. A9 Stillorgan Centre, Dublin, Layout Plan.

Plate A10 Tivoli Centre, Yardley, Birmingham; perspective view before construction.

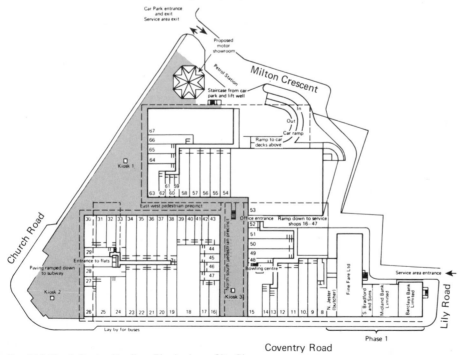

Fig. A10 Tivoli Centre, Yardley, Birmingham, Site Plan.

Plate A11 Walkden Centre, Manchester.

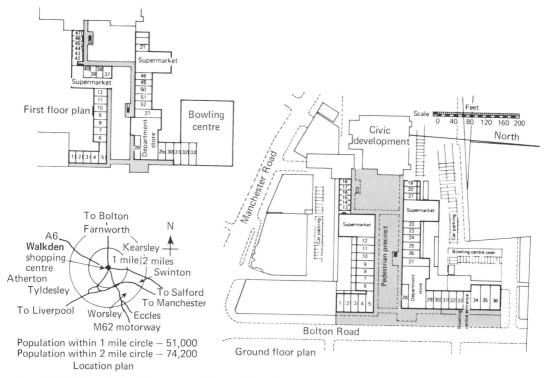

Fig. A11 Walkden Centre, Manchester, Site and Floor Plans.

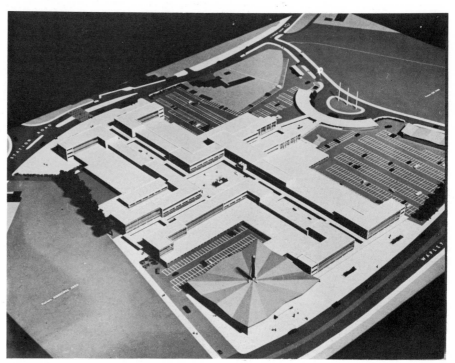

Plate A12 Yate Centre, Gloucestershire.

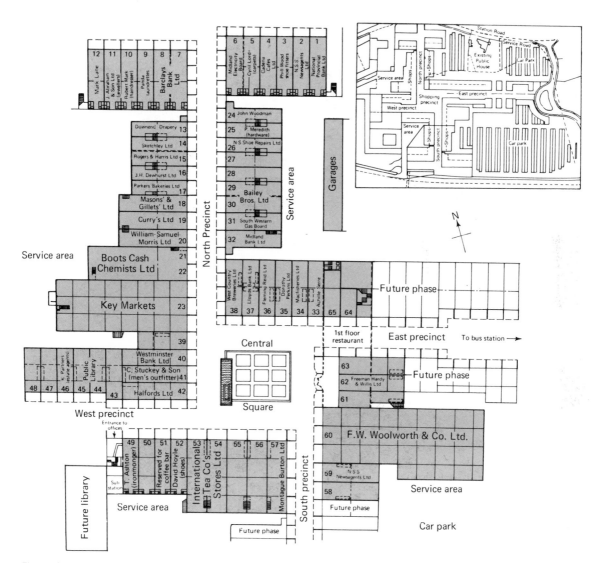

Fig. A12a and b Yate Centre, Gloucestershire, Site Plan, and Merchandising Layout.

Plate A13 Kilkenny Centre, Adelaide, Australia.

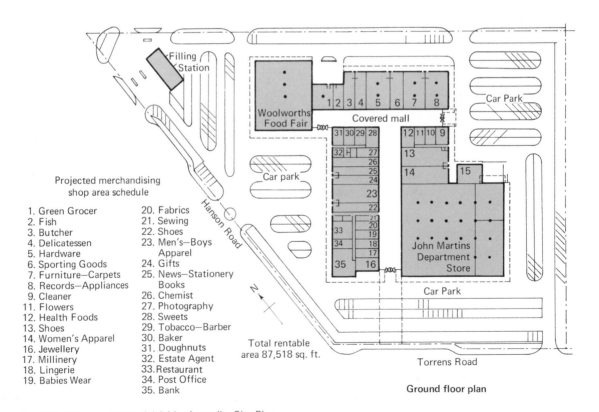

Projected merchandising
shop area schedule

 1. Green Grocer
 2. Fish
 3. Butcher
 4. Delicatessen
 5. Hardware
 6. Sporting Goods
 7. Furniture—Carpets
 8. Records—Appliances
 9. Cleaner
11. Flowers
12. Health Foods
13. Shoes
14. Women's Apparel
16. Jewellery
17. Millinery
18. Lingerie
19. Babies Wear

20. Fabrics
21. Sewing
22. Shoes
23. Men's—Boys
    Apparel
24. Gifts
25. News—Stationery
    Books
26. Chemist
27. Photography
28. Sweets
29. Tobacco—Barber
30. Baker
31. Doughnuts
32. Estate Agent
33. Restaurant
34. Post Office
35. Bank

Total rentable
area 87,518 sq. ft.

Ground floor plan

Fig. A13 Kilkenny Centre, Adelaide, Australia, Site Plan.

Plate A14 Northland Centre, Detroit, U.S.A.

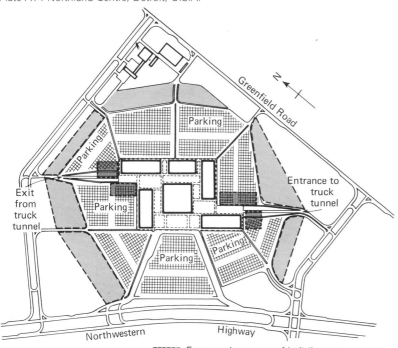

Future enlargement of building area
Future enlargement of parking area

Fig. A14 Northland Centre, Detroit, U.S.A., Site Plan, illustrating the areas reserved for future expansion.

Appendix B

classification of American shopping centres

Table B1 CLASSIFICATION OF AMERICAN SHOPPING CENTRES

Author and source	Author's classification	Average total floor area in ft²	Range of floor areas in ft²	Site size in acres	Number of parking spaces	Parking spaces per 1,000 ft² of floor area	Population served	Number of families served	Major tenant(s)	Number of smaller units
Urban Land Institute Technical Bulletin No. 30	Neighbourhood	40,000	30,000–75,000	4–10	360	8·1	7,000–20,000	1,000	Supermarket	8–10
	Community	150,000	100,000–300,000	10–30	1,300	8·17	20,000–100,000	5,000	Variety or junior department store	
	Regional	400,000	400,000–1m	over 40	4,000	7·73	Over 100,000		1 or 2 department stores	
Pearson T.P.I. Journal Sept./Oct. 1957	Local			5–10			3,500–5,500	1,000–5,000	Supermarket	10–15
	District			10–15			20,000	5,000	Department store	20–40
	Regional			35–75			100,000–200,000	30,000–50,000		50–100
Percival T.P.I. Journal Sept./Oct. 1965	Neighbourhood		10,000–25,000				5,000–10,000		Supermarket	10–20
	Community		40,000–140,000				10,000–30,000		Junior department store	40–60
	Regional		Up to 1m				100,000–250,000		1 or 2 department stores	100
Reynolds T.P. Review April 1958	Convenience		20,000–40,000	2–5	200–400	10	7,000–15,000		Supermarket	
	Local		50,000–100,000	5–10	500–800	8	30,000–50,000		Variety store	
	District		150,000–200,000	50	1,000–2,000	8	50,000–200,000		Junior department store	
	Regional		500,000–1m	100	2,500–8,000	7	250,000–1m		1 or 2 department stores	
Waide	Neighbourhood	54,000			400	8			Junior department store	
T.P.I. Journal Sept./Oct. 1963	Community	163,000			1,100	7			Department store	
	Regional	500,000			3,000	5–6			1 or 2 department stores	

Appendix C
examples of projection and computer techniques of market potential analysis

The following tables and notes indicate the calculations necessary for the assessment of floor space on a hypothetical basis of 5,000 households. The calculations apply only to retail shops and do not cover service trades, such as catering establishments, launderettes, dry cleaners, hairdressers, shoe repairs or service stations.

    This example is reproduced by permission of the Modern Merchandising Methods Department of the National Cash Register Company Ltd.

Table C1   PROJECTED NATIONAL AND FAMILY EXPENDITURE

	1	2	3	4	5	6	7	8
Commodity group	Total national expenditure (£m)		Increase or decrease (%)	Projected increase to	to	Average family expenditure		
	1958	1963		1970 (%)	1981 (%)	1958	1970	1981
Food and household preparations	4,227	4,365	3·26	7·82	15·00	87s 7d	94s 5d	100s 1d
Alcoholic drinks	913	1,079	18·20	43·60	83·70	4s	5s 9d	7s 4d
Tobacco and cigarettes	1,031	1,041	0·97	2·30	4·50	13s	13s 4d	13s 7d
Shoes	248	269	8·45	20·30	38·80	5s 10d	7s	8s
Men's wear	408	446	9·31	22·30	42·80	8s 1d	9s 11d	11s 6d
Women's wear	799	932	16·65	40·00	76·50	13s 6d	19s	24s
Furniture and floor coverings	362	399	6·08	14·60	28·00	5s 10d	6s 9d	7s 6d
Household textiles	150	175	12·00	28·80	55·20	2s 4d	3s	3s 7d
Radio and electrical	388	511	31·70	76·00	146·00	3s 10d	6s 10d	9s 8d
Hardware	155	161	3·87	9·30	17·75	3s 5d	3s 9d	4s
Books	51	56½	10·80	25·90	49·70	1s 1d	1s 4d	1s 7d
Newspapers/ magazines	187	165	−11·77	−28·20	−54·00	3s 10d	2s 9d	1s 9d
Chemist's goods	219	260	18·71	44·80	86·00	4s 10d	7s	9s
Miscellaneous and recreation	489	636	30·00	72·00	138·00	4s 4d	7s 6d	10s 5d
Sweets and chocolate						4s 2d	4s 2d	4s 2d

APPENDIX C

1   The comparison of 1958 and 1963 spending figures is taken from the Consumers' Expenditure Table (at 1958 prices) of the National Income and Expenditure Report of 1964 (Central Statistical Office). This document was chosen partly because the tables of national spending should reflect a more accurate trend than individual family spending figures, and partly because it is the only document which presents figures for spending adjusted for constant prices (1958 is the base).

2   The 1963 figures have been reduced by 3·9 per cent because this is the estimated overall population increase between 1958 and 1963. In this way, the figures for the 2 years become comparable as regards population as well as regards value.

3   The projected increases to 1970 and 1981 are simple the percentage increases on 1958 arrived at from extrapolation of the increases or decreases between 1958 and 1963.

4   The family expenditure figure in column 6 is that derived from the 1958 figures in the *Ministry of Labour Survey*, and columns 7 and 8 represent the figures in column 6 adjusted by the percentages in columns 4 and 5. There is an exception, however, in the case of alcohol. The expenditure figures in the *Ministry of Labour Survey* include spending in licensed premises. They have therefore been reduced so that they only cover spending in retail shops. This figure has now been based on off-licence sales as quoted by the Census of Distribution 1961.

5   No separate figures for sweets and chocolate are available from the Income and Expenditure Survey. The only figures which can be a guide in this direction are those of the Ministry of Labour which are not adjusted for price increases. Therefore, the projection to 1970 and 1981 has been assumed to remain constant, because any increases in actual family spending as shown by the Family Expenditure Survey could well be accounted for by price increases.

6   A noteworthy drop in volume of expenditure on newspapers and magazines will be seen. It seems unlikely that only half the number of newspapers and magazines will be bought in 1981. It may, therefore, be more reasonable to assume that there will be no increase on 1963, but that it will remain constant at that level. Expenditure for 1970 and 1981 thus becomes 3s 10d less 11·77 per cent = 3s 5d.

Table C2   PROJECTED SPENDING AND SPACE REQUIREMENTS

Type of trade	1 Average family spending 1970	2 1981	3 Spending of 5,000 families 1970	4 1981	5 Sales per square foot Mean	6 High Average	7 Shop space per 5,000 families (ft²) Specialists 1970	8 1981	9 %	10 General Stores 1970 (ft²)	11 1981 (ft²)
			£	£							
Food	94s 5d	100s 1d	23,600	25,000	26s	30s	15,700	16,700	—	—	—
Off-licences	5s 9d	7s 4d	1,425	1,830	—	20s	1,425	1,830	—	—	—
Confectionery/Tobacco/ Newsagency	18s 10½d	19s 1½d	4,700	4,700	—	50s	1,880	1,900	—	—	—
Shoes	7s	8s	1,750	2,000	10s 10d	15s 3d	1,880	2,150	18	420	470
Men's wear	9s 11d	11s 6d	2,480	2,790	12s	16s	2,540	2,860	18	560	630
Women's wear	19s 10d	24s	4,960	6,100	10s 6d	14s	4,840	5,920	32	2,260	2,780
Furniture/Furnishings	6s 9d	7s 6d	1,685	1,850	8s 3d	10s 3d	2,470	2,710	25	820	900
Household textiles	3s	3s 7d	750	900	9s 4d	13s	600	690	49	600	690
Radio/electrical	6s 10d	9s 8d	1,710	2,415	10s	15s	2,050	2,900	10	230	320
Books/stationery	5s 7d	7s 5d	1,400	1,850	11s	17s	1,320	1,740	20	330	440
Chemists, photo dealers	7s	9s	1,750	2,250	17s 2d	21s 9d	1,430	1,840	11	189	230
Jewellery, fancy goods, etc.	3s 3d	4s 7d	815	1,150	11s	14s 6d	790	1,110	30	330	480
Hardware	3s 9d	4s	950	1,000	7s	9s 3d	1,480	1,560	28	570	600

Columns 1 and 2
are merely columns 7 and 8 from Table C1 carried over.

Columns 3 and 4
are totals of spending by 5,000 families derived by multiplying columns 1 and 2.

Columns 5 and 6

The two sales conversion factors are derived from a comprehensive survey of department stores, and indicate the sales per square foot experienced in individual departments. It is felt that they should reflect sales per square foot in a normal shop handling similar merchandise. Column 5 is the overall mean average for the whole sample; column 6 is the average of the upper quartile and can be considered as a reasonable figure for more efficient operations. The exceptions to his source are food, sweets and tobacco, and off-licences. The food figures are those from the last *Self-Service and Supermarket* survey, and the off-licence and sweets and tobacco figures are those suggested by reputable companies.

Columns 7 and 8

are based on the relationship between columns 6 and 3 and 4 respectively. The higher sales conversion factor has been used because modern methods of trading will make more efficient use of space. A very important factor which must be considered in this connection is the extent of shopping in the listed commodity groups which is at the moment done through general stores (i.e. department and variety stores). It is important to note that these figures represent selling area only. There are no facts to suggest the extent of total area, but based on supermarket experience, it would not be unreasonable to assume that space for storage, administration and staff services would be as much again.

Column 9

is the proportion of commodity sales going into general stores in those groups where this proportion is fairly substantial.

Columns 10 and 11

are thus proportions of space in general stores based on the 1961 percentage (column 9). There may be variations in habit, in that there may be tendencies toward the general store, but there are no facts to point the direction of such tendencies.

EXAMPLE OF COMPUTER METHOD OF MARKET ASSESSMENT The following flow diagram and input data indicate the various stages necessary to analyse the existing retail structure of a region using a computer technique.

This example is reproduced by permission of the West Midlands Shopping Research Group of the Town Planning Institute, whose publication *Predicting Shopping Requirements* gives a more detailed analysis of the development of the technique.

INPUT DATA FOR COMPUTER PROGRAM The box numbers refer to the stages in the flow diagram where this information will be required.

Box 1 1 Define study area. This should be sufficiently generous to ensure the inclusion of the entire hinterland of each centre under review.

Box 2 2 Define appropriate population units and calculate the population in each. Unit size should relate to type of trade and sizes of centre being considered. No unit should contain more than one shopping centre and these should be centrally located if possible.

Box 3 3 Calculate expenditure per head per annum in the area concerned, including allowances for local variations, socio-economic groupings, etc.

Boxes 4 and 5 4 Multiply expenditure per person by population for each unit to give the total generated expenditure per unit. Divide this into four groups as follows:
Accessibility trade (a) Convenience sales.
(b) Durables sales.
Attraction trade (a) Convenience sales.
(b) Durable sales.

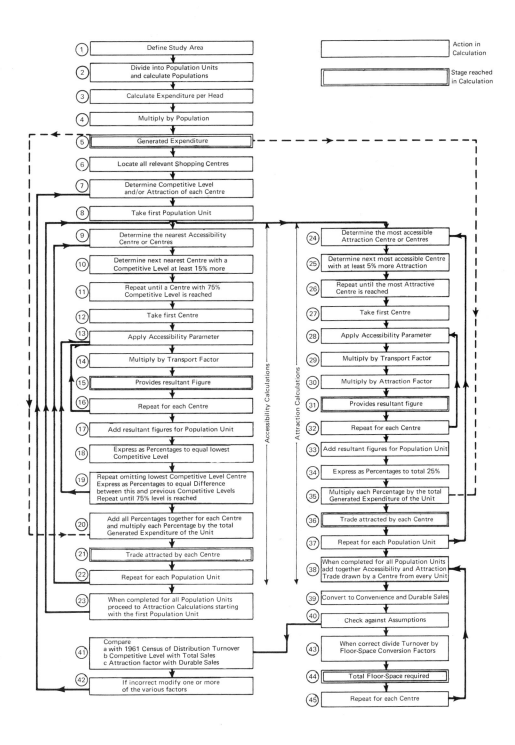

① Define Study Area

② Divide into Population Units and calculate Populations

③ Calculate Expenditure per Head

④ Multiply by Population

⑤ Generated Expenditure

⑥ Locate all relevant Shopping Centres

⑦ Determine Competitive Level and/or Attraction of each Centre

⑧ Take first Population Unit

Action in Calculation

Stage reached in Calculation

Accessibility Calculations

⑨ Determine the nearest Accessibility Centre or Centres

⑩ Determine next nearest Centre with a Competitive Level at least 15% more

⑪ Repeat until a Centre with 75% Competitive Level is reached

⑫ Take first Centre

⑬ Apply Accessibility Parameter

⑭ Multiply by Transport Factor

⑮ Provides resultant Figure

⑯ Repeat for each Centre

⑰ Add resultant figures for Population Unit

⑱ Express as Percentages to equal lowest Competitive Level

⑲ Repeat omitting lowest Competitive Level Centre Express as Percentages to equal Difference between this and previous Competitive Levels Repeat until 75% level is reached

⑳ Add all Percentages together for each Centre and multiply each Percentage by the total Generated Expenditure of the Unit

㉑ Trade attracted by each Centre

㉒ Repeat for each Population Unit

㉓ When completed for all Population Units proceed to Attraction Calculations starting with the first Population Unit

Attraction Calculations

㉔ Determine the most accessible Attraction Centre or Centres

㉕ Determine next most accessible Centre with at least 5% more Attraction

㉖ Repeat until the most Attractive Centre is reached

㉗ Take first Centre

㉘ Apply Accessibility Parameter

㉙ Multiply by Transport Factor

㉚ Multiply by Attraction Factor

㉛ Provides resultant figure

㉜ Repeat for each Centre

㉝ Add resultant figures for Population Unit

㉞ Express as Percentages to total 25%

㉟ Multiply each Percentage by the total Generated Expenditure of the Unit

㊱ Trade attracted by each Centre

㊲ Repeat for each Population Unit

㊳ When completed for all Population Units add together Accessibility and Attraction Trade drawn by a Centre from every Unit

㊴ Convert to Convenience and Durable Sales

㊵ Check against Assumptions

㊸ When correct divide Turnover by Floor-Space Conversion Factors

㊹ Total Floor-Space required

㊺ Repeat for each Centre

㊶ Compare
a with 1961 Census of Distribution Turnover
b Competitive Level with Total Sales
c Attraction factor with Durable Sales

㊷ If incorrect modify one or more of the various factors

Fig. C1. Flow diagram for calculating shopping turnover and floor space.

Box 6   5 Locate all shopping centres, i.e. all groups within the study area having a competitive level of 30 per cent or more, and any large centres outside the area which might draw trade.

6 Numbers of shops in each centre.

7 Types of shops in each centre.

Boxes 7, 9 10 and 11   8 Competitive level of each centre. This is the level to which accessibility needs can be met or the percentage of per capita accessibility expenditure which a centre could supply. It is obtained by taking the different shops in the centre and calculating the percentage of the total trade in terms of expenditure per head they could take.

9 Distance from each population unit to every centre to which people may go.

Boxes 9, 10 and 11   10 List of all relevant centres for each population unit obtained from items 7 and 8.

11 Information on car ownership in study area.

12 Information on public transport from each population unit to each centre.

13 Information on parking facilities for each centre.

14 Convert item 9 into time, allowing for the information in items 11, 12 and 13, i.e. add in an allowance for time taken to park.

Box 13   15 Accessibility parameter based on journey time.

Boxes 14 and 29   16 Transport factor obtained from items 11 and 12. If direct public transport services are available, then the factor is taken as 1·00. If not, then car ownership rate per household is used. If a centre is within half a mile, it is assumed to be within walking distance and a factor of 1·00 is applied.

Boxes 17 and 33   17 Figures could be extracted at this stage to give traffic flows, parking requirements and public transport demand.

Boxes 24, 25 and 26   18 The most accessible centre is included first and then any others having a similar accessibility. The most attractive centre can be determined from boxes 6 and 7.

Box 30   19 Attraction factors are obtained from durable turnover figures contained in the Census of Distribution. If not available, durable turnover can be estimated or the factor based on facilities which can be obtained from item 6.

Box 39   20 Apply known percentages to convert turnover into convenience and durable sales.

Box 43   21 Apply floor space conversion factors.

Appendix D
tenant types in shopping centres

Table D1   TENANT TYPES IN SHOPPING CENTRES

Tenant type	Breda	Cowley	Drumchapel	Elephant and Castle	Gem, Nottingham	Oadby	Stillorgan	Walkden	Yate	Northland, Detroit
Department store		1	1				1			1
Variety store		1	1	1				1	1	1
Co-operative		1	1						1	
Supermarket/food hall	d	3	2	1	d	d	4	2	2	1
Baker/confectioner	d	4	2	1	d	d	1	2	2	3
Butcher	d	1	2	1	d	d	2	2	1	
Fishmonger	d	1	1				1		1	
Greengrocer	d	2	1	1	d	d	2	2	1	
Grocer/other foods	d	1	1		d	d	1		1	5
Sweets/tobacco	d		1	2	d	d	1	3		3
Off-licence	1	1		1	d		2	1		
Men's wear	d	6		4	d	d	2	3	3	8
Women's wear	d	7		2	d	d	5	3	2	17
Children's wear	d				d	d	1	1	1	4
Shoes		5	3	2	d	d	2	1	5	13
Car accessories	d			1	d	d	1		1	
Carpets	d	1			d	d	1	1	1	
Drapery	d		2		d	d		1		1
Electrical goods	d	3			d	d	1		1	
Florist	1	1				d	1			1
Furniture/furnishings		1	1	3	d	d		2	1	2
Gifts/souvenirs	d			4			1			1
Hardware	d	1		1	d	d	1	1	3	
Jewellery/watches	d	1		1	d	d	1	1	1	6
Leather goods/luggage	d				d	d				
Linens	d	1	1			d			1	1
Newsagent/bookseller	1	2	2	2	d	d	2	2	2	3
Paints/decorations		1	2	1	d	d		1	2	2
Photographic goods	d	2				d	1			1
Radio/television	1	1		1	d			1	1	
Television rentals		3	2	5			2	1		1
Records/music	d				d	d	1	1		
Sewing machines			1					1		2
Sports goods		1				d				3
Toys	d				d	d			1	
Chemist/toiletries	d	1	2	2	d	d	2	1	2	1
Cleaners	1	5	2	1			2	2	1	
Hairdresser		1	2	1			3		1	4
Launderette		1	1	1			1		1	
Optician		2	1	1			1			1
Shoe repairs			1		d	d	1	1	1	
Travel agent		1	1	1			1	1		1
Restaurant		1		4		d	1		1	6
Café			1		d				1	
Coffee bar	1									4
Bank	1	2	2	3			1	2	5	1
Bingo hall			1							
Bowling centre								1		
Filling station	1			1		1				1
Gas board office		1	1	1					1	
Electricity board office		1							1	
Professional offices		3		1			1		2	11
Public house		1								
Public library									1	
Betting office		1							1	
Post office		1							1	1

NOTE: Numbers indicate the number of units allocated to each trade. 'd' indicates a department in supercentre types.

The following list indicates the types of tenant suitable for regional centres. The extent to which these store types are included in any particular project would depend on the local circumstance in each case.

1 Department store
Major department store
Junior or branch department store

2 Variety store

3 Food stores
Supermarket
Bakery/confectionery
Dairy products
Fishmonger
Fruit and vegetables
Health foods
Meats/delicatessen
Off-licence
Sweets

4 Clothing stores
Men's wear
Men's accessories
Men's shoes
Women's wear
Women's accessories
Furs
Lingerie
Maternity wear
Millinery
Women's shoes
Women's speciality wear
Youth shop
Children's wear
Children's shoes
Infant's wear
Beachwear
Casual wear
Sports wear

5 Furniture and home furnishing
Furniture
Antiques
Appliances
China, glass and pottery
Drapery
Floor coverings
Interior decoration
Lamps and shades
Radio and television

6 Hardware stores
Hardware
Do-it-yourself
Electrical goods
Paints and wallpapers
Plumbing supplies

7 Other stores
Art supplies
Car accessories
Fabrics
Florist
Garden equipment and furniture
Gifts and cards
Hobby shop
Jewellery
Kitchenware
Knit shop
Leather goods and luggage
Linen and lace
Music and records
Newsagent/tobacconist
Office equipment
Perfumes and cosmetics
Pet shop
Photographic and tape recording
Silverware and cutlery
Souvenirs
Sports goods
Stamps and coins
Stationery and books
Toys

8 Eating facilities
Café
Cafeteria
Cocktail lounge
Coffee bar
Public house
Restaurant
Snack or sandwich bar

9 Services
Beauty salon
Dry cleaners and dyers
Estate agency
Filling station and servicing facilities

Hair dressing
Launderette
Optician
Shoe repairs/heel bar
Studio photographer
Travel agency/ticket office

10 Institutional tenants
Banks
Post Office
Professional offices
Public utility offices

further acknowledgements

The author wishes to thank the following individuals and companies for their valuable assistance, and also the respective authors and publishers who have been named where applicable for permission to include extracts and information from their works.

B. Andrews Esq., (Manager, Northland Centre, Detroit, U.S.A.).

Architectural Press Ltd., (*Architect's Journal and Architectural Review*).

Arndale Developments Ltd., Bradford.

The Austin-Smith/Salmon/Lord Partnership, (Architects, Gem Supercentre, Nottingham).

The Automobile Association, (*Parking: Who Pays?*).

U. Aylmer Coates Esq., C.B.E., B.Arch., F.R.I.B.A., P.P.T.P.I., County Planning Officer, Lancashire County Council, (Haydock Centre).

Birds Eye Foods Ltd., (*What's in Store?*).

Boissevain and Osmond, (Architects, Elelephant and Castle Centre).

Business Intelligence Services Ltd.

Business Week, (McGraw-Hill Publications).

R. G. Clarke Esq., A.M.T.P.I., A.M.I.Mun.E., County Planning Officer, Kent County Council, (*The Influence of Car Ownership on Shopping Habits*).

John Costello and Associates, (Architects, Stillorgan Centre, Dublin).

R. K. Cox, Esq., B.Sc.(Econ.), A.S.C.C., (*Retail Site Assessment*).

E. L. Cripps Esq., B.Sc., A.R.I.C.S., A.M.T.P.I., formerly of Bedfordshire County Council Planning Department.

D. R. Diamond Esq., Former Editor, *Urban Studies Journal*.

Dunlop Heywood and Company, (Haydock Centre).

Eno Foundation for Highway Traffic Control, Saugatuck, Connecticut, U.S.A.

Estates Gazette.

Evening Echo, Bournemouth, (Hampshire Centre).

Faber and Faber (*Garden Cities of Tomorrow*).

S. R. Fisher Esq., A.R.I.B.A., M.T.P.I., of Messrs, Leach, Rhodes and Walker, (Architects, Haydock Centre).

William Furness Associates, ('Speedramp' systems).

Gem Supercentres Ltd.

Goadsby and Harding, (Agents, Hampshire Centre).

B. Green Esq., Manager, Breda Centre, Belfast.

L. E. Gregory Esq., Dip.Arch.(Dist.), Liv'l., F.R.I.B.A., (Architect, Hampshire Centre, Bourne-mouth).

Grimly and Sons, Birmingham, (Terminus Centre, Wylde Green).

V. Gruen Esq., F.A.I.A., (Architect, Northlands Centre, Detroit; author, with L. Smith, of *Shopping Towns U.S.A.* and of *The Heart of Our Cities*).

Her Majesty's Stationery Office, (Census and other References).

John Hinton Esq., (Ormesby Centre, Middlesbrough).

International Council of Shopping Centres Inc., (Gordon D. McDonald Esq., Director of Research).

Colin Johnson Partnership, (Architects, Ormesby Centre, Middlesbrough).

Professor R. H. Kantorowich, M.A., B.Arch., A.R.I.B.A., A.M.T.P.I., (*Regional Shopping Centres: a planning report on North-West England, parts One and Two*—the Haydock Report), published by the Department of Town and Country Planning, University of Manchester.

R. V. Killick Esq., Estates Manager, Safeway Food Stores Ltd.

Lancashire Evening Post, (Gem Centre, Preston).

D. R. Leaker Esq., A.R.I.B.A., A.R.I.A.S., J.P., Chief Architect and Planning Officer, Cumber-nauld Development Corporation, (*Retail Trade Report* and *Revision*).

Leonard Hill Books Ltd., (*British Shopping Centres*).

T. A. Lester Esq., Dip.Arch., A.R.I.B.A., and R. B. Todd Esq., Dip.Arch., A.R.I.B.A., of Elder, Lester and Partners (Architects, Thornaby Centre).

J. R. Libbey Esq., Editor, *Stores and Shops Journal.*

Marketing Trends Ltd.

O. Marriott Esq., Financial Editor, The Times, (*The Property Boom*).

John Mather and Partners, (Architects, Breda Centre, Belfast).

McGraw-Hill Book Co. Ltd., New York, (*The Selection of Retail Locations* by Richard L. Nelson and *Design for Modern Merchandising*, edited by Kenneth C. Welch).

Metropolitan Railway Surplus Lands Co. Ltd. (Haydock Centre).

Michell and Partners (Architects, High Market Scheme).

P. A. Mold Esq., Public Relations Officer, G.E.M. Super Centres Ltd.

B. E. Moore Esq., Editor, *Self-Service and Supermarket Journal.*

Multiple Shops Federation, (F. J. E. Robotham Esq., Real Estate Officer).

D. Murray Esq., Dip.Arch., A.R.I.B.A., A.M.T.P.I., City Architect and Planning Officer, Oxford, (Cowley Centre, Oxford).

Ordnance Survey, (Local Accessibility Maps).

S. Penn-Smith, Son and Partners, (Architects, Oadby Centre).

Pergamon Press Ltd., (*The Changing Pattern of Distribution*).

Pilkington Brothers Ltd., (High Market project).

Public Relations of Ireland Ltd., (Stillorgan Centre, Dublin).

Ravenseft Properties Ltd. (Whitgift Centre, Croydon).

Dr. W. J. Reilly, (*The Law of Retail Gravitation*).

Reinhold Publishing Corporation, (*Shopping Centres: Design and Operation* by G. Baker and

B. Funaro, and *Shopping Towns U.S.A.*, by V. Gruen and L. Smith).

Miss J. P. Reynolds, Editor, *The Town Planning Review*.

Brian Ring, Howard and Partners, (Architects, Terminus Centre, Wylde Green, Sutton Coldfield).

J. B. Ross Esq., F.R.I.C.S., M.T.P.I., County Planning Officer, Northumberland County Council, (*Trends in Retail Distribution*).

Royal Institute of British Architects, (*R.I.B.A. Journal*).

Royal Institution of Chartered Surveyors, (*R.I.C.S. Journal*).

B. L. Saidman Esq., Wingate Investments Ltd., (Terminus Centre, Wylde Green, Sutton Coldfield).

R. J. Simpson Esq., F.S.V.A., William Willett Ltd., (Elephant and Castle Centre).

W. K. Smigielski Esq., Ing. Arch., M.T.P.I., City Planning Officer, Leicester City Council, (*Leicester Traffic Plan*).

N. A. H. Stacey and A. Wilson, (*The Changing Pattern of Distribution*).

R. W. Stephenson Esq., Executive Editor, The Supermarket Association.

Stone, Toms and Partners, (Architects, Yate Centre).

Sir Percy Thomas and Son, (Architects, Chester Centre).

Town Planning Institute, (*T.P.I. Journal* and *Summer School Report*).

Urban Land Institute, Washington, U.S.A.

D. N. T. Wales Esq., A.A.I., Messrs. Donaldson and Sons, (Elephant and Castle Centre).

J. V. Wall Esq., F.R.I.B.A., Borough Architect, Teesside (Thornaby-on-Tees Centre).

West Midlands Shopping Research Group, (*Predicting Shopping Requirements*).

Woolco Department Stores, (Bournemouth, Oadby and Thornaby-on-Tees stores).

The author is also grateful to the following developers, architects and other organizations for permission to include the various plans, diagrams and illustrations.

PLATES IN
APPENDIX A

A1 **Breda Centre, Belfast**
C. and A. Anderson, (Developers).
John Mather and Partners, (Architects).
A2 **Cowley Centre, Oxford**
D. Murray Esq., Dip.Arch., A.R.I.B.A., A.M.T.P.I., City Architect and Planning Officer, Oxford.
Photograph by courtesy of *Oxford Mail and Times*
A3 **Cross Gates Centre, Leeds**
Arndale Developments Ltd., (Developers).
A4 **Drumchapel Centre, Glasgow**
Arndale Developments Ltd., (Developers).
Photograph by courtesy of Bryan and Shear Ltd., Glasgow.
A5 **Elephant and Castle Centre, London**
William Willett (Elephant and Castle Ltd.), (Developers).
Boissevain and Osmond, (Architects).
Photograph by courtesy of Associated Iliffe Press, London.
A6 **Gem Centre, Nottingham**
Gem Supercentres Ltd., (Developers).
The Austin-Smith/Salmon/Lord Partnership, (Architects).
Photograph by courtesy of John Maltby Ltd., London.

A7 **Hampshire Centre, Bournemouth**
Woolco Department Stores, (Developers).
L. E. Gregory, Dip.Arch.(Dist.), Liv'l, F.R.I.B.A., (Architect).
Photograph by courtesy of J. W. Kitchenham Ltd., (K. Hoskin).
A8 **Woolco Store, Oadby, Leicester**
Woolco Department Stores Ltd., (Developers).
S. Penn-Smith, Son and Partners, (Architects).
Photograph by courtesy of Practical Press Ltd., London.
A9 **Stillorgan Centre, Dublin**
Metropolitan Estate and Property Co. (Ireland) Ltd., (Developers).
John Costello and Associates, (Architects).
Photograph by courtesy of Pieter Stroethoff, Dublin.

A10 **Tivoli Centre, Yardley, Birmingham**
The Murrayfield Real Estate Co. Ltd., (Developers).
James A. Roberts Esq., A.R.I.B.A., (Architect).
A11 **Walkden Centre, Manchester**
Arndale Developments Ltd., (Developers).
Photograph by courtesy of C. H. Wood (Bradford) Ltd.
A12 **Yate Centre, Gloucestershire**
Metropolitan Estate and Property Co. Ltd., (Developers).
Stone, Toms and Partners, (Architects).
Photograph by courtesy of the Gloucestershire Gazette.
A13 **Kilkenny Centre, Adelaide, Australia**
Arndale Developments (Australia) Pty. Ltd., (Developers).
John Graham Company, (Architects).
A14 **Northland Centre, Detroit, U.S.A.**
J. L. Hudson Co. Ltd., (Developer).
Victor Gruen and Associates, (Architects).
Photograph by courtesy of Reinhold Publishing Corporation, New York.

PLATES IN THE 1.1 **Gem Store, Preston**
TEXT Gem Supercentres Ltd., (Owners).
Photograph by courtesy of the *Lancashire Evening Post*.
1.2 **Gem Store, Preston**
Gem Supercentres Ltd., (Owners).
2.1 **Frolunda Torg Centre, Gothenburg, Sweden**
AB Göteborgsbostader, (Developers).
Klemming and Thelaus, (Architects).
Photograph by courtesy of *Stores and Shops Journal*.
3.1 and 3.2 **High Market Scheme**
Pilkington Brothers Ltd., (Sponsors).
Gordon and Eleanor Michell, A./A.R.I.B.A., (Architects).
3.3 **Ormesby Market, Middlesbrough**
Hinton's Stores, (Developers).
Colin Johnson Partnership, (Architects).
Photograph by courtesy of Dennis Wompra Studios, Middlesbrough.
3.4 **Piccadilly, London**
Photograph by courtesy of *Evening Standard*, London.
3.5 **High Street, Inverness**
Photograph by courtesy of Murrayfield Real Estate Co. Ltd.
9.1 **Breda Centre, Belfast**
C. and A. Anderson, (Developers).
John Mather and Partners, (Architects).

10.1 **Northland Centre, Detroit, U.S.A.**
J. L. Hudson Co. Ltd., (Developer).
Victor Gruen and Associates, (Architects).
10.2 **Drumchapel Centre, Glasgow**
(As Plate A4).
10.3 **Yate Centre, Gloucestershire**
Metropolitan Estate and Property Co. Ltd., (Developers).
Stone, Toms and Partners, (Architects).
11.1 **Yate Centre, Gloucestershire**
Metropolitan Estate and Property Co. Ltd., (Developers).
Stone, Toms and Partners, (Architects).
Photograph by courtesy of South West Picture Agency, Bristol.
11.2 **Thornaby-on-Tees Centre, Middlesbrough**
County Borough of Teeside.
Elder, Lester and Partners, (Architects).
Photograph by courtesy of Dennis Wompra Studios, Middlesbrough.
11.3 **Elephant and Castle Centre, London**
William Willett (Elephant and Castle) Ltd., (Developers).
Boissevain and Osmond, (Architects).
Photograph by courtesy of Practical Press Ltd., London.
12.1 **Elephant and Castle Centre, London**
(As Plate 11.3).
12.2 **'Speedramp'**
Richard Sutcliffe Engineering Systems Ltd., (Manufacturer).
William Furness Associates, (Public Relations).
Gillinson, Barnett and Partners, (Architects).
13.1 **Gem Centre, Nottingham**
Gem Supercentres Ltd., (Developers).
The Austin-Smith/Salmon/Lord Partnership, (Architects).
Photograph by courtesy of H. Tempest Industrial Ltd., Nottingham and Design
Advertising Ltd., Leeds.
13.2 **Hampshire Centre, Bournemouth**
Woolco Department Stores (Developers).
L. E. Gregory, Dip.Arch.(Dist.), Liv'l, F.R.I.B.A., (Architect).
Photograph by courtesy of J. W. Kitchenham Ltd., (K. Hoskin).
13.3 **Safeway Store, Muirend, Glasgow**
Safeway Food Stores Ltd., (Developers).
Photograph by courtesy of R. Shankland Esq., Glasgow.
13.4 **Breda Centre, Belfast**
C. and A. Anderson, (Developers).
John Mather and Partners, (Architects).
Photograph by courtesy of R. Clements Lyttle Studios, Belfast.
13.5 **Cowley Centre, Oxford**
(As Plate A2).
14.1 **Hampshire Centre, Bournemouth**
(As Plate A7).
14.2 **Gem Centre, Nottingham**
(As Plate A6).
14.3 **Breda Centre, Belfast**
(As Plate A1).
14.4 **Elephant and Castle Centre, London**
(As Plate 11.3).
14.5 **Gem Centre, Nottingham**
(As Plate A6).

14.6 **Chester Centre**
Grosvenor Estate Commercial Developments Ltd., (Developers).
Sir Percy Thomas and Son, (Architects).
Photograph by courtesy of Stewart Bale Ltd., Liverpool.
14.7 **Frolunda Torg Centre, Gothenburg, Sweden**
(As Plate 2.1).
14.8 **Whitgift Centre, Croydon**
Ravenseft Properties Ltd., principal subsidiary company of the Land Securities
Investment Trust Ltd.
Fitzroy Robinson and Partners, (Architects), and L. V. Barber Esq.
14·9 **Elephant and Castle Centre, London**
William Willett (Elephant and Castle) Ltd., (Developers).
Boissevain and Osmond, (Architects).
Photograph by courtesy of *Evening Standard*, London.
14.10 **Arndale Centre, Doncaster**
(As Plate A11).

FIGURES IN APPENDIX A

A1 **Breda Centre, Belfast**
C. and A. Anderson Ltd., (Developers).
John Mather and Partners, (Architects).
A2 **Cowley Centre, Oxford**
D. Murray Esq., Dip.Arch., A.R.I.B.A., A.M.T.P.I., City Architect and Planning
Officer, Oxford.
A3 **Cross Gates Centre, Leeds**
Arndale Developments Ltd., (Developers).
A4 **Drumchapel Centre, Glasgow**
Arndale Developments Ltd., (Developers).
A5 **Elephant and Castle Centre, London**
William Willett (Elephant and Castle) Ltd., (Developers).
Boissevain and Osmond, (Architects).
Architectural Press Ltd.
A6 **Gem Centre, Nottingham**
Gem Supercentres Ltd., (Developers).
The Austin-Smith/Salmon/Lord Partnership, (Architects).
Architectural Press Ltd.
A7 **Hampshire Centre, Bournemouth**
Second Covent Garden Property Co. Ltd., (Developers).
L. E. Gregory Esq., Dip.Arch.(Dist.) Liv'l, F.R.I.B.A., (Architect).
A8 **Woolco Store, Oadby, Leicester**
Woolco Department Stores Ltd., (Developers).
S. Penn-Smith, Son and Partners, (Architects).
A9 **Stillorgan Centre, Dublin**
Metropolitan Estate and Property Co. (Ireland) Ltd., (Developers).
John Costello and Associates, (Architects).
A10 **Tivoli Centre, Yardley, Birmingham**
Murrayfield Real Estate Co. Ltd., (Developers).
James A. Roberts Esq., A.R.I.B.A., (Architect).
A11 **Walkden Centre, Manchester**
(As Fig. A3).
A12 **Yate Centre, Gloucestershire**
Metropolitan Estate and Property Co. Ltd., (Developers).
Stone, Toms and Partners, (Architects).

A13 **Kilkenny Centre, Adelaide, Australia**
Arndale Developments (Australia) Pty. Ltd., (Developers).
John Graham Company, (Architects).
A14 **Northland Centre, Detroit, U.S.A.**
J. L. Hudson Co. Ltd., (Developer).
Victor Gruen and Associates, (Architects).
Plan by courtesy of Reinhold Publishing Corporation, New York.

3.1 **Haydock Centre**
Metropolitan Railway Surplus Lands Co. Ltd., (Developer).
Leach, Rhodes and Walker, (Architects).
3.2 **Ormesby Centre, Middlesbrough**
Hinton's Stores, (Developers).
Colin Johnson Partnership, (Architects).
4.1 **Community Centre**
Plan by courtesy of *Town Planning Institute Journal,* issue of Sept/Oct. 1965,
'Shopping Centres in Britain' by R. N. Percival, page 332.
5.1 **Haydock Centre**
Plan by courtesy of Department of Town and Country Planning, University of
Manchester, from *Regional Shopping Centres—a planning report on North-West
England.*
5.2 **Haydock Centre**
(As Fig. 5.1).
6.1 **Cumbernauld Town Centre**
D. R. Leaker Esq., A.R.I.B.A., A.R.I.A.S., J.P., Chief Architect and Planning Officer,
Cumbernauld Development Corporation.
6.2 **West Midlands Study**
Figure by courtesy of West Midlands Shopping Research Group, from *Predicting
Shopping Requirements.*
6.3 **West Midlands Study**
(As Fig. 6.2).
10.1 **Marion Centre, Adelaide, Australia**
Arndale Developments (Australia) Pty. Ltd., (Developers).
10.2 **Terminus Centre, Wylde Green, Sutton Coldfield**
Wingate Investments (Sutton Coldfield) Ltd., (Developers).
Brian Ring, Howard and Partners, (Architects).
10.3 **Yate Centre, Gloucestershire**
(As Fig. A12).
11.1 **Northland Centre, Detroit, U.S.A.**
J. L. Hudson Co. Ltd., (Developer).
11.2 **Town Centre, Thornaby-on-Tees**
County Borough of Teeside.
Elder, Lester and Partners, (Architects).
13.1 **Northland Centre, Detroit, U.S.A.**
(As Fig. 11.1).
13.2 **Hourly Parking Requirements**
Urban Land Institute, from *Parking Requirements for Shopping Centres.*
13.3 **Accumulation Pattern**
(As Fig. 13.2).
13.4 **Yate Centre, Gloucestershire**
(As Fig. A12).

Frontispiece

The Hammerson Group of Companies (Joint developers).

Bernard Engle and Partners (Architects).

Photograph by courtesy of John Maltby Ltd.

bibliography of books

ADLER, M., *Modern Market Research*, Crosby Lockwood, 1956.
ALEVIZOS, J. P. and BECKWITH, A. E., *Downtown and Suburban Shopping Habits*, Boston University, 1954.
AMERICAN SOCIETY OF PLANNING OFFICIALS, *Criteria and Standards for Shopping Centres*, 1953.
   Site Design, Parking and Zoning for Shopping Centres, 1954.
   Pedestrian Malls, 1958.
ASSOCIATION OF LAND AND PROPERTY OWNERS, *Shops in Redevelopment Areas*, 1966.
ATKINS, C. R., *People and the Motor Car*, University of Birmingham, 1964.
AUBERT-KRIER, J., *Monopolistic and Imperfect Competition in Retail Trade*, Hutchinson, 1949.
AUTOMOBILE ASSOCIATION, *Parking: Who Pays?*, 1967.
BARNUM, H. G., KASPERSON, R. and KIUCHU, S., *Central Place Studies: A Bibliography of Theory and Applications*, Regional Research Institute, 1965
BAKER G. and FUNARO, B., *Shopping Centres—Design and Operation*, Reinhold, 1951/1956.
   Parking, Reinhold, 1958.
BEDFORDSHIRE COUNTY COUNCIL, *Leighton-Linslade Central Area Shopping Survey*, 1965.
BERRY, B. J., *Geography of Market Centres and Retail Distribution*, Prentice-Hall, 1967.
BESTOR and JONES, *City Planning: A Basic Bibliography*, Californian Council of Civic Engineers and Land Surveyors, 1962.
BOARD OF TRADE, *Report on the Census of Distribution and Other Services*.
BOHRMAN, C. G., *Present Tendencies in the Planning of Shopping Centres*, South African Institute of Town Planners Summer School, 1959.
BRIERLEY, J., *The Parking of Motor Vehicles*, C. R. Books, 1962.
BRITTON, J. N. H., *Regional Analysis and Economic Geography*, Bell, 1967.
BUCHANAN, C. D., *Mixed Blessing: The Motor Car in Britain*, Leonard Hill, 1958.
   Traffic in Towns, H.M.S.O., 1963, Penguin, 1964.
BUILDING MANAGERS ASSOCIATION, *The Percentage Lease*, Chicago, 1955.
BURNS, W., *British Shopping Centres*, Leonard Hill, 1959.
CANOYER, H. G., *Selecting a Store Location*, Department of Commerce, Washington, D.C., 1946.
CHAPIN, F. S. and WEISS, S. F., *Urban Growth Dynamics*, Wiley, 1962.
CHRISTALLER, W., *Central Places in Southern Germany*, (Translated by C. W. Baskin), Prentice-Hall, 1966.
COVENTRY PLANNING DEPARTMENT, *Shopping in Coventry*, 1964.
COX, R. K., *Retail Site Assessment*, Business Books, 1968.
CUMBERNAULD DEVELOPMENT CORPORATION, *Retail Trade Provision Report*, 1960.
   Revision of Retail Requirements, 1964.
DAVIS, D., *History of Shopping*, Routledge and Kegan Paul, 1966.
DICHTER, E., *Handbook of Customer Motivations*, McGraw-Hill.
DICKINSON, R. E., *City, Region and Regionalism*, Kegan Paul, 1947.
DODGE CORPORATION, *Design for Modern Merchandising*. (Edited by K. C. Welch), 1954.
DUNCAN, D. J. and PHILLIPS, C. F., *Retailing Principles and Methods*, Irwin, 1951.

'E. AND O.E.', *Planning. The Architects' Handbook*, Iliffe and Sons.
ENO FOUNDATION FOR HIGHWAY TRAFFIC CONTROL, *Parking Lot Operation*, 1948.
    Highway Traffic Estimation, 1956.
    Traffic Design of Parking Garages, 1957.
    Locating Controlled Regional Shopping Centres, 1965.
FORD, P. and THOMAS, C. J., *Shops and Planning* (*Southampton Survey*), Blackwell, 1953.
GAMBLE, C., *Parking at Shopping Centres*, Florida Planning and Zoning Association.
GARRISON, W. L., *et al.*, *Studies of Highway Development and Geographic Change*, University of
    Washington, Seattle, 1959.
GEOGRAPHIA LTD., *Marketing and Media Surveys.*
GOTTMAN, J., *Megalopolis*, 20th Century Fund Inc., 1961.
GRAY, J. G., *Pedestrian Shopping Streets in Europe*, 1965.
GRUEN, V., *The Heart of Our Cities*, Thames and Hudson, 1965.
GRUEN, V. and SMITH, L., *Shopping Towns U.S.A.*, Reinhold, 1960.
GUTKIND, E. A., *The Twilight of Cities*, Macmillan, 1962.
HAGGETT, P., *Locational Analysis in Human Geography*, Arnold, 1965.
HALL, M., KNAPP, J. and WINSTON, C., *Distribution in Great Britain and North America*, O.U.P., 1961.
HIGHWAY RESEARCH BOARD, Washington, D.C., *Parking as a Factor in Business*, Special Report 11,
    1953.
    Shopper Attitudes, Special Report 11-A, 1953.
    Travel to Commercial Centres, Bulletin 79, 1953.
    Urban Traffic Congestion, Bulletin 86, 1954.
    Shopping Habits and Travel Patterns, Special Report 11-B, 1955.
    Highway Capacities Manual, 1956.
    Parking and Buying Habits of a Department Store's Customers, Special Report 11-C, 1956.
    Parking and its Relationships to Business, Special Report 11-D, 1956.
    Travel Characteristics in Urban Areas, Bulletin 203, 1958.
    Land Use and Development at Highway Interchanges, Bulletin 288, 1961.
    Shopping Centres and Parking, Highway Research Record 130, 1966.
HILL, T. B. and LICHFIELD, N. and ASSOCIATES, *Regional Shopping Report, Southend-on-Sea*, 1965.
HOLLAND COUNTY COUNCIL, *The Borough of Boston—A Survey of the Catchment and Retail
    Shopping Areas*, 1965.
HOLMES, J. D. L., *Selected and Annotated Bibliography of the Planned Suburban Shopping Centre*,
    University of Texas, 1957.
HORNBECK, J. S. (Editor), *Stores and Shopping Centres*, McGraw-Hill, 1962.
INSTITUTE FOR CENTRE-PLANAEGNING, *By Centre Menneske*, Denmark, 1965.
INTER-COUNTY REGIONAL PLANNING COUNCIL (U.S.A), *Standards for New Urban Develop-
    ment*, Denver, 1960.
INTERNATIONAL COUNCIL OF SHOPPING CENTRES INC., *Chain Store Leasing Guide* (No.
    44/08).
    Merchants' Associations (No. 44/01).
    Shopping Centre Bibliography (No. 44/02).
    Enclosed Malls (No. 44/03, 44/06 and 00/09).
    New Techniques of Financing, (No. 00/09).
ISARD, W., *Methods of Regional Analysis*, Wiley, 1960.
JEFFERYS, J. B., *Retail Trading in Britain*, 1850–1950, C.U.P., 1954.
JEFFERYS, BRAVINGTON and KNEE, *Retailing in Europe*, Macmillan, 1962.
JEFFERYS and KNEE, *Retailing in 1970*, Macmillan, 1962.
JOHNSON-MARSHALL, P., *Rebuilding Cities*, Edinburgh University Press, 1965.
JONASSEN, C. T., *Shopping Centres versus Downtown*, Ohio State University, 1955.
KASPER, K., *International Shop Design*, Thames and Hudson, 1967.
KENT COUNTY COUNCIL, *The Influence of Car Ownership on Shopping Habits*, 1964.
KETCHUM, M., *Shops and Stores*, Reinhold, 1948/1957.
KING COUNTY PLANNING DEPARTMENT, SEATTLE, *Locational Tendencies and Space Require-
    ments of Retail Business*, 1963.
KLOSE, D., *Multi-storey Car Parks and Garages*, Architectural Press, 1965.
LEVY, H., *The Shops of Britain*, Routledge, 1948.
LING, A. G., *Runcorn New Town*, Runcorn Development Corporation, 1967.
LOMAS, G. *et al.*, *Population Growth and Planning Policy in the West Midlands*, Cass, 1965.
LOSCH, A., *Economics of Location*, G. Fisher Verlag, 1944.
LUCK, WALES and DONALD, *Market Research*, Prentice-Hall, 1961.
MANCHESTER UNIVERSITY, *Regional Shopping Centres in North-West England*, (*The Haydock
    Report*), Part One, 1964; Part Two, 1966.
MARKETING TRENDS LTD., *Supermarkets and the British Housewife*, 1966.

MARRIOTT, O., *The Property Boom*, Hamish Hamilton, 1967.
MC CLELLAND, W. G., *Costs and Competition in Retailing*, Macmillan, 1966.
MEYER, J. R., KAIN, J. F. and WOHL, M., *The Urban Transporation Problem*, O.U.P., 1965.
MITCHELL, R. B. and RAPKIN, C., *Urban Traffic—A Function of the Land Use*, Columbia University Press, 1954.
MULTIPLE SHOPS FEDERATION, *The Planning of Shopping Centres*, 1963.
    Shopping Centres in North-West Europe, 1967.
    Standards for Service Areas in Shopping Centres, 1968.
MUMFORD, L., *The Highway and the City*, Harcourt, Brace and World Inc., 1963.
NATIONAL CASH REGISTER COMPANY LTD. (U.S.A.), *Expenses in Retail Businesses*, 1955.
NATIONAL CASH REGISTER COMPANY (G.B.), *Thoughts on Future Shopping Requirements*.
NATIONAL INSTITUTE OF REAL ESTATE BROKERS, *Percentage Leases*, 1957.
NATIONAL RESEARCH BUREAU (CHICAGO), *Directory of Shopping Centres*, 1960.
NATIONAL RESEARCH COUNCIL (WASHINGTON), *Parking as a Factor in Business*, 1956.
NELSON, R. L., *The Selection of Retail Locations*, McGraw-Hill, 1958.
NORTHUMBERLAND COUNTY COUNCIL, *Trends in Retail Distribution*, 1963.
OWEN, W., *Cities in the Motor Age*, Viking Press, 1959.
OXFORD CITY COUNCIL, *Cowley Centre Plan*, 1965.
PAIN, G. M., *Planning and the Shopkeeper*, Barrie and Rockliff, 1967.
PASDERMADJIAN, H., *The Department Store*, Newman books, 1954.
PROCTER, A., *What Parking means to Business*, The Automotive Safety Foundation, Washington, 1955.
PARNES, L., *Planning Stores that Pay*, McGraw-Hill.
RANELL, J., *The Core of the City*, Columbia University Press, 1956.
RATCLIFFE, R. V., *The Problem of Retail Site Selection*, University of Michigan, 1939.
REILLY, W. J., *The Law of Retail Gravitation*, 1929.
RITTER, P., *Planning for Man and Motor*, Pergamon, 1963.
SAMUELS, H., *The Law relating to Shops*, Knight, 1965.
SIMMONS, J., *The Changing Pattern of Retail Location*, Chicago University, 1964.
SMIGIELSKI, W. K., *Leicester Traffic Plan*, 1964.
SMITH, P. E., *Shopping Centres—Planning and Management*, National Dry Goods Association, 1956.
SMITH, W., *Future Highways and Urban Growth*, Automobile Manufacturers Association, 1961.
    Parking in City Centres, Automobile Manufacturers Association, 1965.
SNIBBE, R., *Small Commercial Buildings*, Reinhold.
SOCIAL SURVEYS LTD., *Harlow: Its Shopping Facilities, with Particular Reference to the Need and Demand for a Department Store*, 1957.
SOMAKE, E. and HELLBERG, R., *Stores and Shops Today*, Batsford, 1956.
STACEY, N. A. H. and WILSON, A., *The Changing Pattern of Distribution*, Pergamon, 1958 and 1965.
STANTON, E. M., *Branch Stores*, National Dry Goods Association, 1956.
TETLOW, J. and GOSS, A., *Homes, Towns and Traffic*, Faber and Faber, 1965.
THOMPSON, J. WALTER, *The Shopping Centre in the United States*, 1954.
TOWN PLANNING INSTITUTE, *Planning Research*.
TRIPP, A., *Town Planning and Road Traffic*, 1942.
TUNNARD, C. and PUSHKAREV, B., *Man-made America: Chaos or Control*, Yale University Press, 1964.
URBAN LAND INSTITUTE, *Shopping Centres—An Analysis* (Mott and Wehrly), Technical Bulletin No. 11, 1949.
    Market Analysis of Shopping Centres (Hoyt), Technical Bulletin No. 12, 1949.
    Shopping Centres—Planning Principles and Tested Policies, (J. R. McKeever), Technical Bulletin No. 20, 1953.
    Conservation and Rehabilitation of Major Shopping Districts, (Nelson and Aschman), Technical Bulletin No. 22, 1954.
    Shopping Habits and Travel Patterns, (Vorhees and Stegmaier), Technical Bulletin No. 24, 1955.
    Shopping Centes Re-studied, (McKeever), Technical Bulletin No. 30, 1957.
    A Re-examination of the Shopping Centre Market, (Hoyt), Technical Bulletin No. 33, 1958.
    Parking Requirements for Shopping Centres, (Vorhees), Technical Bulletin No. 53, 1965.
    Store Location and Customer Behaviour, (C. and N. J. Gruen), Technical Bulletin No. 56.
    The Community Builders Handbook, 1954.
    The Dollars and Cents of Shopping Centres, 1961, 1963, and 1966.
    Indices of the Impact of a Regional Shopping Centre, E. W. Finder, New York University (J. C. Nichols Foundation Research Study).
    Operation Shopping Centres, 1961.
    Standard Manual of Expense Accounts for Shopping Centres.
WARDROP and DUFF, *Factors affecting Road Capacity*, Road Research Laboratory, 1956.
WEST MIDLANDS SHOPPING RESEARCH GROUP, *Predicting Shopping Requirements*, 1967.
WESTWOOD, B. and N., *The Modern Shop*, Architectural Press, 1955.

bibliography of magazines, periodicals and papers

AMBROSE, P. J.,   'A shopping model of the south coast conurbation', Paper at University of Sussex, 1966.

American Builder   'Planning to build a shopping centre?' July 1954, p. 101–102.

American City   'Baltimore will build a new market', H. Hews, Aug. 1949, p. 80–81.
'The modern urban commercial centre', T. C. Robinson, May 1951, p. 103–104.
'How to expand shopping centre zones', H. D. Bovert, Jan. 1956, p. 116–117.
'Shoppers' paradise mall', D. H. Lutes and E. R. Turner, May 1958, p. 112–113.

American Federation of Arts   'Shopping centres of tomorrow', V. Gruen, 1954.

American Institute of Architects Journal   'Toledo takes a step', J. N. Noble, 1959, p. 55–57.
'Shopping centre shelters for fall-out protection', M. Flatow and R. J. Nordhaus, Feb. 1962, p. 78–83.
'Shopping streets and the pedestrian rediscovered', M. R. Wolfe, May 1962, p. 33–42.
'Comprehensive architectural practice: shopping centres', C. Gamble, Aug. 1962, p. 55–62.
'Shopping centres of the future', Aug. 1963, p. 87–91.
'Urban parking lots: eyesores or assets?' L. W. Keck, Feb. 1965, p. 55–58.

American Institute of Planners Journal   'Development of planned shopping centres', H. T. Fisher, 1951.
'An historical review of the gravity and potential concepts of human interaction', G. A. P. Carrothers, Vol. 22, 1956, p. 94–102.
'Public policy and the outlying shopping centre', E. M. Horwood, April 1958, p. 215–222.
'Shopping streets and the pedestrian rediscovered', M. R. Wolfe, Feb. 1962, p. 78–83.
'Future of retailing in the downtown core', G. Sternlieb, May 1963, p. 102–112.
'Market areas of shopping districts', D. A. Peterson, Nov. 1963, p. 297–301.
'Downtown mall experiment', S. F. Weiss, Feb. 1964, p. 66–73.
'A retail market potential model', T. R. Lakshmanan and W. G. Hansen, May 1965, p. 134–143.

AMERICAN INSTITUTE OF REAL ESTATE APPRAISERS   *Real Estate Appraisal Practice*, 1958.

AMERICAN MARKETING ASSOCIATION   'Forecasting shopping goods sales in proposed suburban centres', H. J. Casey (Convention Paper, June 1956).

AMERICAN PLANNING AND CIVIC ASSOCIATION   'Modern shopping centres', K. C. Welch, 1948–49.
'The impact of new shopping centres upon established business districts', H. T. Fisher, 1950.
'Location of shopping centres', K. C. Welch, 1951.
'Economics of urban and suburban shopping centres', H. T. Fisher, 1952.
'Regional shopping centres', A. Rubloff, 1953.

BIBLIOGRAPHY

American Sociological Review	'Research note on the hypothesis of a median location', T. E. Hoult, May 1954, p. 536–538.
	'The growth of metropolitan suburbs (1940–50)', L. F. Schnore, April 1957.
	'Suburbanisation of the retail trade (1948–51)', H. D. Tarver, Aug. 1957.
Appraisal Journal	'Planning suburban shopping centres', T. McReynolds, 1951.
	'Shops, stores and shopping centres', L. W. Ellwood and R. Armstrong, April, July and Oct. 1952.
	'Appraising shopping centres', A. K. Beman, April 1957.
	'How shopping centres are financed', F. D. Hall, July 1957.
	'Outlying shopping centres versus downtown retail trade', R. Nelson, Oct. 1957.
	'Retail store locations', J. A. Lowden, Oct. 1958.
	'Shopping centre leases', J. B. Tully, Oct. 1958.
Architect and Building News	'Suburban shopping centres in Sweden', J. L. Berbiers, 31 July 1952, p. 147–151.
	'Shops at Lincoln', 7 Aug. 1952, p. 176–181.
	'The design of shopping centres in Britain today', G. Sheard, 30 Sept. 1954.
	'Elephant and Castle centre', 20 July 1960, p. 69–72 and 27 July 1960, p. 111–120.
	'Urban survival and traffic', 26 April 1961.
	'Farsta shopping centre', Dec. 1961, p. 855–864.
	'Redevelopment at South Bromley', Feb. 1962, p. 306–317.
	'Lulea shopping centre, Sweden', 26 Sept. 1962, p. 220–223.
	'Bull Ring centre, Birmingham', O. Luder, 26 Aug. 1964, p. 400–410.
	'Offices and shops, Tolworth', 10 Feb. 1965, p. 265–269.
	'Elephant and Castle centre', 29 Dec. 1965, p. 1210–1216.
	'Cole Brothers department store, Sheffield', 19 Jan 1966, p. 101–106.
	'Yate Centre', 13 April 1966, p. 653–654.
Architect and Engineer	'What makes a successful shopping centre?' F. E. Cox, July and Aug. 1954.
Architects Journal	'Bristol', D. R. Childs and D. A. Boyne, 2 Oct. 1952, p. 396–405.
	'Shops, Tile Hill, Coventry', 21 Feb. 1957, p. 293–304.
	'Motropolis' (special issue), 1 Oct. 1959.
	'Shopping centre at Grangemouth', 25 Feb. 1960, p. 321–334.
	'Elephant and Castle centre', 21 July 1960, p. 28.
	'Shopping facilities at Cumbernauld', 1 Dec. 1960, p. 783–789.
	'Car parking at Cumbernauld', 15 Dec. 1960.
	'Moving pavements', A. Goss, 5 Jan. 1961, p. 18–19.
	'Birmingham's new shopping centre', S. Greenwood, 18 May 1961.
	'Coping with cars', N. Seymer, 11 July 1962.
	'"Hollow ring" town centres', G. E. Carter, 1 Aug. 1962.
	'Cumbernauld town centre', G. Copcutt, 5 Dec. 1962.
	'Traffic in Towns', 4 Dec. 1963, p. 1175–1190.
	'The South-east Study', 15 April 1964, p. 833–838.
	'Off-centre at Leeds', 3 June 1964, p. 1238.
	'Analysis of the Smeed Report', D. H. Crompton, 1 July 1964, p. 8.
	'The out-of-town shopping centre', 30 Dec. 1964, p. 1532–1533.
	'Planning in the North-west', 17 Feb. 1965, p. 387.
	'Shopping centre in the North-west', (Letter by R. H. Kantorowich), 10 March 1965, p. 568.
	'Gem shopping centre, Nottingham', 5 May 1965, p. 1071–1082.
	'Elephant and Castle shopping centre', 28 July 1965, p. 205–216.
	'Bootle shopping centre', 29 Sept. 1965, p. 728–729.
	'Shop spaces' (briefing guide), 2 Feb. 1966, p. 429–442.
	'Shop spaces' (fixtures/equipment), 16 Feb. 1966 (Sheet 1370).
	'Shop spaces' (design of foodshops), 23 Feb. 1966, p. 549–560.
	'Shop buildings' (design guide), 2 March 1966, p. 597–630.
	'Shop buildings' (legal requirements), 9 March 1966.
	'Shop buildings' (furniture, goods handling and shopfronts), 16 March 1966.
	'Review of parking buildings', 6 July 1966.
Architectural Design	'American shopping centres', July 1959, p. 258–269.
	'Charlotte Street scheme, Portsmouth', June 1964, p. 281–282.
	Elephant and Castle centre', May 1965, p. 210.
	'Nordweststadt centre, Frankfurt', Feb. 1966, p. 86–88.
Architectural Forum	'Suburban shopping districts', Aug. 1950, p. 106–109.
	'Shoppers' World (and others)', Dec. 1951, p. 180–199.

'Sophisticated supermarkets', Sept. 1952, p. 136–140.
'New thinking on shopping centres', V. Gruen and L. Smith, March 1953.
'How to plan successful shopping centres', V. Gruen and L. Smith, March 1954, p. 144–147.
'Big shopping centre with no "Mr. Big"', June 1954.
'Northland shopping centre', June 1954, p. 102–119.
'Shopping centres —How many are enough?' Aug. 1954, p. 41–43.
'Two pocket shopping centres', Jan. 1956, p. 140–143.
'New supermarket plan', June 1956, p. 154.
'A breakthrough for two-level shopping centres', O. Tanner, Dec. 1956.
'Three shopping centres in Detroit', Oct. 1957, p. 110–119.
'How to plan successful shopping centres', March 1958, p. 409–424.
'Closed to traffic', O. Tanner, Feb. 1959, p. 88–93.
'Atlanta shopping centre', Oct. 1959, p. 120–127.
'Knoxville centre', April 1962, p. 128–129.
'Must shopping centres be inhuman', J. W. Rouse, June 1962, p. 104–107.
'Shopping centre Mexico City', June 1962, p. 114–115.
'Village shopping centre, Cleveland', June 1962, p. 116–119.
'Randhurst shopping centre', Nov. 1962, p. 106–111.
'Southdale centre', March 1963, p. 132.
'Fort Worth shopping centre', July 1963, p. 96–99.
'Caution advised on shopping centres', March 1964, p. 120–129.
'Market Street East centre, Philadelphia', Nov. 1966, p. 34–43.

Architectural Record   'Markets in the meadows', March 1949.
'Regional shopping centres', K. C. Welch, March 1951.
'Valuation of neighbourhood shopping centres', L. Smith, Oct. 1951, p. 508–517.
'Traffic problems in shopping centres', K. C. Welch, Oct. 1952, p. 223–228.
'Shopping centres', Oct. 1953, p. 178–201.
'Commercial buildings, signs and symbols', Sept. 1956.
'Building for retailing', Sept. 1957.
'Observations on shopping centres', R. Bennett, Sept. 1957, p. 217–219.
'Shopping can be a pleasure', Sept. 1957.
'Skokie centre', Sept. 1957, p. 220–227.
'Toronto centre', Sept. 1957, p. 229–232.
'Shops and the market place', M. Ketchum, Oct. 1958, p. 193–212.
'Retailing and the automobile', V. Gruen, March 1960, p. 192–210.
'Shopping centres by the John Graham office', March 1960, p. 221–224.
'Lloyd centre, Portland', Dec. 1960, p. 123–128.
'Facilities for retailing', May 1961, p. 165–188.
'Four American shopping centres', June 1962, p. 163–182.
'Role of outdoor lighting in shopping centre design', W. H. Kahler, June 1962, p. 188–191.
'Basic necessities of store design', L. J. Israel, June 1964, p. 157–176.
'Can cities compete with suburbia?' C. B. Wurster, Dec. 1964, p. 149–156.
'Department stores and shopping centres in the United States', May 1965, p. 187–210.
'World's largest shopping centre opens', Dec. 1965, p. 138–143.
'Shopping centres and stores', April 1966, p. 149–170.
'Elements of shopping centre design', L. Douglass, April 1966, p. 160–163.
'Architecture for selling', May 1967, p. 171–186.
'New approach for shopping centres', V. Gruen, April 1968, p. 167–168.

Architectural Review   'Regional shopping centres', July 1951, p. 56.
'District centre at Coventry', July 1956, p. 24–32.
'Hubs without wheels' (Vallingby and Harlow), June 1958, p. 373–392.
'Paramus centre, New Jersey', V. Gruen, July 1958, p. 196–198.
'Shopping precincts: townscape', C. Forehoe and K. Browne, 1959.
'Parking terminals', M. Brawne, Aug. 1960, p. 124–134.
'Elephant and Castle centre', Jan 1961, p. 54–55.
'Cambridge shopping centre', March 1961, p. 201–202.
'Hayesford Park centre', March 1964, p. 172–173.
'Super-markets', E. Beazley, Nov. 1966, p. 329–334.
'Elephant and Castle centre', T. Bendixon, April 1967, p. 280–285.

Architecture and   'Suburban shopping centres', July 1960, p. 20–25.
Design (Rhodesia)

Architecture in Australia	'Shopping centre, Sydney', Jan.–March 1958, p. 60–64. 'Shopping centres in Australia', Dec. 1961, p. 49–73. 'Two shopping malls in Australia', March 1964, p. 74–81.
Arkitektur	'Shopping centre, Lulea', No. 2, 1959, p. 50–53. 'Farsta centre', March 1961. 'New Town centres', No. 8, 1965, p. 267–276.
Arts and Architecture	'Shopping centres of tomorrow', V. Gruen, Jan. 1954.
ASSOCIATED MERCHANDISING CORPORATION (U.S.A.)	'Future shopping centres', V. Gruen (Address given by V. Gruen, 30 April 1968).
Australian Planning Institute Journal	'Suburban centres', S. J. Munro, July 1966, p. 68–71. 'A survey of Chadstone shopping habits', P. J. Rimmer and R. J. Johnston, July 1966.
AUTOMOBILE ASSOCIATION	'Shopping century 21', *Drive*, Autumn 1967, p. 30–34, 36–41, 46–47.
Bau	'Shopping centres and their planning', No. 2, 1966, p. 27–34.
Bauen + Wohnen	'Shopping centres in America', Aug. 1958, p. 226–269. 'Shopping centre, Berne', Oct. 1963, p. 300–307. 'Regional shopping centres', Nov. 1963, p. 465–470. 'Shopping centre, St. Gallen', Nov. 1963, p. 471–473. 'Pedestrian shopping centre, Amstelveen', March 1964, p. 88–93. 'Shopping centre Vienna', Sept. 1965, p. 361–364.
Bauwelt	'Design and planning of shopping centres', No. 47, 1966, p. 1361–1379.
BIRD, ALFRED AND SONS LTD.	'"Mrs. Housewife and Her Grocer" (Surveys)', 1957, 1960, 1966.
Board of Trade Journal	4 Sept., 2 and 30 Oct. 1959. 15 Feb. and 4 Oct. 1963. 23 Feb. 1968.
Bournemouth Evening Echo	'Supplement on Hampshire centre, Bournemouth', 14 March 1968.
BRITISH ROAD FEDERATION	'Bulletin No. 366', Aug. 1967. 'Car Parking', 1968.
Build (Dublin)	'Stillorgan shopping centre, Dublin', Dec. 1966, p. 24–27.
The Builder	'Shopping precinct, Glenrothes', 13 Jan. 1956, p. 53–56. 'Shopping centre boom continues', May 1956. 'Shopping centre, Canterbury', Aug. 1958, p. 352–353. 'Shopping precinct, Leicester', 13 March 1959, p. 486–487. 'Shopping centre, Grangemouth', 26 Feb. 1960, p. 404–408. 'Shopping and office centre, York', 2 June 1961, p. 1038–1039. 'Shopping precinct, Coalville', 27 March 1964, p. 653–656. 'Bull Ring, Birmingham', 10 July 1964, p. 61–66. 'Shopping centre, Drumchapel, 23 Oct. 1964, p. 895.
Building	'Comparison of concrete costs at Elephant and Castle centre', 24 June 1966, p. 147–148 and 150.
Building, Engineering, Lighting (Australia)	'Roselands shopping centre, Sydney', Sept. 1965, p. 70–75.
Business Economic Review	'The shopping centre revolution and its impact', S. Shaw, April 1958.
BUSINESS INTELLIGENCE SERVICES	'Assessing the value of shop locations' (Notes of seminar, 9 March 1967). '1 Evaluating local purchasing power', M. Thorncroft. '2 The hierarchy of shopping centres', M. Thorncroft.

'3 The form of shopping centres', T. Donaldson.
'4 The cost of locations', V. Flood.

Business Week   'Shopping attitudes', J. P. Alevizos and A. E. Beckwith, 24 Oct. 1953, p. 41–42 and 44.

Cambridge   'Parking space for cars —assessing the demand', G. J. Roth, Paper No. 5, 1965.
University
Occasional Papers

Canadian Architect   'The market place', J. Acland, Oct. 1958, p. 31–37.
                                   'The business of shopping centres', J. F. Harris, Oct. 1958, p. 42–44.
                                   'Canadian shopping centres', Oct. 1958, p. 45–57.
                                   'Shoppersville, Montreal', Jan. 1959, p. 58–59.
                                   'Rockland centre', Feb. 1960, p. 50–75.
                                   'Ottawa centre', May 1964, p. 60–63.
                                   'Yorkdale centre, Montreal', June 1964, p. 39–52.

Canadian Institute of   'Eliot Lake centre, Ontario, June 1960, p. 256–258.
Architects Journal   'Stockholm city centre', Feb. 1961, p. 52–57.
                                   'Yorkdale centre, Montreal', June 1964, p. 37–54.

Casabella   'From the department stores to the shopping centres', A. Cortesi, No. 257, 1961, p. 15–24.
                                   'The growth of shopping centres in America', M. Brunati, No. 311, 1966, p. 12–31.

Chain Store Age   'What to look for in shopping centres', V. Gruen, July 1948.
                                   'Yardstick for shopping centres', V. Gruen, Feb. 1950.
                                   'How to measure a trading area', W. Applebaum and R. F. Spears, Jan. 1951.
                                   'Check that centre', S. O. Kaylin, 1955.
                                   'Shopping centre supplement', May 1962.
                                   'Annual shopping centre survey', May issues 1953–1966.

Chartered Auctioneer   'The retailing revolution', T. L. Burfield, May 1963, p. 217–226.
and Estate Agent   'Commercial redevelopment', R. S. Stewart, Feb. 1966, p. 89–100.

Chartered Surveyor   'Planning of shopping centres', M. L. Fenton-Jones, Aug. 1962, p. 76–80.
                                   'Assessment of shopping needs', L. Smith, Jan. 1964, p. 322–329 and March 1964, p. 482–487.
                                   'Assessment of shopping needs', R. Turton, June 1964, p. 633–634.
                                   'Revolution in retailing', J. P. Walmsley, Nov. 1964, p. 247–254.
                                   'Bull Ring, Birmingham', J. M. Robson and J. A. Hepburn, April 1965, p. 528–532.
                                   'Shopping centres (assessment of floor space)', C. Clarke, April 1965, p. 532–533.
                                   'Cowley centre, Oxford', B. J. Wratten, Sept. 1965, p. 126–131.
                                   'Retail trading in small towns', R. Turton, Jan. 1966, p. 374–377.

Daily Telegraph   'Architects want ban on through traffic', 22 June 1965.
                                   'Stranded in Southwark: One white elephant', 12 April 1967.
                                   'Urban housewives take to out-of-town shopping', S. Bevan, 12 Feb. 1968.
                                   'Woolworths too long in the bargain basement', 15 Feb. 1968.
                                   'Cash-and-carry comes to market', 25 May 1968.
                                   'Continued growth of supermarkets', 20 June 1968.
                                   'Development on "mediaeval square" design', (Manchester), 20 June 1968

Design   Issue on shops, Nov. 1962.

Design (Bombay)   'Ramakrishnapuram district centre, New Delhi', Oct. 1965, p. 12–25.

The Director   'Woolworths step into one-stop shopping', Feb. 1967, p. 237–239.

DSIR   'Factors affecting the amount of travel', J. C. Tanner, 1961.

EAST SUFFOLK   'Advice to applicants seeking planning permission (No. 2: Car parking)'.
COUNTY COUNCIL

The Economist   'Shopping the American way in Germany', 2 April 1966, p. 34.
                                   Issues of 1 June 1960, 8 July 1961, 17 Feb. 1962, 18 Jan. 1964, 20 June 1964.

BIBLIOGRAPHY

Economic Geography 'The functional bases of the central place hierarchy', B. J. L. Berry and W. L. Garrison, 1959.
'Future directions in retail area research', D. L. Thompson, Vol. 42, 1966.
'Form and function in the geography of retailing', S. B. Cohen and G. K. Lewis, Jan. 1967, p. 1–42.

Ekistics 'Function of the American shopping centre (Urban design conference)', J. W. Rouse, Aug. 1963, p. 96–105.

Electrical Supervisor 'Electrical services at the Bull Ring, Birmingham', J. P. Cutting, Jan. 1966, p. 4–10.

Estates Gazette 'The planning of shopping centres', M. L. Fenton-Jones, 17 Dec. 1961 and 25 Aug. 1962.
'Out-of-town shopping—solution or mistake?' O. Luder, 20 Feb. 1965, p. 651–652. Reply by J. V. Butterfill, 13 March 1965, p. 943–945.
'Out-of-town shopping centres', H. M. D. Norton, 19 Feb. 1966, p. 675, 677 and 679.
'Shops and shopping districts', C. Darlow, 17 Dec. 1966, p. 1029–1033.
'No parking, no shopping', 15 July 1967, p. 231.
'Central area redevelopment', J. H. Bartlett, 15 July 1967, p. 249, 251 and 253.
'Planning for urban expansion', R. S. McConnell, 2 Sept. 1967, p. 861, 863 and 865.
'Shopping trends', 16 Sept. 1967, p. 1035.
'Development of Runcorn shopping centre', 21 Oct. 1967, p. 307.
'Redevelopment of town centres', A. L. Strachan, 2 Dec. 1967, p. 929, 931 and 933.
'Streets paved with cars', 20 Jan. 1968, p. 205.

Fabian Research Series 'The future of retailing', R. W. Evely, No. 177, 1955.

Financial Times 'Annual review', 17 July 1961.
'A new pattern for shopping—in or out-of-town', 22 Aug. 1962.
'Developing new shops', 28 Dec. 1962.
'The new shopping centre', 19 July 1963.
'Brave new world turns sour for shop developers', 6 Sept. 1966.
'Making a success of shopping centres the Solihull way', 18 Nov. 1966.
Issues of 27 Oct. 1962, 4 Dec. 1962, 8 Feb. 1963 and 20 May 1963.

Geographical Journal 'Urban hinterlands in England and Wales', F. H. W. Green, No. 116, 1950, p. 64–88.
'A classification of service centres in England and Wales', W. I. Carruthers, No. 122, 1957, p. 371–385.
'Urban hinterlands: Fifteen years on', F. H. W. Green, June 1966, p. 263–266.

Glass Age 'Cowley centre, Oxford', Nov. 1965, p. 42–43.

The Grocer 'Gem sells out to Asda', 19 Nov. 1966, p. 33.
'Planners' curbs on advertising', 19 Nov. 1966, p. 64.
'Traders fighting Woolco plan', 26 Nov. 1966, p. 30.
'Asda's 80% slice in Gem', 26 Nov. 1966, p. 33.
'Woolco man looks at Fame operation', 26 Nov. 1966, p. 74.
'Two more Woolco sites', 4 March 1967, p. 30.
'More of these stores on the northern scene in '68?' C. Beddall, 17 Feb. 1968, p. 40 and 44.

Grocers Gazette 'British group buy control in Gem', 19 Nov. 1966, p. 5.
'Bartfield says "No Finance Trouble"', L. Millard, 19 Nov. 1966, p. 7.
'The Shops Act 1950', 19 Nov. 1966, p. 30 and 32.
'Planners want curbs on advertisements', 19 Nov. 1966, p. 36.
'Three more Woolcos on the way', 4 March 1966, p. 5.

The Guardian 'The political battle of the roads', T. Bendixon, 24 Oct. 1966.
'Leicester traffic plan', 25 Nov. 1966.
'Advantages of sale and lease-back', R. Mallinson, 11 Jan. 1967.
'Neighbourhood shopping', A. Adburgham, 10 Feb. 1967.
'Annual statement by Woolworth', F. L. Chapin, 16 Feb. 1967.

Harvard Business Review 'Relation of consumer's buying habits to marketing methods', M. T. Copeland, 1922–23.
'Dynamic planning for retail areas', V. Gruen, Nov. 1954.
'The personality of the retail stores', P. Martineau, Jan. 1958.

Heating and Ventilating Engineer 'Air-conditioning at the Bull Ring, Birmingham', S. Greenwood, Dec. 1964, p. 312–316.

Hobart Papers   'Revolution in retailing', C. Fulop, Paper No. 9, 1961.
                                      'Paying for parking', G. J. Roth, Paper No. 33, 1965.

Housing Review,   'Principles for the development of shopping facilities', G. C. Turner, July/Aug. 1957, p. 136–143.

Institute of Landscape   'Shopping precincts at Coventry', Nov. 1957, p. 12–14.
Architects Journal   'The landscape architect and the shopping centre', R. Zion, May 1961, p. 7–9.

Institution of Municipal   'Provision of car parks in shopping and commercial centres', Oct. 1961.
Engineers Journal   'Elephant and Castle centre', Jan. 1966, p. 93–118.

Interior Design and   'Interiors of Merrion centre, Leeds; Lulea, Sweden; Malmo, Sweden and Elephant and Castle, London',
Contract Furnishing   May 1965, p. 229–244.

International Lighting   'Farsta centre, Sweden', H. H. Mollander, May 1961, p. 220–223.
Review

International Road Safety   'Two-tier shopping development in Britain', J. W. Dark, Summer 1962, p. 5–14.
and Traffic Review

Irish Times (Dublin)   'Stillorgan shopping centre, Dublin', supplement, 1 Dec. 1966.

Journal of Marketing   'The mechanics of constructing a market area map', F. Strohkarck and K. Phelps, Vol. 12, 1948.
                                      'New laws of retail gravitation', P. D. Converse, Oct. 1949.
                                      'The wheel of retailing', S. C. Hollander, July 1960.
                                      'Defining and estimating a trading area', D. L. Huff, 1964.
                                      'Guidelines for a store-location strategy study', W. Applebaum, Oct. 1966, p. 42–45.

Journal of Planning and   'The redevelopment of shopping areas', W. J. Leaper, Feb. 1963, p. 87–94 and March 1963, p. 168–175.
Property Law

Journal of Regional   'Consumer behaviour in an urban hierarchy', R. L. Johnston and P. J. Rimmer, No. 7, 1967.
Science   'An econometric forecasting model for a region', F. W. Bell, No. 7, 1967.

Journal of Retailing   'The rise of shopping centres', Spring 1955.
                                      'Shopping centres and local government—collision or co-operation', Summer 1955.
                                      'Impact of shopping centres locally and downtown', G. H. Stedman, Summer 1956.
                                      'Subjective distance', D. L. Thompson, Spring 1963.

Lancashire Evening Post   'Gem discount centre, Preston', Supplement, 10 April 1968.

LANCHESTER COLLEGE, Report on conference, 'Planning for Shopping Facilities', 20/21 April 1967.
COVENTRY

Land Economics   'Shopping centres in urban redevelopment', R. M. Lillibridge, May 1948.
                                      'Shopping centre trade areas', D. L. Huff, Feb. 1963.
                                      'A programmed solution for approximating an optimum retail location', D. L. Huff, Aug. 1966, p. 293–304.
                                      'An urbanisation pattern for the U.S.: some consideration for the decentralisation of excellence', Feb. 1967.
                                      'Modern proposals for the physical decentralisation of community', Feb. 1967.
                                      'A behavioural approach to determining optimum location for the retail trade', D. N. J. and C. Gruen,
                                      Aug. 1967.

Landscape Architect   'The landscape architect and the shopping centre', Oct. 1957, p. 6–12.
                                      'Shopper's World centre', S. N. Shurcliffe, July 1958, p. 145–151.

Landscape Architecture   '"Paradise" in a small town', W. M. Ruff, July 1958, p. 215–218.
                                      'New shopping centres', H. A. Anthony, Summer 1960, p. 214–218.

L'Architecture d'Aujourd'hui 'Shopping centres, Malmaison, Denver, Copenhagen, Lulea and Sao Paulo', No. 85, 1959, p. 32–93.

L'Architecture Française   'Shops and shopping centres', No. 278–280.

La Technique des Travaux   'Macy store, New York', Jan. 1967, p. 25–34.

Libre Service   'Selling in 1995', May 1966.
Actualités

McGOVERN, P. D.   'Livingston town centre: A report on the size and phasing of a new regional centre', 1965.

MINISTRY OF   'Town centres—approach to renewal', 1962.
HOUSING AND   'Town centres—cost and control of redevelopment', 1963.
LOCAL GOVERNMENT   'Town centres—current practice', 1963
                         'Parking in town centres', 1965.
                         'Planning investment and town centre redevelopment', Circular 50/66.

MINISTRY OF   'The transport needs of Great Britain in the next twenty years', 1963.
TRANSPORT   'Road pricing, the economic and technical possibilities', 1964
                         'National travel survey 1964 (preliminary report 1967).
                         'Urban traffic engineering techniques', 1965.
                         'Roads in urban areas', 1966.
                         'Cars for cities', 1967.
                         'Better use of town roads', 1967.

Municipal Engineering   'Thornaby centre', J. L. Watson, 16 Aug. 1963, p. 1237–1238.
                         'Cowley centre, Oxford', 17 Sept. 1965, p. 1927.
                         'Highways superintendent and new shopping centres', J. S. Miles, 24 Sept. 1965, p. 2016–2019.
                         'Seacroft centre, Leeds', 13 May 1966, p. 977.
                         'Design factors in providing for traffic-free shopping precincts', P. S. Chester, 31 March 1967, p. 599.
                         'Parking', F. W. Dawkes, 17 May 1968, Supplement.

Municipal Journal   'Town planning at the local level', J. Tyrwhitt, 10 Feb. 1950, p. 382–384.
                         'Romford development', 28 May 1958, p. 1261.
                         'Scottish shopping centre', 28 Aug. 1959, p. 2348–2349.
                         'Lichfield development', 6 Nov. 1959, p. 3077.
                         'Elephant and Castle centre', 16 Sept. 1960, p. 2890–2891.
                         'West Bromwich centre', 30 Dec. 1960, p. 4098–4099.
                         'Jarrow centre', 10 Feb. 1961, p. 405.
                         'High Wycombe centre', 7 April 1961, p. 1105–1107.
                         'Gateshead centre', 11 Aug. 1961, p. 2583.
                         'Locating retail premises in urban redevelopment', A. J. Brown, 18 Oct. 1963, p. 3169–3173.
                         'Coalville centre', 3 Jan. 1964, p. 27.
                         'Walkden centre', 10 Jan. 1964, p. 88.
                         'Solihull centre', 11 Nov. 1966, p. 3671.

NATIONAL CASH   'Shopping centres in America and Britain', 1962.
REGISTER CO. LTD.   'The story of shopping centres'.

NATIONAL COMMITTEE 'Planned neighbourhood shopping centres', M. Villanueva, 1945.
ON HOUSING (U.S.)

NATIONAL ECONOMIC 'Conditions favourable to further growth', 1963.
DEVELOPMENT OFFICE 'Newsletter on out-of-hours deliveries', 5 July, 1967.
                         'Press notice on out-of-hours deliveries', 13 Dec., 1967.

NATIONAL INSTITUTE 'Outlying shopping centres: Planning and operation', L. Smith, May 1951.
OF ESTATE BROKERS
(U.S.)

New Scientist   'Shopping in 1985', A. P. McAnally, 16 Sept. 1965, p. 702–705.
                         'Beating the weather in Minnesota', C. Marwick, 30 Nov. 1967, p. 549–550.

New Society   'Great supermarket revolution', P. Coldstream, 1 Nov. 1962.

New York Times   'Shopping centre goes to the shopper', C. B. Palmer, 29 Nov. 1953.

The Observer   'The pressure cooked in Chester', I. Nairn, 6 Nov. 1966.
                         'The Woolworth riddle', J. Davies, 22 Jan. 1967.
                         'Store men tread warily in flight to suburbia', R. Elgin, 26 Feb. 1967.

Official Architecture and   'New proposals for Coventry', A. G. Ling, Nov. 1955, p. 563–569.
Planning   'Town planner and the shopkeeper', Sept. 1958, p. 414–416.
                              'Shopping Precinct. Shrewsbury', Jan. 1958, p. 37–38.
                              Issue on shopping and shopping centres, Aug. 1967.
                              'The future of city centres', R. S. McConnell, Sept. 1967, p. 1266–1275.

Opinion and Comment   'Retail store location', P. D. Converse, University of Illinois, May 1951.

OXFORD CITY   'Cowley centre report', Feb. 1965.
COUNCIL

Practical Builder   'Developing shopping centres', J. C. Nichols, Dec. 1945.

Productivity Review   'Retailing (Review No. 28)', British Productivity Council, 1957.

Property Developer (1964)   'Comparisons of American and British commercial developer', W. J. N. Oswald, p. 73–79.

PUBLIC WORKS AND   'English Motorways: Development and progress', H. N. Ginns, 18 Nov. 1966.
MUNICIPAL SERVICES
CONGRESS

Regional Science   'Gravity models and trip distribution theory', M. Schneider, No. 5, 1959.
Association   'Retail location and consumer behaviour', B. J. Berry, H. G. Barnum and R. J. Tennant, No. 9, 1962.
                              'Land values and spatial structure', E. von Boventer, No. 18, 1967.
                              'Location games', W. Isard and T. E. Smith, No. 18, 1967.

Retail Business   'Review of Catering', Feb. 1966.
                              'Specialist food shops and U.S. discount houses, 1966', Dec. 1966.
                              'Too many supermarkets', Feb. 1967.
                              'Annual review of retailing', March 1967.
                              'Retailing in a cold climate', May 1967.
                              'Consumer durable shops', June 1967.
                              'Ten years of retailing', March 1968.

Royal Institute of British 'Shopping and the town centre', July 1963, p. 288–290.
Architects Journal

Scottish Geographical   'Analysis of shops and service trades in Scottish towns', J. B. Fleming, Vol. 70, No. 3, Dec. 1954, p.
Journal   97–106.

Scottish Journal of Political 'Development of new shopping centres: area estimation', D. R. Diamond and E. B. Gibb, June 1962,
Economy   130–146.

Self-Service and   'The supermarket industry today and tomorrow', R. W. Stephenson, March 1964, p. 5–7 and 70.
Supermaket Journal   'Supermarkets in Britain', March 1964, p. 91–92 and 95–96.
                              'Stepless escalators', April 1964, p. 75.
                              'On the brink of a new retail era', Aug. 1964, p. 14.
                              'No membership for Gem stores', Sept. 1964, p. 17.
                              'Allways plan an out-of-town', Sept. 1964, p. 15.
                              'Cars destroy loyalty', B. Gendal, Sept. 1964, p. 92.
                              'Supermac N.I.', Nov. 1964, p. 57–58.
                              'Gem store, Nottingham', Dec. 1964, p. 30–32.
                              'Tolworth centre', Jan. 1965, p. 22–27.
                              'America in Britain today', A. Offord, Feb. 1965, p. 92–93.
                              'Review of Haydock Report', Feb. 1965, p. 95.
                              'Gem very disappointed', March 1965, p. 21 and 25.
                              'Bolton Co-op goes out-of-town', April 1965, p. 94–95.
                              'A revolution in store design', May 1965, p. 66.
                              'Free bus to Gem centre', May 1965, p. 143.
                              'Supermac', July 1965, p. 76–77.
                              'Britain's first punched card supermarket', Aug. 1965, p. 20–21.
                              'One stop shopping is not enough', Jan. 1966, p. 52 and 57.
                              'The importance of the fridge', March 1966, p. 19.
                              'American shopping, Ormesby style', March 1966, p. 44–46.

'Site evaluation', March 1966, p. 75–76 and 79–80.
'The Waitrose showpiece', April 1966, p. 24–26.
'Floor spaces in supermarkets', June 1966, p. 19.
'Appraisal of the U.S. food retailing scene', June 1966, p. 41.
'Self-service outlets', June 1966, p. 49 and 51.
'Fame and Gem discuss link-up', July 1966, p. 21.
'Selling in 1985', July 1966, p. 30 and 32.
'Self service shops in Germany', July 1966, p. 60.
'Late night shopping', Sept. 1966, p. 46, 48 and 70.
'Distribution of supermarkets', Oct. 1966, p. 78.
'Woolworths launch U.S.-style department stores', Nov. 1966, p. 21.
'Fame stores', Nov. 1966, p. 22–23.
'Supermarket earnings', Nov. 1966, p. 65.
'Preview of the 1970's', Nov. 1966, p. 82, 83 and 91.
'The chain that never was (Gem)', Dec. 1966, p. 15.
'Naafi builds a shopping centre', Dec. 1966, p. 18–19.
'Gem taken over by Asda', Dec. 1966, p. 21.
'Self-service drug stores', Dec. 1966, p. 44–45.
'Changes in shopping habits', July 1967, p. 17 and 23.
'Convenience stores', 2 Nov. 1967, p. 1 and 16.
'Out-of-town centre at Wroxham', 9 Nov. 1967, p. 8–9.
'Convenience stores', 16 Nov. 1967, p. 46.
'Operation "Moondrop" (out-of-hours deliveries)', 30 Nov. 1967, p. 16.
'Latest news on supermarkets', 7 Dec. 1967, p. 33 and 37.
'Operation "Moondrop"', 4 Jan. 1968, p. 16–17 and 11 Jan. 1968, p. 8–9.
'Drive-through shops', 18 Jan. 1968, p. 22.
'Hard lessons from the property boom', 1 Feb. 1968, p. 22–23, 25–26, 28.
'Out-of-town supermarkets recommended at Canterbury', 8 Feb. 1968, p. 16.
'Fewer stores take more money', 29 Feb. 1968, p. 31.
'The look of shops tomorrow', 7 March 1968, p. 31 and 37.
'There's life in the Elephant yet', M. Fairchild, 21 March 1968, p. 6–9 and 12.

Shopping Centre Age   'Shopping centres of the future', March 1963.
                            'Planning shopping centre profits', n.d.

Shop Property   'Yate centre', July 1967, p. 20–21.
                            'Location: The retailer's dilemma', T. Rhodes, Oct. 1967, p. 5 and 7.
                            'Evaluating local purchasing power', M. Thorncroft, Jan. 1968, p. 9 and 24.
                            'Thornaby town centre development', Jan. 1968, p. 17.
                            'Shopping centre, Edgbaston, Birmingham', Jan. 1968, p. 20.
                            'Cross Gates centre, Leeds', Jan. 1968, p. 26.
                            'Staple Hill centre, Bristol', March 1968, p. 11.
                            'Greywell centre, Havant', March 1968, p. 16.
                            'Parly II regional centre, Paris', June/July 1968, p. 18.

Sociological Review   'Buying and selling—the sociology of-distribution', C. Sofer, July 1965, p. 183–209.

STEVENAGE   'Survey of shopper parking', n.d.
DEVELOPMENT
CORPORATION

Stores and Shops Journal 'The rise of the shopping centre', Ellsworth and Sewell, Feb. 1958.
                            'Taking shops to people', Feb. 1958.
                            'Bull Ring, Birmingham', July 1964, p. 34.
                            Features on shopping centres, Aug. 1964, p. 34 and Dec. 1964, p. 37.
                            'Gem centre, Nottingham', Jan. 1965, p. 37.
                            'How many days a week?', Feb. 1965, p. 23.
                            'Chaos or order? Retailing and the challenge of the motor age', Lord Sainsbury, Feb. 1965, p. 28–31.
                            'Woolworth developments', March 1965, p. 22–24.
                            'Where do we go from here?', Sir Rex Cohen, April 1965, p. 24–28.
                            'Supermac', April 1965, p. 36–37.
                            'Elephant and Castle centre', May 1965, p. 38–41.
                            'The American shopping centre', June 1965, p. 24 and 26.
                            'The quiet revolution in U.S. and U.K.', June 1965, p. 30–31.

'Thornaby centre', June 1965, p. 59 and 62.
'Park Farm centre, Derby', Aug. 1965, p. 29–31.
'Choosing a shopping development', C. A. Orndahl, Sept. 1965, p. 65, 66 and 70.
'An American symposium', Nov. 1965, p. 24–31.
'Gem discounts', Nov. 1965, p. 33.
'Towards the 1970's', Dec. 1965, p. 16–19.
'Macy's New York', Feb. 1966, p. 34–35.
'Roselands centre, Sydney', May 1966, p. 35.
'The trend towards concessionaire trading', C. Wilson, June 1966.
'Traffic and the retailer', J. S. Berry, Oct. 1966, p. 28 28–31.
'Re-thinking the shopping centre concept', Dec. 1966, p. 17–18.
'Woolworths go discount', Dec. 1966, p. 20.
'Aston centre, Birmingham', Dec. 1966, p. 56.
'Scandinavia's biggest shopping centre', Feb. 1967, p. 19–21.
'Second phase at Cumbernauld', Feb. 1967, p. 45.
'Winsford centre', May 1967.
'Montreal's underground shopping centre', March 1968.

Sunday Times   'Bull Ring, Birmingham', O. Marriott, 14 March 1965.
                        'Gem swing into discount policy', P. Clarke, 12 Sept. 1965.
                        'Tolworth centre', R. Troop, 10 Oct. 1965.
                        'When the city centre boom falters', O. Marriott, 31 Oct. 1965.
                        'Dublin shopping out-of-town', O. Marriott, 6 March, 1966.
                        'Promotions for shopping centres', R. Troop, 29 May 1966.
                        'Stockport development', R. Troop, 29 May 1966.
                        'The stores take stock', P. Wilsher, 2 Oct. 1966.
                        'Woolworth plan chain of Woolco suburban stores', O. Marriott, 9 Oct. 1966.
                        'Birmingham's suburban centre', R. Troop, 30 Oct. 1966.
                        'The big shopping explosion', R. Troop, 20 Nov. 1966.
                        'Solihull centre', R. Troop, 18 Dec. 1966.
                        'No jazz, no stamps, no gimmicks', E. Good, 12 Feb. 1967.
                        'Botley centre, Oxford', R. Troop, 12 Feb. 1967.
                        'Hammerson development, Southend', R. Troop, 19 Feb. 1967.
                        'Growth ban forces U.S. supermarkets overseas', H. Unger, 14 May 1967.
                        'Profit and loss at the corner shop', O. Stanley, 30 July 1967.
                        'High Wycombe centre', R. Troop, 30 July 1967.
                        'Woolworth's big store gamble', G. Nuttall, 8 Oct. 1967.
                        'Can the Lavender Hill mob beat retailers to the draw?', R. Lewis, 2 June 1968.
                        'Victory for Laing in the Bull Ring', R. Garrick, 23 June 1968.

Supermarket Merchandising 'Are shopping centres failing?', A. Rubloff, Feb. 1964.

Supermarket News   'Supermarkets in shopping centres', 4 Jan. 1954, p. 13–24.

The Surveyor   'The despised corner shop', W. Burns, 25 Sept. 1954.
                        'Planning of shopping centres', W. Burns, 13 Aug. 1955, p. 797–798.
                        'Romford development', 3 May 1958, p. 461–462.
                        'Stevenage town centre', 31 May 1958, p. 553–554.
                        'The town planner and the shop keeper', O. W. Roskill, 23 Aug. 1958, p. 847–850.
                        'Bull Ring, Birmingham', 30 Jan. 1960, p. 107–108.
                        'Swindon centre', 8 Oct. 1960, p. 1,125–1,127.
                        'Stockport development', 25 March 1961, p. 323–324.
                        'Feltham precinct', 9 Dec. 1961, p. 1463–1464.
                        'Cowley centre, Oxford', 16 Dec. 1961, p. 1487–1488.
                        'Planning for retail trade in Ipswich', 3 Nov. 1962, p. 1,327–1,328.
                        'Cowley centre to relieve traffic congestion in Oxford', 18 May 1963, p. 653–654.
                        'Greenmarket centre, Newcastle upon Tyne', 23 Jan. 1964, p. 23–25.
                        'Haydock centre', 17 Oct. 1964, p. 17–24.
                        'Planning for walking and riding', P. Ritter, 7 Nov. 1964, p. 34–35.
                        'Blackburn centre', 21 Nov. 1964, p. 25–27.
                        'Bangor centre', 28 Nov. 1964, p. 27–30.
                        'The regional shopping centre', J. Brierley, 12 Nov. 1966, p. 131–132.
                        'Shopping centres — traffic and economic aspects', H. D. Peake, 28 Jan. 1967, p. 24–26.

Technical Valuation   'Economic factors and their analysis', L. Smith, 1954.

BIBLIOGRAPHY

THOMPSON, J
WALTER & CO. LTD.
'Shopping in suburbia', 1963.
'The changing face of supermarket shopping', 1964.
'How many nations?', 1964.
'Pin-pointing the affluent household', 1964.
'The new housewife survey', 1967.

Time
'Macy's store, Queens, New York', 9 July 1965.

The Times
Special report on supermarkets, 9 July 1967.
'A true out-of-town shopping centre (Bournemouth)', G. Ely, 15 April 1968.

Town and Country
Planning
'Shops: their place in new and redevelopment areas', D. Gibson, Dec. 1950, p. 495–500.
'Shopping centres: some factors in design', W. Burns, May 1954, p. 242–245 and June 1954, p. 308–311.
'Planning for shopping', June 1957, p. 265–267.
'The American shopping centré', L. H. Wilson, Sept. 1961, p. 359–365.
'The future of central retail cores', C. D. Morley, Sept. 1962, p. 355–358.
'Shopping demands and shop design (Forum)', W. L. Waide, July 1963, p. 306–308.
'The economist in planning', H. Cole, Oct. 1963, p. 403–405.
'Cambridge: shopping growth and population distribution', D. E. Keeble, April 1967, p. 184–189.

Town Planning Institute
Journal
'Shopping centres', C. J. Craven, April, 1939, p. 198–200.
'The provision of shops in a new town', W. G. Bodie, Nov. 1953, p. 269–271.
'Planning for shops', D. S. R. Overton, Dec. 1954, p. 9–12.
'Shopping centres in Canada', N. Pearson, Sept./Oct. 1957, p. 231–235
'The isolated corner shop in residential areas', J. S. Cheer, Dec. 1957, p. 16–18.
'The problem of the parked car', W. Burns, July/Aug. 1958.
'Civic design and the shopping centre', L. H. Wilson, July/Aug. 1958, p. 104–202.
'Town planning and the retail trade', O. W. Roskill, Summer School Report, 1958, p. 6–16.
'Car parking in city centres', G. F. Chadwick, April 1961, p. 84–90.
'The design of shopping centres', J. S. Harris, Sept./Oct. 1961, p. 245–251.
'Car parking in American central areas', G. F. Chadwick, June 1962.
'Changes and trends in American central areas', V. J. Robinson, June 1962.
'Changes in shopping habits', W. L. Waide, Summer School Report, 1962, p. 86–87.
'King's Lynn study report', R. J. Green and R. M. Beaumont, Dec. 1962, p. 311–314 and March 1963, p. 80–81.
'Changing shopping habits and their impact on town planning', W. L. Waide, Sept./Oct. 1963, p. 254–264.
'Studying traffic in towns', P. Wood, Sept./Oct. 1963, p. 265–271.
'Retail trading centres in the Midlands', G. M. Lomas, March 1964, p. 104–119.
'Regional shopping centres (Review of Haydock report)', Jan. 1965, p. 40.
'The relationship of parking demand with the level of trading', J. S. Wyeth, April 1965, p. 147–150.
'Shopping centres in Britain', R. N. Percival, Sept./Oct. 1965, p. 329–333.
'Local changes in shopping potential', H. Bliss, Sept./Oct. 1965, p. 334–337.
'Regional shopping centre at Haydock', Sept./Oct. 1965, p. 346–347.
'Assessment of shopping needs', R. N. Percival, Summer School Report, 1965, p. 107–109.
'West Midlands shopping study', Interim Report, April 1966, p. 146–149.
'Forecasting shopping demand', T. Rhodes and R. Whitaker, May 1967, p. 188–192.
'Shopping in Enfield', Sept./Oct. 1967, p. 374.
'A note of forecasting shopping demand', H. F. Andrews, Sept./Oct. 1967, p. 352–354.
'A further note on forecasting shopping demand', T. Rhodes and R. Whitaker, Nov. 1967, p. 415–416.
'Review of Haydock study (Part Two)', Nov. 1967, p. 425.
'The nodal structure of the Solent region', W. K. D. Davies and G. W. S. Robinson, Jan. 1968, p. 18–22.
'Planning and the shopkeeper (Review of book by Gillian Pain)', M. M. Dunne, Jan. 1968, p. 31–32.
'Shopping centres in North-West Europe (Review of publication by Multiple Shops Federation)', R. Turton, Jan. 1968, p. 32.
'Predicting shopping requirements (Review of West Midlands Shopping Research Group book)', Feb. 1968, p. 96–97.
'Some comments on "The nodal structure of the Solent region",' D. Thorpe, April 1968, p. 177–178.
'The study of nodal structures: a rejoinder', W. K. D. Davies, May 1968, p. 233–234.
'Data requirements for urban land use models', T. Rhodes, June 1968, p. 281–283.
'Parking in urban centres', June 1968, p. 285–286.

Town Panning Review·
'The Lijnbaan, Rotterdam', April 1956, p. 21–26.
'Transport—maker and breaker of cities', C. Clarke, Jan. 1958, p. 237–250.
'Suburban shopping in America', J. P. Reynolds, April 1958, p. 43–59.

'Pedestrian conveyors', J. P. McElroy, July 1961, p. 125–140.
'Service facilities in Greater London', W. I. Carruthers, April 1962, p. 5–31.
'Suburban shopping in Liverpool', H. R. Parker, Oct. 1962, p. 197–223.
'Traffic generated by a Wilmslow store', E. M. Stone, July 1963, p. 119–145.
'Shopping in the North-West', J. P. Reynolds, Oct. 1963, p. 213–236.
'The traffic problem in towns', R. J. Smeed, July 1964, p. 133–158.
'An economic approach to traffic congestion', G. J. Roth, April 1965, p. 49–61.
'Quantitative measure of accessibility', F. Savigear, April 1967, p. 64–72.
'Assessment of shopping potential and the demand for shops', J. P. Lewis and A. L. Traill. Jan. 1968, p. 317–326.
'Analysis of intra-urban shopping patterns', P. J. Ambrose, Jan. 1968, p. 327–334.
'The changing role of department stores', H. R. Parket, April 1968, p. 55–64.

Traffic Engineering

'Traffic impact of regional shopping centres', V. Gruen, March 1953.
'Planning for shopping', V. Gruen, Jan. 1956.
'Why malls?', R. L. Munro, Aug. 1967.
'Discussion on malls', S. R. McMinn, Dec. 1967.

Traffic Engineering and Control

'Road capacity in city centres', R. J. Smeed, Nov. 1966, p. 455–458.
'Travel estimates from Census data', H. J. Wotton and G. W. Pick, July 1967.
'Forecasting by land/use traffic model technique', H. B. Barke and A. N. Crowther, Aug. 1967.
'Traffic generation of a large department store', J. Gantwort, Oct. 1967.
'The case for road pricing', J. M. Thompson, March 1968.
'Journey speed and flow in central urban area', March 1968.

Traffic Quarterly

'Parking needs in shopping centres', D. K. Jackson, Jan. 1951, p. 32–37.
'Traffic planning opportunities in shopping centre design', H. T. Fisher, Oct. 1951, p. 383–392.
'Department stores and parking', C. O. Pratt, Jan. 1952.
'Parking plans for shopping centres', K. C. Welch and B. Funaro, Oct. 1952, p. 416–426.
'Decentralisation of retail trade', S. C. McMillan, April 1954.
'Maintaining the health of our central business districts', L. Smith, April 1954, p. 111–122.
'Appraisal of shopping centres', K. C. Welch, Oct. 1954, p. 384–396.
'Defining urban trade areas', J. D. Carroll, April 1955.
'Shopping centre traffic problems., April 1955.
'The law of retail gravitation applied to traffic engineering', H. J. Casey, July 1955, p. 313–321.
'Two regional centres in one town', I. A. Germain, July 1955, p. 360–379.
'Retail structure of the urban economy', E. J. Kelly, July 1955, p. 411–430.
'Suburban shopping centre effects on highways and parking', H. Hoyt, April 1956, p. 181–189.
'Canadian shopping centres', H. Shuffrin, July 1956, p. 289–305.
'The regional centre and downtown', K. C. Welch, July 1958, p. 371–388.
'Shopping centre design', L. Douglass, July, 1958, p. 409–424.
'Can cities survive in the automobile age?', E. J. Logue, April 1959.
'The downtown shopping centre', F. Forman, Oct. 1959, p. 495–503.
'Lincoln Road Mall, Miami', M. N. Lipp, July 1961, p. 441–447.
'Recent trends in the decentralisation of retail trades', S. C. McMillan, Jan. 1962, p. 75–94.
'Future trip length', W. R. Mills, April 1963, p. 203–218.
'Effects of the automobile on patterns of urban growth', H. Hoyt, April 1963, p. 293–301.
'Suburban town centres', M. L. Hancock and W. O. Billing, April 1964, p. 233–249.
'Pedestrian in the city', B. Benepe, Jan. 1965, p. 28–42.
'Nuisances of traffic in residential areas', D. M. Winterbottom, July 1965, p. 384–395.
'A new look at highway capacity', July 1966, p. 322–346.
'Characteristics of shopping centres', W. D. Stoll, April 1967, p. 159–177.
'Malls and their problems', S. P. Walsh, July 1967, p. 321–328.

UNIVERSITY OF CALIFORNIA

'Shopping centres: planning and design for traffic and traffic generation', G. H. Harding, 1960.
'Shopping centre study results', J. Shaver, 1962.

UNIVERSITY OF CHICAGO

'Commercial structure and commercial blight', B. J. L. Berry, Research Paper No. 85, 1963.

UNIVERSITY OF HULL

'Retail distribution in Eastern Yorkshire in relation to central place theory', J. R. Tarrant, Occasional Paper in Geography No. 8, 1967.

UNIVERSITY OF YALE

'Traffic characteristics at regional shopping centres', D. E. Cleveland and E. A. Mueller, 1961.

Urbanistica	'Satellite towns of Stockholm', G. Gentili, Sept. 1958.
Urban Land	'Shopping centres—look before you leap', J. C. Nichols, June 1948.
	'Shopping centres that offer new ideas', Dec. 1951.
	'A case for contrast in suburban shopping', Feb. 1952.
	'Department store trends in the development of shopping centres', L. Smith, March 1952.
	'The current trend in new shopping centres', H. Hoyt, April 1953.
	'Estimating productivity for planned regional shopping centres', J. W. Rouse, Nov. 1953.
	'Branch store policies', R. Armstrong, May 1954.
	'The status of new suburban centres', H. Hoyt, June 1955.
	'Commercial real estate relationships—downtown and suburban', L. Smith, March 1956.
	'Parking and its relationship to business', J. T. Stegmaier, May 1956.
	'Impact of suburban shopping centres', H. Hoyt, Sept. 1956.
	'Analysing the shopping centre market', L. Smith, Jan. 1957.
	'Sales in leading shopping centres and shopping districts', H. Hoyt, Vol. 20, 1961.
	'Symposium on small shopping centres', Jan. 1961 and March 1962.
	'U.S. Metropolitan retail shopping patterns: Exodus of department stores from central business districts, 1958–1963; sales trends in shopping centres', H. Hoyt, April 1966.
Urban Studies	'The main provincial towns as commercial centres', E. L. Hammond, Nov. 1964, p. 129–137.
	'Urban form, car ownership and public policy', J. F. Kain and M. E. Beesley, Nov. 1964, p. 174–203.
	'Forecasting car ownership and use', J. F. Kain and M. F. Beesley, Nov. 1965, p. 163–185.
	'Comments on forecasting car ownership and use', J. C. Tanner, June 1966, p. 143–146.
	'Shopping assessment at Haydock and elsewhere', H. R. Cole, June 1966, p. 147–156.
	'On the nature of analytical models', L. Loewenstein, June 1966, p. 112–119.
	'Cost-benefit in town planning', N. Lichfield, Nov. 1966, p. 215–249.
	'Centrality and the central place hierarchy', W. K. D. Davies, Feb. 1967, p. 61–79.
	'Effects of consumer income differences on the business provisions of small shopping centres', Ross L. Davies, June 1968, p. 144–164.
	'The main shopping centres of Great Britain in 1961: their locational and structural characteristics', D. Thorpe, June 1968, p. 165–206.

index